Brutal Fantasies

Brutal Fantasies

*Imagining North Korea
in the Long Cold War*

CHRISTINE KIM

Duke University Press   *Durham and London*   2025

© 2025 DUKE UNIVERSITY PRESS. All rights reserved
Project Editor: Ihsan Taylor
Typeset in Garamond Premier Pro by Copperline Book Services

Library of Congress Cataloging-in-Publication Data
Names: Kim, Christine, [date] author
Title: Brutal fantasies : imagining North Korea in the long
Cold War / Christine Kim.
Description: Durham : Duke University Press, 2025. |
Includes bibliographical references and index.
Identifiers: LCCN 2025004860 (print)
LCCN 2025004861 (ebook)
ISBN 9781478032397 paperback
ISBN 9781478029021 hardcover
ISBN 9781478061229 ebook
Subjects: LCSH: Other (Philosophy) in literature | Other
(Philosophy) in motion pictures | Korea (North)—Foreign
public opinion | Korea (North)—In popular culture | Korea
(North)—Social conditions—20th century | Korea (North)—
Politics and government—1948–1994
Classification: LCC DS932.2 .K45 2025 (print) |
LCC DS932.2 (ebook) | DDC 951.9304—dc23/eng/20250430
LC record available at https://lccn.loc.gov/2025004860
LC ebook record available at https://lccn.loc.gov/2025004861

Cover art: Apartment buildings, Pyongyang, 2010. Photograph
© Eric Lafforgue. All rights reserved 2025 / Bridgeman Images.

Contents

Preface
vii

Acknowledgments
xi

INTRODUCTION
Cultural Fantasies of the Inhuman
1

1
DYSTOPIC SPECULATION
Stylizing Transpacific Villains
25

2
THE INHUMAN FIGURE OF HUMAN RIGHTS
Life Writing, Testimonies, and
Escape from Camp 14
51

3
IMPERIAL DIASPORAS
South Korean Diasporic
Exceptionalism, North Korean Terror,
and *How I Became a North Korean*
81

EPILOGUE
Situating North Korea Within
Socialist Lifeworlds
109

Notes
119

Bibliography
141

Index
153

Preface

From 2012 to 2014, when I first began thinking about North Korea, there were many stories circulating in the media about how bizarre a place it was. These included tales about a unicorn lair near Pyongyang being discovered by archaeologists, the execution of Jang Song Thaek (uncle of current leader Kim Jong Un) by being fed to a pack of 120 dogs, the existence of a North Korean girl group called Moranbang that included a member who was allegedly Kim Jong Un's mistress, and state-sanctioned haircuts for men and women. These news items were often written in a tone of disbelief or even incredulity and lacked political or historical context; and in this way, they encouraged readers to view North Korea as odd, even humorous. The idea that North Korea could be the target of such casual mockery was almost shocking, given that only a decade earlier it was widely depicted as a dangerous and tyrannical force or what US President George W. Bush called part of the Axis of Evil. These emerging representations of North Korea as comically odd and evil were also quite different from characterizations I had encountered while growing up. At community gatherings, in church sermons, and at extended family events, North Korea was occasionally invoked as an object of loss, sympathy, or even pity through references to starving people, some even relatives, who endured harsh conditions and who needed those of us in North America to send aid and missionary support.

Reflecting on these various depictions and thinking about how they changed during my lifetime, I found it almost impossible not to notice how North Korea was routinely and blatantly Orientalized within the US cultural imagination, albeit in distinct ways, by Korean diasporic and non-Korean diasporic Americans. It also became quite apparent that these characterizations of North Korea as strange, dangerous, melancholic, and pathetic—in short, as Other and, as I will suggest, as inhuman—bore a strong resemblance to how Asian Americans have long been racialized. Recognizing these similarities between how North Koreans and Asian Americans were racialized was a powerful moment for me, one that has taken years to digest. Such depictions often paint North Korea as a relic from the Cold War era, a time characterized by volatile dictatorships, constant nuclear threats, and antiquated cultural and political practices. These kinds of representations, of course, stand in sharp contrast to those of the United States, which has long proclaimed itself to be a global peacekeeping force. Such imaginings of North Korea as a place of absolute difference—whether found in scholarship or in Western media and culture—presume a measure of objective distance that have made it difficult for me to find a place to insert my own story. But gaining insight into both the structure of knowledge production about North Korea and the affinities between North Korea and Asian America has let me begin to sketch out a different set of racial geographies in which it is possible to consider North Korea in terms of relationality and make space for diasporic positionalities.

I have also realized the personal implications of what began as a project about trying to understand the Orientalized representations that have circulated in Canada and the United States and that structure diasporic relations to North Korea. My maternal grandparents were from North Hamgyong-do province in what is now North Korea; my grandfather's hometown is Chongjin, and my grandmother's is Hoeryong. My mother's older brother and sister were born in the northern part of Korea, and the family migrated southward between the end of 1944 and 1947, when my mother was born in Seoul. In 1971, my mother migrated to Canada, and her parents and siblings eventually followed. This is a history of North Korean relations that I became aware of only late into the writing of this book, and by chance when my cousin's wife mentioned that she could tell that my grandmother was originally from the north because of the way she seasoned her food. After this family visit, I confirmed the story with my mother, who provided details about her parents' hometowns and the differences between their class backgrounds and upbringings. She did not share much else about their migration, however, noting that anyone who would know more details had since passed away. My parents and grandparents had never spoken much about their childhood experiences to my brother and me, and the memories they shared had been limited to those about hardship during and after the war and abbreviated versions of the journeys that eventually brought them to Canada. Until very recently, the possibility that my family history could be traced back to anywhere but South Korea had never entered my mind. I had always assumed that ours was a straightforward story of postwar migration from South Korea to Canada.

In Canada, my parents owned a corner store in Rexdale, a working-class suburb of Toronto, and I have often thought of myself as having lived a version of Ins Choi's *Kim's Convenience* without realizing how the specter of North Korea has also been present in my own life, or perhaps to be more precise, how I have lived the intertwining of North and South Korea in the shadows of US empire through the pressures I felt growing up, the foods I ate, the tenor of my family's gatherings, the particular ways we experienced everyday happiness and even joy, and the many silences with which we lived. In reflecting upon these untold family histories, I have been struck by how they illustrate the contrast between the complex histories of the Korean diaspora and our selective practices of narrating—within texts such as the ones described above and in everyday stories—our relations to the various regions of Korea. I will never know if these stories of migration were not shared because my grandparents thought they were unimportant or because they felt it was too difficult to remember the people and places no longer accessible. But the truth might also be that they knew I would not be able to fully comprehend the nuances of their stories and decided not to try sharing them.

I offer this story as the kind of "autobiographical example" that Saidiya Hartman, Christina Sharpe, Y-Dang Troeung, and many others theorize, one that uses "one's own formation as a window onto social and historical processes, as an example of them,"[1] and to reflect upon how diasporic subjectivities can disrupt familiar migrant tropes by attempting to inhabit historical elisions. I also share this story not because it is unique, but precisely because so many diasporic Koreans in Canada and the United States have similar, if not precisely identical, ties to what is now North Korea.

Thinking about our varied relations to North Korea and how they are shaped by contemporary racial politics, Cold War legacies, and the current global order constitutes the core of this project. As a book directly concerned with knowledge production about North Korea, *Brutal Fantasies* addresses the relations of power that structure North Korea and North America (primarily the United States but also with points of articulation with Canada and other parts of the US empire) with the intention of better understanding how the long Cold War continues to inform the global order, diasporic relations, and conceptions of the human in an uneven yet remarkably persistent fashion. It also asks what kind of archive twentieth- and twenty-first-century representations of North Korea offer us, both for knowing North Korea and for understanding the structures of knowledge production that have shaped how the global order is imagined, and how we as readers can position ourselves in relation to these structures. In doing so, my hope is that this book can open up space to engage with the more complex relations and the more nuanced stories that exist between and about North Korea and North America.

Acknowledgments

In the decade that it has taken to imagine, research, write, and rewrite this book, I have had the good fortune to be surrounded by a network of extraordinary people. I cannot thank them enough for their care which, offered in the form of support, encouragement, and generous critique, made it possible for me to complete this project. My first and foremost acknowledgment is to my family: Yusuf, Zahra, and Zidan; my parents, Kim Jung Ah and Kim Youn O; my brother and sister-in-law, Eric and Lillian. Their love, humor, and support are everything.

I am grateful to all the intellectual companions who have enriched my thinking and living over the years by engaging in conversation, reading countless drafts of my work, and creating formal and informal spaces for scholarly work. I thank friends from writing groups, transpacific cultural studies, Asian Canadian intellectual communities, Inter-Asia cultural studies, Canadian studies, Simon Fraser University (SFU), and the University of British Columbia (UBC) for sustaining me with their brilliance, generosity, and kindness: Y-Dang Troeung, Danielle Wong, Chris Lee, Helen Leung, Kimberly Bain, David Chariandy, Christopher Patterson, Candida Rifkind, Andrew Burke, Sophie McCall, Colette Colligan, Robert Diaz, Jane Park, Guy Beauregard, Andy Wang, Audrey Yue, John Erni, Jin-me Yoon, Kirsten McAllister, Vinh Nguyen, Madeleine Thien, Ayesha Chaudry, Rumee Ahmed, David Khang, Yiwen Liu, Cheryl Narumi Naruse, Deanna Reder, and David Coley.

As this book neared completion, my department hosted a manuscript workshop for it. I am grateful to Crystal Baik and Hentyle Yapp for their encouraging and insightful critiques and for being exactly the right readers for this book. Thank you also to UBC's Department of English Language and Literatures, my former head Patsy Badir, and Kihan Yoon-Henderson for supporting the workshop.

My deep gratitude to Ken Wissoker for being a superb editor. Under his editorial guidance, I was able to find my voice. I will always be thankful for his insights, encouragement, and patience as I wrote this book. My appreciation also goes to Kate Mullen, Ihsan Taylor, Stephanie Attia, and the rest of the wonderful team at Duke University Press. Many thanks to my indexer, Paula Durbin-Westby.

This book has benefited enormously from the labor of many research assistants. In addition to compiling research materials, reading drafts, discussing ideas, and copyediting, they have supported this project with their enthusiasm and by offering keen insights. Many thanks to Kihan Yoon-Henderson, Dylan Jackson, Tina Kong, Ethan Eu, Joshua Trichilo, and Jade Shan. I am also indebted to Bev Neufeld, SFU's extraordinary research grants facilitator, whose feedback on numerous drafts of a grant proposal was enormously helpful in conceptualizing this project. My gratitude also to Selma Bidlingmaier for tracking down and sending me a copy of Sung-Hyung Cho's *Verliebt, Verlobt, Verloren* from Germany, and to Ulrike Zöllner for her assistance in translating the German dialogue in the film into English for me so I could watch it. I am grateful to Krys Lee, who generously shared her time with me to talk about her work. My thanks to Andy Wang, Guy Beauregard, John Erni, Audrey Yue, JP Catungal, and the Vancouver Institute for Social Research for giving me the opportunity to present parts of this project.

An earlier version of part of chapter 2 was published as "Figuring North Korean Lives: Reading at the Limits of Human Rights," in *The Subject(s) of Human Rights: Crises, Violations, and Asian/American Critique*, ed. Cathy Schlund-Vials, Guy Beauregard, and Hsiu-Chuan Lee (Philadelphia: Temple University Press, 2020), 217–32. Thank you to the editors and to Temple University Press for publishing my contribution as part of their collection.

This book is supported in part by funding from the Social Sciences and Humanities Research Council. It is also supported by UBC's Scholarly Publication Fund Award.

Introduction

CULTURAL FANTASIES OF

THE INHUMAN

In his post-9/11 State of the Union address, President Bush gave an impassioned speech updating the American public on the measures that had been taken to liberate women and children from the Taliban government and to protect the world from terrorists trained in Afghanistan camps. Firm, even jubilant at times, about the actions the US would continue to take to further its war on terror, President Bush noted that while the US had dealt with the threat of Afghanistan, there were several other regimes that it had its eye on. Naming North Korea, Iran, and Iraq as part of "an axis of evil" that "pose[d] a grave and growing danger" to global peace, he described North Korea as "a regime arming with missiles and weapons of mass destruction, while starving its citizens."[1] Yet it is worth underscoring that this representation condemning the state as a force of absolute evil within a post-9/11 landscape is only one of many incarnations that North Korea has taken within the Western cultural imagination during the late twentieth and early twenty-first centuries.[2] As Cold War thrillers such as *The Man-*

churian Candidate (novel 1959; film 1962) illustrate,³ North Korea's ideologies and its relationships with the major Communist powers China and the former USSR meant that it was viewed as part of the Red Scare in the post–World War II period. Since then, the US media, feature films, documentary films, memoirs, novels, human rights commissions, and human rights testimonies have tended to depict North Korea as dangerous, given its leaders' erratic behavior in making nuclear threats; needy, because of its malnourished population; and melancholic, with countless Korean families remaining separated by the impenetrable demilitarized zone (DMZ). These repetitions convey at once the absolute foreignness and relative inconsequentiality of North Korea for North American publics. These familiar, perhaps even banal, representations reveal much about the unconscious structures of the contemporary global order and the affects that signal racialized alterity.⁴ This book attempts to explore why North Korea is known in these terms within North America as it traces the consequences of this knowledge production.

Brutal Fantasies examines everyday representations of North Korea for how they articulate and also contest the assumptions of distance and difference that underpin understandings of the global order by foregrounding questions about perspective, positioning, context, and narrative fashioning. While representations of North Korea reinforce the West's perception that the country is a time capsule from the Cold War era, those same discourses depict Canada and the United States as part of a dynamic and modern landscape. And yet, as I argue in this book, there are ways of reading North Korea that challenge this narrative of modern "EuroAmerica and its 'shadow'" by critiquing its assumptions and effects while also recognizing the other complex relations that exist between North Korea and the United States.⁵ By opening with these observations, my intention is to highlight how North Korea gets read as a signifier of a bygone era and to ask what is at stake—intellectually, affectively, and materially—in these representations as they are made part of dominant narratives of the Cold War as well as of the narratives told by the Korean diaspora.

The West, in many ways, is an inadequate shorthand that I use to signal a particular post-1945 formation in which various discourses of capitalist modernity, liberalism, the Cold War, human rights, colonialism, imperialism, and race intersect without always coalescing in a consistent or even harmonious fashion. While these forces are at work in geographies outside the West, they are mobilized most often by Western countries and used, to name just one purpose, to disavow sites such as North Korea as illiberal.⁶ Rather than perceiving the unknown dimensions of North Korea as aspects to be recovered and mapped, I argue that the fantasy of an unknowable and illiberal North Korea is integral to how it functions as part of a discursive formation in the United States and, more broadly, in the Global South. This illiberal differentiation is tied to a practice of viewing North Korea through a Cold War analytic even as we, in the Global North, understand ourselves to be in a post–Cold War era. Moreover, as I will demonstrate, these fantasies are part of a larger constellation of Cold War affects that racialize diasporic Asians in the United States. Fantasy production, as Neferti Tadiar demonstrates through her study of the neocolonial relations between the Philippines and the United States, "names a socio-symbolic logic or dreamwork obtain[ed] in the organization of the international community and the scene of its exchanges (the affairs of the world market and international relations)," structured by universal ideals such as security and global civil society.[7] Fantasies of North Korea operate in a similar fashion to affirm the hegemonic desires of the current global order or, as Leslie Bow defines fantasy, as "a screen for projecting cultural and political desires."[8] By defining the appropriate purveyors of freedom and violence for the rest of the world, these fantasies of North Korea generate a sense of global intimacy for those seeking to qualify the human through liberal understandings of agency.

Central to this project is the concept of the inhuman that I take up in two primary ways (and return to later in this introduction to provide more critical context). In the first, North Korea is an inhuman figure that is bizarre, cruel, and melancholic, thereby marking the limits of the human as imagined in a postwar world—the human idealized in terms of dignity, freedom, sociability, culture or political life[9]—and embodying qualities, values, and behaviors that are antithetical to those of the universal human. But North Korea is also constructed as an inhuman figure in a second sense as it functions as techne, or what Pheng Cheah in his study of globalization, the human, and the inhuman defines as "a technical attitude toward other human beings [that] reduces them to objects for instrumental use."[10] In this other sense, the inhuman is reduced to its function or purpose, acting "as a means rather than as an end in itself."[11] Thus we might think of North Korea as a kind of stock figure that sits in the background of many Cold War and post–Cold War narratives, inhuman in terms of how it is both crafted as a figure and instrumentalized in these narratives. Used to emplot, to borrow Hayden White's term, a dominant narrative of the Cold War, the figure of North Korea plays a crucial role in the transformation of "what would otherwise remain only a chronologically ordered series of events with the formal coherency of the kind of plot structures met with in narrative fiction."[12] Often functioning as a device to further plot or reinforce narrative structures, North Korea adds urgency to stories of humanity but is rarely ever taken up as the main subject of them.

In these narratives, whether they take the form of internet memes about Kim Jong Un or news items about the devastating conditions defectors have fled, the threat of nuclear weapons or, more recently, the launching of air balloons with bags of waste attached over South Korea,[13] North Korea is portrayed as a figure that is variously comic and tragic. Pertinent here are the classical definitions of comedy and tragedy that continue to shape Western storytelling. Aristotle's observations about these genres are useful guides as he notes that comedy takes as its focus men who are "worse than the average" and those who are "ridiculous" and that tragedy is a form that makes us feel both pity and fear in order to then experience catharsis.[14] These deep-seated ideas about comedy and tragedy are crucial for understanding how North Korea is imagined today and also for understanding the kinds of responses they elicit in Western audiences, both for their affective dimensions and for the actions they in turn generate. Given that, as White points out, there is no inherent reason for plotting any sequence of events as tragedy or as comedy since stories are told or written but not found,[15] I ask how these global stories come to take the shape they do. At the same time, I recognize that North Korea does not often sit at the forefront of the United States' imagination and, given its positioning, functions more as a minor tragedy or comedy for the American public. Because there is less pressure to resolve the tensions it poses, North Korea can trigger feelings similar to Sianne Ngai's ugly feelings, ones that are "explicitly *a*moral and *non*cathartic, offering no satisfactions of virtue, however oblique, nor any therapeutic or purifying release."[16] Since literary and cultural forms influence "how the social order and its subjects are imagined, articulated, and effected,"[17] North Korea's abjectness works to reinforce the normativity of Western subjects and values, thereby justifying and even helping to prolong a post–Cold War global order.

These familiar Cold War narratives tend to eclipse other stories that can be told about this period, including a complex network of histories and narratives of the Cold War that Heonik Kwon calls decompositional histories. Taking Vietnam and South Korea as his case studies, Kwon writes a postcolonial account that intends to "break out of the global abstraction of the cold war and attend to its diverse, contrary historical realities across locales."[18] This version not only draws attention to neglected histories but also revisits long-standing assumptions that shape how the Cold War is known. For instance, we are reminded that while the beginnings of the Cold War are often debated by historians, "there is a strong consensus in contemporary literature that the end of the cold war is a fait accompli, a universal historical reality."[19] But while 1989 may have signaled the end of the Cold War for those who understood it primarily as an ideological conflict between the United States and the Soviet Union, in places that experienced active fighting and lived the Cold War "both as a politically bifurcating and radicalizing social order and as a geopolitical order,"[20] not all aspects of it are over. Following Kwon and many new Cold War studies scholars who examine the multiple temporalities of the Cold War as well as the range of structures, relations, and events it produced, I consider how this bifurcated structure continues to affect human rights and diaspora via the figure of North Korea, even as the twenty-first century has set aside the paradigm of the Cold War in favor of neoliberalism and globalization.

At the heart of this project is a belief that representations of North Korea are deeply entangled with the racial logics that construct Asia as a distant region and Asians in the United States as foreign others. *Brutal Fantasies* argues that as objects of knowledge for the United States, North Korea and diasporic Asians are constructed within scholarly and popular imaginations through shared logics whose terms of emergence and circulation are tied to histories of imperialist expansion that reached new heights through Cold War racializing projects. As Christina Klein notes, US postwar expansion generated a discourse of racial tolerance and inclusion that served as its official ideology.[21] But these changes to US immigration policies took place during the late 1960s and early 1970s as the US continued to engage in proxy wars in Asia and Africa. Rather than signaling a change in how Asian migrants were viewed within and outside of the United States, "national inclusion was premised on the very notion that their lives were expendable in order to safeguard the freedoms promised by the nation-state."[22] Klein and other scholars such as Nikhil Pal Singh and Heonik Kwon note that this rhetoric of racial inclusion was tied to a commitment to quash communism rather than to a genuine desire to promote equality. As Singh historicizes US multiculturalism within the contexts of American imperialism and the culture wars since the 1940s, he argues that "anti-communism was the modus operandi for a political project in which a racial animus and an imperial ambition remained paramount."[23] Thus the color line that W. E. B. Du Bois called the problem of the twentieth century was actually a doubled line as it "turned out to be as much about the color of human belief and thought as about the physical color of the human body."[24]

In the case of Korean migrants who relocated to the United States, or to an allied country such as Canada, during the post–Korean War era, many would have believed that the price of racial inclusion was an embrace of capitalist and democratic ideals and a public distancing of oneself from communism and, by extension, from North Korea. Stories such as those told by Eun-Joung Lee in the Legacies of Korean War online archive about how she had not known about her father's blacklisting from the South Korean university system (which was one of the reasons for her parents' migration to the United States) draw attention to the censuring of North Korea–related discussions, even within familial spaces.[25] The effects of this epistemological structure on the relations between North Korea, North Korean migrants, and Korean diasporas can be seen in the limited place of North Korea within diasporic stories. The structures of the Cold War shaped migrant lives in the United States and beyond by rendering uncomfortable, and perhaps even taboo, topics such as Korean politics during the Cold War, or the friends and kin who remained in North Korea.[26] Exceptions existed, as shown in Jason Lee's short documentary film, *Letters from Pyongyang*, which focuses on Korean Canadians and others in diasporic Korean communities who got in touch with overseas committees in hopes of finding out what happened to their loved ones in North Korea.[27] As a result of his efforts, Lee and his father were eventually granted permission to visit North Korea and meet with their remaining relatives. But the casting of North Korea as a minor villain in Cold War narratives has impacted how the Korean diaspora narrates North Korea more often as an imagined entity than as part of a common set of histories or experiences. As a notable lacuna within diasporic memory, North Korea is frequently configured as a distant site of loss, sympathy, or curiosity for younger generations who know of it mostly as the focus of humanitarian efforts or of religious missions undertaken by Korean and non-Korean church groups that try to save North Korea from itself.[28]

Valuable insights can be gleaned if we approach North Korea in terms of what Lisa Yoneyama calls "transwar connectivity," a phrase she coins to describe "the *ability* to make connections, to perceive affinities and convergences of geohistorical elements that have worked together to constitute mid-twentieth-century violence."[29] Critiquing the tendency of the Japanese public to read Okinawa's experiences under the expansion of the Japanese colonial empire during the nineteenth-century and the US military presence in the twenty-first century as discrete rather than as intertwined histories—in other words, neglecting their transwar connectivity—Yoneyama's *Cold War Ruins* asks how remembering their connections "might generate an unlearning that critically unsettles the way we believe we know our history."[30] Yoneyama is one of a number of scholars who trace what we might call the long Cold War in terms of repressed knowledges, along with others, such as Oswaldo de Rivero, who contributes insight into how the rhetoric of development that permeated twentieth-century discussions of emerging nation-states masked the inherent unviability of the majority of these economies. Thomas Borstelmann attends to the intertwining of US civil rights and global decolonization movements with their respective traditions of white supremacy. Sunny Xiang reads Cold War documents and literature through tone in order to explore the Cold War not only for its "new structures of governmentality, but also [as] an imperial poetics that operationalized diminution and occlusion."[31] And Randall Williams identifies the continuities between the pre– and post–World War II eras, noting that rather than rectifying violence, human rights is "the privileged epistemic form for political violence."[32] This body of scholarship illuminates the constancy of a global order rooted in colonialism, imperialism, and racial capitalism whose terms and mechanisms for domination have been shifting throughout the twentieth and twenty-first centuries. The figuration of North Korea as inhuman offers another opportunity to consider what is at stake in the "epistemic repression"[33] of the connections between multiple systems of violence, domination, colonialism, and imperialism. North Korea as a prompt asks what might be discerned if we read the Cold War and post–Cold War eras together and as constituting a long Cold War, a formation rooted in earlier colonialisms and imperialisms whose effects are, to borrow, Xiang's words, "often quotidian and still ongoing."[34]

I read diaspora's relationship to North Korea as an instance of racial affect in which difference is constructed relationally and naturalized through feeling. In *The Melancholy of Race*, Anne Anlin Cheng directs attention to how racialization operates on a psychic level in order to ensure that scholars attend not only to the social and legal dimensions of race but also to "the more immaterial, unquantifiable repository of public and private grief that has gone into the making of the so-called minority subject and that sustains the notion of 'one nation.'"[35] Racial melancholia offers a means of understanding how the "loss" of North Korea is intertwined with—and perhaps to a degree even structures—diasporic subjectivity through a complex dynamic of rejection, attachment, and internalization.[36] But racial melancholia is not the only affect through which North Korea is constructed in terms of racial difference, neither by diasporans nor by non-diasporans. If, following Alexander Weheliye, we define "race not as a biological or cultural classification but as a set of sociopolitical processes that discipline humanity into full human, not-quite-humans, and nonhumans,"[37] we can see how other reactions such as shock, disgust, and confusion also reinforce a sense of distance and difference from North Korea.

To conceptualize diasporic Asians and North Korea, then, as part of the same racial formation is also to reflect upon how we encounter these representations and how they circulate as comparable forms of anti-Asian racist sentiment that exceed geographical regions. At stake in refusing to accept North Korea as an uncomplicated signifier of inhuman Asianness is a commitment to understanding how North Korea ties together the longer histories of the dehumanization of Asians in US settler colonial projects with the disposability of Asian life during the hot wars of the Cold War period. In other words, North Korea offers a means of reading the racialization of Asians in settler colonialism and the Cold War through each other. Thus, another way of complicating Cold War analytics is to attend to the particular intertwining of race and ideology as well as to understanding North Korea in relation to local knowledges and national histories other than just EuroAmerica's. Imagining Asian America or Korean diasporas in relation to North Korea requires acknowledging complex, often even conflicting, personal and intellectual connections to unexpected sites and communities. But the payoff of understanding North Korea in terms of intimacies and unruliness is that it yields new ways of understanding the Cold War and post–Cold War eras and their racializing projects.

Messy Objects, New Methodologies

Brutal Fantasies comes out of thinking that is informed by conversations taking place in Asian American studies, Asian Canadian studies, Global Asias, Inter-Asia cultural studies, and Asian diaspora studies. While these are overlapping spaces in which many of the same scholars and texts circulate, their different structures and geographies illuminate the messiness of Cold War logics in novel ways. Read together, these various approaches to Asias and Asian diasporas prompt a reckoning with colonialisms, imperialisms, Cold Wars, and globalizations as multiple and simultaneous, thus countering tendencies to conceptualize history in the singular, linear, and homogeneous terms inherited from area studies. I offer this book as a contribution to these conversations as it intends to name moments that frustrate, or even refuse, area studies framings and universal paradigms of the human in order to pivot toward different conversations about North Korea. Intending to recognize the minor inhuman as a figure that is not simply strange but also at times strangely familiar, I focus on North Korea as an assemblage of geopolitical speculations that seem to be about place and people but that in fact say more about the power dynamics embedded in who gets to read and frame North Korea itself.

This project asks how North Korea can be conceptualized outside of the militarized frameworks of academic area studies while sharing the critical energies of Global South projects. In posing this question, *Brutal Fantasies* engages in conversation with scholars who address Cold War illegibilities. For example, Lisa Yoneyama, Jodi Kim, Laura Kang, and Y-Dang Troeung engage, respectively, with transwar justice and redress culture, with the entanglement of US imperialism and Cold War logics in Asia, with Asian women as a prompt for reconfiguring post–Cold War forms of victimization and violence, and with the erasure of Cambodian refugee lifeworlds.³⁸ This body of scholarship reasserts the need to think about how the Cold War disrupted the lives of people situated in Asia and other non-Western countries, and how it continues to reverberate in those spaces and for their diasporas.

Inspired by these various intellectual and regional approaches to Asias and Asian diasporas as well as by postcolonial, queer, materialist, and Black studies theorists to understand North Korea and diasporic Asians in the United States through concepts of the human and the intimate, my intention is to think relationally rather than comparatively. This is a departure from much of the critical and popular discourse that frames North Korea as a security problem by focusing on nuclear weapons and the need for disarmament. To approach North Korea in terms set by area studies is to imagine it as an unknowable entity in order to manage it, thereby disciplining North Korea in both senses of the word. The colonial dimensions of the post–World War II US disciplinary formations of area studies were intended "to train young men and some women in the necessary language, so they'd be able to interrogate the enemy and to secure the necessary data to carry on a successful war. In other words, it was directed toward winning the war and defeating the enemy."³⁹ The Cold War project of controlling regions required a militaristic weaponization of knowledge, especially language acquisition and cultural "mastery," to infiltrate the local community from a position of power.

And while the end of the Cold War led to "a new raison d'être for area studies, namely the new needs of the contemporary US empire,"⁴⁰ the binary structure it established between the West and the Rest continues to shape knowledge production far beyond the confines of area studies. Tadiar offers a sharp critique of this separation as it emerges in the practice of Western critics who write about gender, race, and sexuality by universalizing Western understandings of difference:

> You know your theoretical acts are local, even as you are aware of the global, but still you cannot seem to retain the fact that this is the place where the brackets are made and placed, the areas conceived and implemented, the global defined (for those areas to demonstrate, resist, or elaborate), which sets the stage for all those other indeterminate "differences" not encapsulated by the ones you know so well to persist in some inchoate form that you are likely to call "cultural."⁴¹

Shu-mei Shih also writes about the persistence of divides as they shape Western critical thought. She notes that even as area studies has undergone certain transformations (as evidenced by its less combative relationship to disciplines and as shaped by the United States' newer and more diffusive need for information), it still acts as a resource for US empire by "continu[ing] to repress the racial logic of the empire vis-à-vis racialized populations out there in the areas as well as its internal racial minorities within the metropole."[42] She turns to "the affective economy of area studies" to map the complicated relations that area studies experts have to their objects of study (and their tendency either to marry their objects or to be hostile toward them) in order to explain Asian studies' tense relations to Asian American studies.[43] As Tadiar's and Shih's observations make painfully clear, current iterations of area studies not only continue to diminish non-white and non-Western bodies and forms of knowledge by centering the West but also influence how non–area studies scholars conceptualize difference more broadly.

This book interrupts this practice of disciplining subjects through difference and distinction by recognizing the messiness of North Korea as an object produced in the post–World War II period. While area studies approaches assume that North Korea constitutes a geopolitical problem that can be solved by knowing and mastering it, I suggest that the impossibility of fully knowing North Korea makes it a moving, but stabilizing, signifier for the global order. North Korea is an object that justifies the actions that national governments and international organizations take toward it by functioning in much the same way that Edward Said described the Orient as operating for Orientalists: "At most, the 'real' Orient provoked a writer to his vision; it very rarely guided it."[44] The structures that produce Orientalism and North Korea as objects of knowledge for Orientalists and area studies experts are designed to maintain the distance between the expert and his object and to ensure that "the Orientalist" remains "outside the Orient, both as an existential and as a moral fact."[45] Such a formulation imagines the Orient and North Korea as discrete and passive entities, relying on experts to interpret them and bestow meaning, rather than as unruly and knowing subjects. But if we expand our gaze as we look toward North Korea to also include the authoritative manner in which Western experts claim North Korea, we can see that this attitude reveals much about the post–Cold War order. Here I am inspired by Kadji Amin's critique of queer studies for how it always reduces its subjects to either good or bad ones as it imagines alternative social worlds. The problem with idealization is that it "tends to be ahistorical, since history, in the Foucauldian sense, is nothing if not the strategic mobility of shifting relational networks within which no one entity can occupy the position of resistance for very long."[46] And while it may be true that subjects can be idealized and resistant only for a finite length of time, the example of North Korea suggests that bad objects can endure indefinitely.

While North Korea is an object of intense scrutiny for area studies, it is comparatively understudied within Asian American studies. With the exception of Christine Hong's voluminous scholarship on North Korea, Korean American studies has tended to engage primarily with South Korea. This is not to say that North Korea has been excluded altogether from the field of Asian American studies; scholars such as Jodi Kim, Daniel Kim, and Crystal Baik include North Korea as part of their book-length studies, and Eleana Kim's *Making Peace with Nature* turns our attention to the discourses of peace, militarism, and ecology as they shape how we know the DMZ.[47] Rather, it is to say that North Korea is not the main focus of Asian American scholarship. Much of the critical energies of Korean American studies are directed toward critiquing the structures of imperialism, militarization, migration, and citizenship that produce the conditions of racialized life for Korean subjects in the United States, often mapping the migrations from South Korea that were produced by the Korean War. North Korea, embedded within socialist worlds and functioning as a figure of illiberalism, is an object less directly useful for critiques of capitalism and liberalism. But what it offers are other ways of understanding Korean diasporas and US imperialism by reframing concepts of resistance, agency, and diaspora. North Korea puts pressure on Asian American studies to decenter the United States as it engages with narratives that neither begin nor end (always) in America in order to produce more expansive conceptions of politics and transnationality.

Mapping the discursive field within which North Korea is located requires negotiations with how it is positioned on the edges of Asian American studies and human rights scholarship, how it is claimed by area studies, and how it looms in the background of critical Cold War studies. As anthropologist Sonia Ryang notes, North Korea is an object that resists conventional methodologies and that requires unorthodox ones.[48] But at the same time, forging a different approach is not a straightforward matter. As a literary and cultural studies scholar situated in Canada, it has been a challenge for me to hold onto my diaspora-centered questions about North Korea while navigating the deep bodies of scholarship that tend to take up North Korea, diaspora, the Cold War, and cultural studies through very different methodologies and objects. My own questions come out of seeing North Korea in what Bruce Cumings calls *parallax* terms. He uses this concept to describe how changing American perceptions of East Asia do not necessarily "represent the reality of shifting power relations" but instead "seem to mark shifting points along a line of observation."[49] Similarly, reading from the vantage point offered by diaspora makes it possible to discern the relations of power that determine prevailing opinions of North Korea and how various disciplines, experts, institutions, and systems of power construct North Korea as an object of knowledge and the material and symbolic effects that these constructions have produced for those in the diaspora, human rights scholars and activists, North Korean migrants, and North Korea as a nation. By taking cultural representations of North Korea as my entry point, I attempt to shift conversations that have fixated on the geopolitical dimensions of North Korea as well as those that center South Korea within investigations into cultural production and diaspora. My intention is to think about why North Korea as an ideation is needed as a geopolitical touchstone and about how North Korea can also act as a very different kind of reference point for those who need it differently.

Toward a Genealogy of the Minor Inhuman

To understand North Korea as a cultural fantasy of the inhuman that accrues meaning as it circulates throughout the United States and sites shaped by US imperialism, I engage with North Korea as a place, a government, and a people, but also as the thing that gets returned to repeatedly, with performative force, as these representations inform how North Korea gets lived. And in this way, I interrupt what Saidiya Hartman in another context refers to as "the violence of abstraction."[50] Akin to Alexander Weheliye's reading of blackness as "the conglomerate effect of different racializing assemblages,"[51] I read the overlapping assemblages that make up North Korea as a cultural fantasy rooted in the multiple logics and historical formations that give rise to how the figure of Asia is imagined as inhuman, a category distinct from, but nonetheless still related to, the subhuman that has often been used to racialize Black and Indigenous subjects.

Reading with Sylvia Wynter, Hortense Spillers, and other Black studies scholars, Weheliye examines the human as a disciplining and racializing category by asking how the deeply sedimented logics of race demand "the barring of nonwhite subjects from the category of the human as it is performed in the modern west."[52] Excluded from the human ("as the postcolonial variant of Fanon's category of les damnés") in order to accommodate the overrepresentation of the Western bourgeoisie, racialized and Indigenous subjects are organized into various subgenres of the human.[53] Race is the principle used to subordinate and exclude certain subjects,[54] with Black and Indigenous peoples functioning "as the physical referent of the projected irrational/subrational Human Other to its civic-humanist, rational self-conception.... All other modes of being human would instead have to be seen not as the alternative modes of being human that they are 'out there,' but adaptively, as the lack of the West's ontologically absolute self-description."[55] By mapping European colonialism from the medieval period to settler colonialism in North America, Wynter makes visible the precise ways in which Black and Indigenous subjects are conceptualized as subhuman while acknowledging the "marked differential in the degrees of subrationality, and of not-quite-humanness, to which each group was to be relegated within the classificatory logic of the West's ethnocultural field."[56]

I want to hold onto Wynter's point that the not-quite-human is a capacious category marked by various classificatory systems in order to ask what version of the not-quite-human North Korea enacts for the West. Just as the different forms of the *subrational* or *subhuman* that racialize Black and Indigenous subjects cannot be understood as equivalent to each other, the *inhuman* offers yet another distinct form of racialization with its own set of cultural logics, racial affects, and geopolitical specificities. Tracing how the Asian has come to be imagined as inhuman requires that we expand our geographies to include sites and powers that lie outside of the circuits of European colonialism and therefore need to be historicized differently. By rerouting our inquiry through North Korea, we produce another genealogy of those excluded from the human; more specifically, engaging with North Korea as a genre of the inhuman reveals how race and racialization are articulated through Cold War ideologies and how the particular forms that these relations take—through, for example, representations of North Korea as an anachronistic nation, North Koreans as starved and dehumanized masses, and North Korean leaders as resembling cult leaders—can be investigated as Asian forms of racialization that exceed North Korea's borders.

Much is revealed if these dynamics of inhumanness embodied by North Korea and North Koreans—as figures to be pitied, feared, or mocked—are positioned in relation to the kinds of techno-Orientalist representations that Jane Park describes in terms of "oriental style"; that Leslie Bow describes as "racist love"; and that David Roh, Betsy Huang, and Greta Niu describe in the context of Asian American studies. For Park, Oriental style is a means of reading the representation of East Asia in Hollywood films in order to understand "the domesticated other we think we know, the other we admire and love and occasionally accept as one of our own; the other we do not realize that we fear and perhaps hate."[57] The central preoccupation for Park is to understand how Orientalism is transformed from yellow peril to yellow future as the Asiatic is associated with twenty-first-century technology and circulates transnationally.[58] Bow takes up these ambiguous feelings by directing our attention to objects such as a cute anthropomorphic cartoon that "operates as a form of visual hate speech, a racial microaggression—that is also somewhat adorable."[59] This critique of racial abstraction helps us understand the split feeling that structures racist love, one "in which attraction masks anxiety."[60] Thus for Bow, techno-Orientalism should be read for how "it also engages a specific affective structure; techno-Orientalism is tech feeling as anti-Asian bias."[61] Roh, Huang, and Niu's collection on techno-Orientalism adds to these interrogations by approaching them from the perspective of Asian American studies. In their introduction, they ask whether "techno-Orientalism [is] still Orientalist if contemporary techno-discourse is being authored principally by Asians, seemingly without regard for the Westerners who look on with a mixture of anxiety and envy?"[62] While much of techno-Orientalism comes out of post-Fordist anxieties about shifting global power and the outsourcing of work to Asia, this diagnosis by Asian American studies often leaves out North Korea. While South Korea offers a site that is useful for analyses of techno-Orientalist fantasy, North Korea remains a problem for this discourse.

Bow's notion of the "*suggestively* human" is a useful analytic for grasping how North Korea becomes a particular genre of the inhuman that is imagined to be unfeeling, trivial, and inconsequential while also being configured as threatening.[63] But the suggestively human in North Korea's case operates somewhat differently from the techno-Orientalist futures that Park, Bow, Roh, Huang, and Niu sketch out, given North Korea's associations with dated rather than with cutting-edge forms of technology. The persistent association of North Korea with nuclear missiles, for example, underscores its Cold War framings, thus making it menacing and inhuman but nonetheless cast in terms of near obsolescence. Unlike the techno-Orientalist imaginaries that configure the Asian in terms of a threatening future, North Korea is a machine-like figure associated with bygone dangers that continue to haunt us.

To take seriously the performative dimensions of North Korea is to ask how and why it becomes for the West a figure of the minor inhuman upon a stage of nations. North Korea is often viewed as embodying a form of inhuman strangeness or cruelty, one that is ever present in the background, like a minor form of white noise that never fully occupies our attention. To describe this form of the inhuman as minor is not to suggest it is insignificant "but rather to indicate the complex relations of power at work" and to ask, as Park does of oriental style, "what kind of cultural work it does in and at the margins."[64] Moreover, to think of "the minor as a method" draws into focus "the epistemological assumptions and ontological conditions that uphold the order of things, the major," and it illuminates the structures that produce the figure of the inhuman as a counterpoint to the political-juridical category of the human that gains prominence in a post–World War II era with the ascendancy of human rights discourses and through the formation of the United Nations with its attendant documents such as the Universal Declaration of Human Rights (UDHR; 1948), the Refugee Convention (1951), and the Refugee Protocol (1967).[65] Within such discourses, the human is figured in universal terms, and the paradigm of liberal human rights is "an antipolitical 'moral discourse' [that] has functioned to evacuate historical and geopolitical contexts, and indeed to imply the obscenity of explanatory frames other than the most immediate."[66] Christine Hong argues that this refusal to contextualize human rights has produced a deep forgetting that "wipes the slate of colonialism clean, adopting a conveniently presentist perspective."[67] To counter this amnesia, we would be wise to heed Randall Williams's call to "shift our analytical perspective from one that assumes that imperialism is a problem *for* international law, to one that grasps their mutually constitutive relationship."[68] Conceptualizing human rights as independent from economic and social rights or from social and historical contexts limits what it can achieve; this limitation can be seen in the driving vision of the UDHR, which outlined a new mode of citizenship that welfare states would then provide, but which overlooked the fact that most of the global population lived under empires rather than in welfare states.[69] By refusing to take the material conditions in which people live into account, human rights discourses abandon equality as a goal. Thus, as Samuel Moyn argues, human rights have "become our language for indicating that it is enough, at least to start, for our solidarity with our fellow human beings to remain weak and cheap."[70] In other words, human rights discourses, by design, idealize the neoliberal subject and exclude all others from consideration. By promoting a liberal moralism that eschews the need for historical framing, human rights discourses continuously produce North Korea as a figure of the minor inhuman. Chapter 2 of this book, by turning to human rights testimonies and North Korean memoirs, examines how human rights discourses shape perceptions of North Korea.

There are many examples that can be drawn from Korean history that make it clear that Koreans were not imagined as the subjects of human rights. For instance, the imposition of an Allied trusteeship on Korea at the end of World War II framed the country as a minor, incapable of self-governance. And, as historian Monica Kim astutely observes, the stakes of the nonrecognition of Korea become apparent if we locate it within the series of anti-colonial movements that took place in the post-1945 era in order to ask how they changed the terms of warfare: "Whether India, Indochina, or Algeria, the demands for sovereign recognition shook the very foundation of Western colonial power and thus its global reach: its prerogative to deny recognition, whether in terms of humanity or the waging of violence. War, we must remember, was a privilege accorded only to recognized states."[71] Here, I would add Hong's observation that "the various human rights vernaculars—anti-colonial, race radical, communitarian, Third World"—that emerged during the Cold War with the intention of making a more inclusive and representative humanism have largely been sidelined within international human rights paradigms.[72] By investigating the ways in which North Korea becomes imagined as a minor inhuman figure rather than as a subject of history, I seek to understand the global order in a post–Cold War era in terms of racial affect, particularly how it manifests in its discourses of Cold War justice, the utopian aspirations of national and global projects, and humanitarian interventions.

Contextualizing the "Hermit Kingdom"

Since many detailed accounts and sophisticated analyses of the division of Korea at the end of the Pacific War and the subsequent Korean War already exist,[73] I limit my retelling of these events to a brief outline. The dominant historical narrative of North Korea and South Korea as it circulates in the West focuses on the Korean War (1950–53), the armistice, and the establishment of the DMZ.[74] What is typically noted in overviews of Korean history are the territorial aspects of the occupations and conflicts, perhaps because they most easily telegraph the lasting impacts of the war. More specifically, much attention is paid to the division of Korea along the 38th parallel at the end of World War II, when Japan surrendered and the United States and the USSR were given the temporary responsibility of governing the South and the North, respectively, until Korea achieved independence. In effect, this meant that while the country was officially freed from Japanese colonialism at the end of World War II, it was immediately reoccupied by US and Soviet forces. Monica Kim critiques the oddness of the United States' claim to having bestowed freedom on Korea through military occupation by asking, "How did one 'occupy' a former colony of a wartime 'enemy' who had surrendered unconditionally?"[75] This situation of occupied liberation continued as the Republic of Korea (ROK) and the Democratic People's Republic of Korea (DPRK) were founded in 1948 (but only the ROK was recognized by the UN, as the DPRK had not participated in the United Nations' [UN's] supervised democratic elections). Two years later, the two nations were at war with each other, and while the physical fighting came to a halt with the signing of the armistice agreement in 1953, the two sides continue to remain at war, their conflicts merely taking on other forms and occurring in other arenas.[76] In her investigation into prisoners of war (POWs), interrogation rooms, and the Korean War, Monica Kim notes "the locus of war in the 'new' postwar era was the interior worlds of individual people," and the pressing question for nations was: "Who would fashion the new human subject for the world after 1945?"[77]

For the purposes of contextualizing my discussion of how North Korea is produced as a cultural fantasy of the inhuman, I highlight a few pertinent details about how Korean histories have been constructed from complex and often unwieldy cultural memories of Korea.[78] The Korean War is often referred to as the forgotten war, and as many critics remind us,[79] it is unlike the heavily televised Vietnam War, which remains a major event in US history. Instead, the Korean War, the first of the proxy wars in Asia, represented an innovation in the sense that it was the first time that the United States used the UN to execute its military campaign. Ryang, Kwon, and other scholars draw attention to factors such as the Western media, international bodies like the UN, and Cold War politics in order to help us comprehend the specific reasons that the Korean War tends to be forgotten. These elements and circumstances are also relevant for understanding forgetting in relation to Korea more broadly, and for examining the kinds of ahistorical readings that tend to be performed of North Korea.

One of the challenges of contextualizing North Korea is that we are acutely aware of how partial our knowledge of it is, and this limited knowledge has become part of a deeply sedimented narrative of North Korea in the West as well as an implicit justification for the creative license often taken with representations of North Korea. This framing is visible in how the history of North Korea since 1948 has been reduced to what Daniel Kim might call a "potted history,"[80] characterized primarily through the reign of three brutal generations of Kims (Kim Il Sung, Kim Jong-il, and Kim Jong Un); the devastating famine of the 1990s; and the perception of North Korean citizens as inhuman beings incapable of thought, feeling, or resistance. Absent from such skeletal overviews are the complex regional dynamics from the past century that would enable more nuanced understandings of the relationship between the North Korean government and its people and that would guide us in imagining North Korea differently. For instance, the ability of the Kim dynasty to remain in power during and after the famine offers one such necessary window. As Hazel Smith explains, the rest of the world expected that dramatic political changes would take place after the Arduous March, as the famine and economic crisis of the 1990s were referred to within the country. However, this did not occur because the dire economic circumstances and repressive political environment made the idea of political protest unappealing and almost impossible. In the context of North Korea, "regime change activity was risky and much less likely to achieve transformation of daily life compared to the marginal improvements that could be gained by engaging in 'grey market' activity."[81] And, while North Koreans may not have worked to overthrow the government, they became increasingly disillusioned with their government whose struggles against US imperialism and adherence to a philosophy of *juche* were far removed from their own desires to overcome their daily struggles with poverty. That North Koreans may be acting pragmatically with the goal of survival is not a narrative that circulates as easily as the one in which the DPRK continues to exert absolute control over a nation of automaton-like citizens who are as incapable of questioning Kim Jong Un as they had been of questioning his father, the Dear Leader, or grandfather, the Great Leader.

Other details of North Korean history serve to counter the presentist understanding of North Korea as incomprehensible and its leaders' decisions as arbitrary and irrational. Using a longer historical lens that extends beyond World War II not only reminds us that Korea has been subjected to the dominance of Japan, China, and the United States for centuries but also reveals how their imperial legacies continue to shape North and South Korea. For instance, despite the formal conclusion of Japanese colonialism at the end of the Pacific War, vestiges were visible for decades afterward in the social conservatism of South Korea.[82] While the post–World War II US occupation supported the Korean Democratic Party (KDP) because it most closely approximated a liberal democratic position, this move overlooked the fact that the KDP was neither representative of the South Korean population nor was there even a basis for liberal politics within South Korea. Under Japanese rule, Korean society had been composed of peasants and a wealthy landowning class and this structure continued to shape South Korean society after World War II.[83] In contrast, North Korea during this period was motivated by an anti-colonial nationalism that attempted to institute major social reforms with respect to gender and class. While the idealism of gender equity and the introduction of laws that addressed divorce and property rights among other things were unable to fully rectify gender inequality in the post–World War II period, they opened the door for future social changes in North Korea. For example, by the 1990s, women had become the main breadwinners in their households, and this position of economic power helped transform the gendered division of labor and other disparities.[84] Assessing North Korea during this period, Cumings argues that in 1946, North Korea was a place where "those who staffed and benefited from it believed it to be a vast improvement over the previous system; [and] those who suffered from it thought it to be a draconian network that denied all freedom to the individual. Both were probably right."[85]

Nevertheless, inspired by this egalitarian vision, many people left the difficult conditions in Japan and even South Korea following the Korean War to go to North Korea and become part of this new society. But families who remained in

South Korea often faced negative long-term consequences when their close relations crossed into North Korea with the hopes of becoming part of its new socialist vision. Deann Borshay Liem and Ramsay Liem's documentary film *Memory of Forgotten War* illustrates this through the stories of people who experienced social and employment barriers because of their familial ties to North Korea and who, as a consequence, migrated to the United States. Through the stories of four Koreans whose families were torn apart by the war, we are given insight into the deep convictions of those who believed in North Korea's anti-colonial projects and supported its utopic aspirations. At the same time, we also learn about the costs borne by relatives who remained in South Korea. The film draws our attention to the political repercussions for those whose relatives had chosen to head North, as they were unable to advance professionally—like Lee Min Yong, who was denied tenure as a lecturer; or Chun Sun Tae, who was unable to become a diplomat[86]—and also to the immense emotional pain of never being able to speak about these losses, not even to close friends.[87] Lee Min Yong recounts how his two brothers and sister who went to North Korea were erased from their family history through a rewriting of the family register; but these excisions proved to be futile as the government still seemed to know about their existence. The four stories recounted in the film illustrate how politically conservative mechanisms such as South Korea's National Security Law have "maintained the hegemony of anti-Communism in South Korea. Its indiscriminate application to suppress dissent of any kind could render any person a *ppalgaengi* (빨갱이) or a Commie."[88] *Memory of Forgotten War* also contradicts multiculturalism's core belief that migrants move because they desire a better life as individuals speak about how they were pushed to emigrate to the United States as a consequence of the barriers imposed by the South Korean government. While the anti-imperial beliefs that drew Lee Min Yong's siblings to North Korea are often oversimplified by the West as North Korean hostility toward the United States—a point reinforced through anecdotes about school children being taught to see America as the enemy—such a framing requires recontextualizing to also include the anti--colonialism directed toward Japan that marked the emergence of the DPRK and that prompted earlier waves of migration from Korea.[89] As Crystal Mun-hye Baik argues, Lee Min Yong himself undermines such approaches through his "framing of the Korean War *beyond* the binary of good and evil as an attempt to speak against and outside of Cold War historical writing."[90] To complicate US-centric understandings of diaspora, chapter 3 of this book positions North Korea in relation to the Korean migrations that occurred before and after 1948.

At the same time, it is worth noting that North Korea was not always, and in many respects is still not, an isolated hermit kingdom. Since its inception,

North Korea has balanced complex economic and political ties to Russia and China while negotiating often-difficult relations to the United States, Japan, and South Korea. North Korea's less well-known global connections include the exchanges of students, labor, and even orphans with socialist countries such as East Germany, Romania, Poland, Hungary, and Russia during the Cold War.[91] The North Korean children's summer camp, Songdowon International Camp, has been in existence since 1960, and hosts children from countries such as Vietnam, Ireland, and Tanzania.[92] Also, what is often neglected is that North Korea was a prosperous regime until the mid-1980s (boasting a stronger economy than South Korea's until then); it offered economic and political assistance to other Global South countries, including Guyana, Cuba, Algeria, Syria, and Cambodia; and it even functioned as a site of refuge for individuals fleeing the Cultural Revolution in China during the 1960s.[93] As historian Moe Taylor's research on the relationship between North Korea and Guyana reveals, Guyanese prime minister and then-president Linden Burnham's concept of cooperative socialism was heavily influenced by North Korea.[94] During this time, North Korea was a shining socialist model for many newly liberated Global South countries. Closer to home, North Korea was also a source of ideological inspiration for many of the Black Panthers, most notably Eldridge Cleaver, who traveled to North Korea and wrote the foreword to *Juche!*, the collected speeches of Kim Il Sung, which Cleaver praises for outlining "new ideas about the world we live in and the possibilities of human ascendency to brilliant heights of achievement and peace."[95] Cleaver argues that there are valuable lessons to be learned by the American public from North Korean struggles, including how to internationalize a struggle that unites oppressed peoples across the globe.[96] And more recently, in the early 2000s, a few human rights organizations were allowed to enter North Korea.[97] Turning to these forgotten aspects of North Korean history, particularly to North Korea's relations to other nonaligned nations, helps to map the complex networks within which North Korea is situated and to remind us that it was once a more prosperous and influential country.

Intimate Archives

North Korea is the embodiment of twentieth- and twenty-first-century global anxieties about race, nation-states, and world systems. As Bruce Cumings notes when he summarizes the representations of North Korea in the US media in the 1990s, "North Korea ended up thrice-cursed, a Rorschach inkblot eliciting anticommunist, Orientalist, and rogue-state imagery."[98] While North Korea is widely assumed to be an enigmatic and impenetrable space, many scholars have argued otherwise, noting that while it is difficult to gather information about North Korea, such a task is not impossible. Researchers have access to UN testimonies by North Korean refugees, North Korean refugee memoirs, US intelligence reports, and archival materials about North Korea held by enemies and allies alike. As Monica Kim's study of the interrogation of prisoners of war during the Korean War shows, much can be gleaned about North Korea by turning to archives and collecting oral histories from outside of North Korea. North Korea is, moreover, not an illogical and unfathomable nation-state but rather "an understandable place, an anti-colonial and anti-imperial state growing out of a half century of Japanese imperialism and another half century of continuous confrontation with a hegemonic United States and a more powerful South Korea."[99] To build upon this reading of North Korea as understandable, this book engages with cultural texts by Korean diasporic authors or produced through collaborations between North Korean and US writers. Through these alternate writings, I trace a genealogy of the many intimacies between North Korea and the US.

Brutal Fantasies critiques those global ways of knowing North Korea that work to normalize a post–Cold War order, and perhaps even to make it aspirational, by turning to filmic, literary, and media depictions of North Korea. Drawing on a different corpus of materials than is conventionally used by area studies, I examine the epistemological structures that construct North Korea as an imagined object for Americans in order to begin to understand the very real effects these representations have produced for North Korea, North Koreans, and Koreans in the diaspora. For this reason, I ground this analysis in an archive of materials largely written in or translated into English and that centers, but is not only limited to, the United States.

Beginning with an examination of fiction and film by non–Korean American and non–Korean British filmmakers and writers for style and genre, I analyze how North Korea is produced as a site of brutality. I then engage with novels and films produced by Korean American and Korean Canadian writers, living both in North America and in South Korea, and memoirs written collaboratively by North Korean migrants and US writers, to frame the memories, histories, and narratives told by North Koreans and diasporic Koreans as a legitimate body of knowledge about North Korea and, moreover, as what Stuart Hall calls a living archive. To read creative texts by diasporic and migrant Koreans as part of a dynamic archive "contradicts this fantasy of completeness. As work is produced, one is, as it were, contributing to and extending the limits of that to which one is contributing."[100] At the same time, these archives provide opportunities to rethink what we believe we know.

Such an approach to archives and knowledge telegraphs clearly that this project neither presumes the kind of objective distance from its objects that area studies demands nor attempts to exert what Gavin Walker and Naoki Sakai call "remote control."[101] By moving away from an approach to North Korea that presumes that what is needed is a true account to set the record straight, *Brutal Fantasies* joins in conversation with other scholars whose work is visibly informed by their deep personal investments. As Vinh Nguyen reminds us as he reflects upon the experience of finding a photograph of his mother in an archive, "Writing that does not eschew the embodied self but makes it a guiding compass becomes a critical mode of living and survival."[102] If we approach North Korea through our relations to it, rather than our distance from it, we can more easily interrogate the designs and desires that shape scholarly knowledge about North Korea, Asia, and Asians.

The Bizarre, the Inhuman Masses, and the Melancholic

By drawing on North Korean defectors' life writing, media representations, films, and fiction produced in the last twenty years, *Brutal Fantasies* analyzes how Cold War and earlier colonial histories continue to exist as illegible but nonetheless powerful affective legacies. The chapters of this book thus examine the affective economy (composed largely of disbelief, fear, and sadness) present in various articulations of this cultural fantasy of North Korea in order to provide ways of conceptualizing North Korea that counter a Cold War frame.

In chapter 1, I consider how the figure of the minor inhuman is written into the US cultural imagination through the genre of what I call dystopic speculation. Through an analysis of Adam Johnson's bestselling and critically acclaimed novel *The Orphan Master's Son* and the Hollywood feature film *The Interview*, I demonstrate how representations of North Korea draw on familiar tropes centered around the bizarre, the strange, and the inhuman qualities of North Korea. As part of this analysis, I consider how American publics turn to works of fiction in order to speculate about North Korea, given the characterization of the country as an otherwise incomprehensible, nonsensical, and hermetic space. However, it is this very speculation about North Korea and appetite for morbid sensationalism that in turn produces, rather than reflects, North Korea's perpetual unknowability within the global imaginary. I consider how representations of North Korea are underwritten by broader Cold War scripts about freedoms and rights as defined by the Global North, and how the generic signifiers of North Korea reinforce Western ideals. The latter part of the chapter complicates these representations of North Korea by positioning North Korea in relation to South Korea and Japan, two US client states. I turn to an analysis of the British film *The Lovers and the Despot* for how it depicts North Korea's kidnapping of South Korean director Shin Sang-ok and actress Choi Eun-hee. Like the other stories examined in this chapter, *The Lovers and the Despot* also writes North Korea as a villainous Cold War figure even as it expands the geographies in which these figurations play out.

Chapter 2 analyzes how North Korea becomes a fantasy of the minor inhuman as it is instrumentalized for the purposes of human rights discourse but never the subject of human rights. I hold onto the questions of positioning and genre examined in chapter 1 as I critique both how human rights discourse is deployed toward North Korea and the demands placed on North Korean subjects to make themselves legible to global humanitarian publics. This chapter tracks how these events collectively spurred new attention toward North Korean defectors and deepened a market for sensationalist life writing, testimony, and biographies relating to North Korea. Then I consider—by way of an analysis of Blaine Harden's *Escape from Camp 14* (based on the biography of Shin Dong-hyuk)—how these works sensationalize North Korean figures based on their very inhumanness, representing the limits to a human rights–based frame. The chapter concludes by turning to a documentary film, *Camp 14: Total Control Zone*, which lets Shin Dong-hyuk explore additional aspects of his story and, moreover, tell his story in terms that do not fit tidily into the frame of human rights.

Chapter 3 begins unfolding the problem of North Korea as a fantasy of the minor inhuman by examining it within the context of Korean diasporas. My intention here is to begin to unravel what North Korea means to the Korean diaspora, both as an affective touchstone and as a structuring principle. At the same time, I also question how the Korean diaspora is typically narrated in terms of the transits between South Korea and the United States, and read through the intertwined frames of the Korean War, US imperialism, and American migration policy. While unquestionably important, this focus obscures more complex social and familial histories that connect many Korean diasporans to North Korea as well as the relations between a US-centered diaspora and a larger network of Korean migrations that prefigure the Korean War. Through a reading of Krys Lee's *How I Became a North Korean*, I consider how privileging certain circuits, discourses of ethnonationalism, and histories of migration produces subjects legible as part of the Korean diaspora and as national citizens as it renders others minor, inhuman, and vulnerable. I argue that the structures that produce legibility are the same ones that transform North Korea from neighbor or kin into distant, disavowed, and exploitable object. This chapter also models a reading of North Korea in terms of intimate connection in order to ask how the Korean diaspora can begin to understand itself in more complex, varied, and networked terms than current Cold War narratives allow.

The book concludes with an epilogue in which I resituate North Korea within a socialist landscape. Drawing primarily on two independent South Korean documentary films, *The Children Gone to Poland* and *Kim Il Sung's Children*, that depict North Korean orphans who were sent to Eastern Europe in the 1950s, I begin to explore the new directions that are made possible when North Korea is no longer reduced to an inhuman figure that is the antithesis of liberalism and US imperialism.

I

Dystopic Speculation
STYLIZING TRANSPACIFIC VILLAINS

Set sometime in the late 1990s or early 2000s, Adam Johnson's Pulitzer Prize–winning novel *The Orphan Master's Son* (2012) tells the story of Pak Jun Do as he struggles to survive amid the atrocities of North Korea under Kim Jong-il's rule. Following Jun Do from his childhood in an orphanage to his final days in an interrogation cell, the novel sketches Jun Do's life as a series of absurd exploits that illustrate the irrational nature of North Korean power and the disposability of average citizens. Written in a style that combines the genres of adventure, dystopia, thriller, satire, and romance, Johnson's novel is divided into two sections. It begins with Jun Do and other orphans who are sent to work as underground tunnel soldiers, searching beneath the demilitarized zone (DMZ) for bombs and South Korean soldiers, when the Arduous March causes their orphanage to close. After spending eight years laboring in these dangerous conditions, Jun Do becomes a soldier known for his ability to deliver knockout taekwondo kicks in the dark and, on this basis, is recruited to assist Officer So and

Gil with kidnapping missions in Japan. After performing countless and mostly random abductions of Japanese individuals, Jun Do is rewarded by being sent to a language school to learn English before being assigned to a fishing boat as a listening officer whose task it is to monitor American, Japanese, and South Korean military transmissions. During one of these listening expeditions, the second mate of the fishing vessel defects, and those remaining on board are forced to concoct a story both to explain the crew member's disappearance and to prove their loyalty. They must all corroborate this story, which does not need to be believable, the fishing captain advises, but it should be useful for Pyongyang's propaganda purposes. The captain turns out to be correct, and their ridiculous story of Jun Do's heroism and self-sacrifice (which involves him surviving a shark attack while attempting to save the second mate who had been thrown overboard by US Naval officers) is certified by North Korean officials after Jun Do withstands the interrogator's beatings. Once Jun Do recovers, he is sent as part of a delegation to Texas in order to negotiate with a US senator about returning a radiation detector (that North Korea had originally stolen from Japan). When the North Korean delegation fails to accomplish its goals, Jun Do is sent to a prison camp, and his story comes to an end.[1] The second section of the novel shifts its attention to Commander Ga, a cruel and powerful North Korean military officer who is married to a famous actress named Sun Moon. The reader later learns that Jun Do has, in fact, become Commander Ga. It is revealed that after killing Commander Ga in self-defense during a violent encounter in Jun Do's prison cell, Jun Do assumed Ga's identity. Jun Do (as the new Commander Ga) falls in love with Ga's beautiful wife, becomes a loving father to their two children, and eventually helps Sun Moon and the children defect to the United States. As this overview indicates, the novel relies primarily on plot rather than on character development to capture and maintain the reader's attention. Plot design is the novel's central method for mediating between the worlds of the reader and the text.

Johnson has defended the outlandish series of events that constitute his fast-paced plot by arguing, "There's a ton of fact in it, but the truth of the place is much more elusive. The true absurdities of North Korea I couldn't even put in, because it was unbelievable. I don't think the Western reader can handle a real portrait of life there."[2] By implying that the fault lies with North Korea as an object that exceeds the limits of the Western imagination, the preposterous plot of *The Orphan Master's Son* is presented as an aesthetic solution to the problem of North Korean incomprehensibility. Lying outside of the novel's scope of consideration is whether this condition of absolute illegibility is produced through the political, racialized, and aesthetic terms by which North Korea is written by the West or by a long Cold War geography that continues to map for distance rather than for proximity between Western readers and North Korea.

I begin this chapter with Johnson's novel because it exemplifies in many respects how the Global North views North Korea, with *The Orphan Master's Son*'s status as a bestseller and the recipient of multiple major literary awards indicating how well it satisfies readerly desires to know North Korea as a brutal fantasy. The novel typifies a tendency to write the North Korean real as a fictionalized construct while bracketing critiques of how and why such representations tend to be mobilized or how they both rely upon and produce racial affects. As such, the novel and surrounding discourse illustrate how knowledge production about North Korea is shaped by matters of style and genre as well as by the enduring legacies of imperialism and the Cold War. This mode that I call dystopic speculation writes North Korea in repetitive and oversimplified terms; it recycles tropes and plots that construct North Korea as a dystopia and produces within the reader a desire to speculate about the inhuman political and economic conditions within the country. This dynamic conditions the West to understand North Korea as simultaneously bizarre and banal by producing a paradoxical sense of knowing, or even mastery, in readers.[3] As a subcategory that includes fictional and nonfictional representations of North Korea, dystopic speculation asserts objectivity while drawing freely on elements of fiction. This chapter critiques how the fiction and nonfiction binary operates within the West's representational practices to abstract North Korea into a racialized metaphor for the unknowable and the ungovernable, or what I call the *minor inhuman*.

Anchored in three texts about North Korea—namely, the Hollywood feature film *The Interview*, Johnson's novel *The Orphan Master's Son*, and the British documentary *The Lovers and the Despot*—this chapter reads these representations in palimpsestic relation for how they write over each other, without completely erasing one another. But unlike more traditional palimpsests, these versions, when read collectively, reveal rather than obscure global anxieties about North Korea. While *The Interview* is a satirical work and *The Orphan Master's Son* combines elements of thriller, speculative fiction, romance, and dystopia, both texts adhere to crucial conventions that characterize dystopic speculation; they confirm Western perceptions of the Cold War and post–Cold War eras by depicting North Korea in terms of depravity, inhumanity, and ignorance. The figure of the North Korean dictator, assumptions of US military and moral superiority, and the docility of North Korea's people are a few of the elements in *The Interview* that reappear in *The Orphan Master's Son*. While Johnson's novel is much more complex than *The Interview*, both fold shared tropes into a familiar narrative of an inhuman North Korea to reinforce what audiences already know or think they know. *The Orphan Master's Son* and *The Interview* draw on the same elements, even as they diverge in that the novel writes them as traumatic moments that constitute a saga, whereas the film turns them into comic punchlines.

This chapter concludes with an examination of *The Lovers and the Despot* in an effort to complicate the narrative framing of North Korea by tracing relationships between North Korea, South Korea, and Japan that, while not routed through North America, are still shaped by their relations to US empire. By locating these representations of North Korea in relation to other depictions and histories that circulate less widely within the United States yet are familiar within Asia, and nonetheless share a tendency to assume the brutality of North Korea, I contend that we gain insight into the kinds of power relations, geopolitical conflicts and manipulations, and imperial ambitions that assumptions of North Korea as bizarre and even unfathomable mask. I contextualize the events depicted in *The Lovers and the Despot* by examining post–World War II Japan and South Korea as US client states. By locating North Korean representations within a formation designed to further US ambitions, I ask what is at stake in writing North Korea as always the villain of Cold War narratives? And how do these discourses that racialize North Korea through incredulity within various spheres of US influence also work to sustain a long Cold War?

Generic Realness

The Orphan Master's Son resolves the contradiction between the unimaginable facts of life in North Korea and the expectations of a Western reader by rewriting North Korea within the horizon of Western values. I deliberately echo Fredric Jameson's language of interpretive methods and horizons here to build on his insight that "texts come before us as the always-already-read; we apprehend them through sedimented layers of previous interpretations, or—if the text is brand-new—through the sedimented reading habits and categories developed by those inherited interpretive traditions."[4] Our habits of knowing frame North Korea as an inhuman place characterized by its odd barbarity; moreover, we read it in relation to a larger plot about freedoms and rights as defined by the Global North and viewed through the "'god trick of seeing everything from nowhere' purveyed by the seemingly pure, objective vision of scientific and capitalist realism."[5] To argue, as Johnson and many reviewers of his novel do, that readers can only feel for an imagined North Korean subject is to relegate North Korea to the status of an unknowable object, meaningful only as an Orientalist fiction about the violation of Western ideals. More generative would be to adopt what Hentyle Yapp calls "a minor method" to approach North Korea, one characterized by hesitation rather than assumption, in an effort to avoid relying on "knowable and immediately available narratives" to determine value and meaning.[6]

Reviews of *The Orphan Master's Son* exhibit this same tendency to read North Korea as a brutal fantasy, and reviewers seem to share Johnson's opinion that "North Korea is the most difficult place on Earth to be fully human."[7] John Cussen's review of Johnson's novel and *Escape From Camp 14* (a memoir of Shin Dong-hyuk's life written by Blaine Harden that I discuss in chapter 2) claims that "a more visceral knowledge of North Korea" is needed if the West is ever to understand North Korea, whose "dystopian perversity overmatches our moral imagination's capacity to comprehend," or North Koreans, whose "plight continues to overwhelm our empathetic abilities."[8] This description frames North Korea in almost sublime terms with the remainder of the review judging the texts for how they guide the reader through this state of being overwhelmed to a place of knowing North Korea. Noting that while Johnson's novel provides insights that nonfiction is incapable of delivering, Cussen argues that *The Orphan Master's Son* ultimately fails to satisfy because it is written in a mode of "faux realism."[9] These competing social and generic expectations reveal how a conflict between what may be real in North Korea and what can be written as realistic for Western readers gives rise to the problem of how to read and write North Korea.[10] As Laura Kang argues, such paradoxes of representation indicate that we should focus less on "an unveiling of some truth that has been misrepresented than [on] a foregrounding of the particular historical circumstances, ideological suppositions, and methodological tactics that enable and constrain that compositional stance."[11]

The politics of cultural representation become increasingly fraught if we consider the expectations for North Korean memoirs and how they are criticized as "unreliable" and "too novelesque to be trusted" when suspected of crossing into fiction.[12] Instead of being praised for their creativity or their ability to anticipate readerly desires, as is Johnson's novel, North Korean memoirs that deviate from oral versions or that contradict information provided by other North Koreans are questioned for their validity and are often used to undermine the credibility of the genre of North Korean memoirs as a whole. Shin Dong-hyuk and Harden's *Escape from Camp 14* and Yeonmi Park and Maryanne Vollers's *In Order to Live* are two notable examples of North Korean life stories that have become controversial on these grounds.[13] These critiques of North Korean memoirs indicate that what the West wants is to encounter these stories as authentic and unmediated ethnographic sources of information.

An examination of the formal dimensions of North Korean representation reveals how dystopic speculative writing about North Korea moves between the literary and cultural realms. Understanding "plot as the syntax of a certain way of speaking our understanding of the world" helps us to understand the genre of dystopic speculation and the worldview that lies behind it.[14] Genre, as a framing device that encourages particular reading practices over others, is one way that narrative guides its readers. In thinking about the stylistic conventions that bind together fiction and nonfiction, I see writing about North Korea as akin to what scholars such as Betsy Huang, Eleanor Ty, and Christl Verduyn have observed about Asian American and Asian Canadian writing as genres that routinely contend with autobiographical and autoethnographic expectations. Within these literatures, repetition and difference produce related forms of Asian racialization, with texts being judged for how they meet rather than challenge readerly preconceptions: "Asian American writing is rarely sui generis, but always expected to be *generic*, its worth measured by how capably the writer executes the essential elements of the expected immigrant narrative and how the immigrant protagonist exemplifies 'what it means to be an Asian immigrant.'"[15]

A genre becomes recognizable because the repetition of "essential elements" gives coherence to a body of writing. In a landmark essay on genre and unoriginality, Wai-Chee Dimock coins the term "*regenreing*, to highlight the activity here as cumulative reuse, an alluvial process, sedimentary as well as migratory."[16] While Dimock argues for repetition as a creative act, Huang takes a contrary approach to "cumulative reuse" by considering how it entrenches "Orientalist 'sediments.'"[17] The question for her becomes, "What narrative strategies are necessary to agitate these entrenched alluvial deposits"?[18] Examining representations of North Korea in light of this tension, North Korea becomes a site imagined through Orientalist sedimentation, written as a place devoid of originality, and characterized by strangeness and oddity. This repetitive mode locks North Korean representation in the Cold War era. To think of North Korea as a set of stylistic conventions is to recognize how its representations are crafted by global audiences and producers rather than by North Korea itself.

I suggest that we hold onto these insights into how North Korea is fashioned through stylistic conventions within the contested terrain of literature and consider them in relation to parallel conversations that have unfolded within the interdisciplinary field of international relations. Unlike literary conversations that ask how aesthetics enable us to comprehend typically inaccessible truths and identify with unfamiliar subjects, discussions within the social sciences have queried whether what passes as knowledge about North Korea is really better understood as fiction, more useful for its insights into international politics than for what it reveals about the country of North Korea itself.[19] To put it another way, how do we come to terms with the fact that what is recognized as objective knowledge about North Korea is actually the result of selective questioning and the dismissal of insights that do not conform to existing debates or collective feeling? Noting that international relations scholars tend to fixate on North Korea as a security concern or as an example of failed nationhood, Shine Choi argues that we would be better served by understandings that recognize North Korea as "a product of encounters between various 'us's' and various 'North Koreas'" and, moreover, that "this various, diverse, fragmented, ambiguous 'us' remains a particular 'us' on one side of politics along the line reified by the Cold War binaries of (neo)liberal US–Western Europe versus the communist-socialist Soviet bloc."[20] To contend with the fiction of North Korea requires attending to the dimensions of power that construct it as a problem for the international community and that, moreover, determine the terms for mediating truth claims.[21]

I share with Shine Choi a desire to interrogate the critical and cultural constructions of North Korea and pay particular attention to the aesthetic and affective aspects that have remained underexamined within scholarship about North Korea. Extending these investigations to include the relations that produce North Korea as a fiction complementary to Cold War era agendas, I understand *Brutal Fantasies* as part of a larger political project that reckons with how the Global South is written. Viewed within this broader context, the inconsistent and contradictory positionings of North Korean defectors and Western literary authors in relation to discourses of truth, fact, and fiction must be read as indications of how power, racialization, and privilege shape representational practices. Only the global elite are able to write North Korea as an ideological fantasy in books that are then embraced for the insights they provide into the everyday conditions of North Koreans. Thus, to ask the question of why Johnson's novel—while perhaps well-researched but nonetheless drawn from a particular archive of English translations—is seen by Western readers as having greater truth value than the stories of defectors is also to ask the question of who gets to define the North Korean real. Johnson's novel illuminates the gendered and racialized script that guides our approach to the documentation of others, such as North Korea defectors, the recent majority of whom are women. North Korea thus poses a *Heart of Darkness*–type problem as it functions as a metaphor for alterity in fiction and nonfiction and promotes a readerly compulsion to speculate as to what constitutes the truth of North Korea. For those of us in the Global North, the brutal and unknowable figure of North Korea indexes the need for global security that protects world order, and we, in turn, ensure that it continues to remain unknowable by dismissing sources that attest otherwise.

Dystopic Speculations

The characterizations of North Korea discussed above strongly resemble those found in news articles, feature films, and documentaries and depict the nation in hyperbolic and even fantastic terms. A brief sampling of news reports from 2012 to 2014 (overlapping with the period during which *The Interview*, *The Orphan Master's Son*, and *The Lovers and the Despot* were released), for instance, illustrates how North Korea is often narrativized in terms of its absolute difference from the West. Widely circulated throughout global media, these stories include a focus on state-legislated haircuts for North Koreans, unicorn caves, North Korean pop singers, and a grisly execution.[22] By providing minimal detail and context, these media depictions often caricaturize North Korea and parody Kim Jong Un by simultaneously villainizing and lampooning him, striking a tone that lies somewhere between international news coverage and tabloid reporting. But as Nicholas Bonner notes, while state-sanctioned haircuts were the norm in North Korea in the 1990s, they were giving way to individual expressions of style in the twenty-first century, a time when foreign brands were sold alongside local ones in the first legitimated North Korean public market.[23] Read within this context, the encouragement of socialist haircuts reads less as an instance of the state flexing its power and more as an attempt to bolster support for North Korean ideals in an increasingly diverse landscape. Even during the era of escalating tensions between US president Trump and North Korean leader Kim Jong Un (as evidenced by their tweets in 2017), public anxieties over the possibilities of nuclear attacks were tempered by an inability to take either leader seriously.

Collectively, these fictional and nonfictional representations produce a highly stylized portrait of North Korea as a dystopia that belongs within the pages of speculative fiction or a Cold War thriller. This perception holds true whether North Korea is being critiqued in journalism, satirized in film, or feared in memoirs. Dystopian literature as a genre requires that we suspend our disbelief in order to engage with the narrative. But in the case of North Korean portrayals, these generic conventions also determine what is understood to be a realistic representation of the everyday. This is visible, for instance, in many media reports that draw on the tropes of the dystopian to represent North Korea in a manner that is simultaneously fascinating and horrifying. And while Johnson's novel presumes to test the limits of what non–North Korean publics can imagine occurring within the country as well as what the regime is capable of, similar reactions on different scales are triggered by the memoirs of North Korean defectors, news stories about the behavior of North Korean leaders, and documentary films about life within the country. Collectively, these literary, filmic, and media representations form what I call a genre of *dystopic speculation* given how remarkably similar they are in terms of tone as well as stance toward North Korea. This is true of an array of popular representations such as Ann Shin's novel *The Last Exiles* (2021), South Korean thrillers like *The Berlin File* (Ryu Seung-wan, dir., 2013), and episodes of the podcast *Real Dictators* (hosted by Paul McGann, 2020) that focus on Kim Jong-il's biography, dystopic speculative texts that are morbidly fascinating for Western audiences.

Because North Korea already signifies the ultimate dystopia, it is difficult for writers such as Johnson to conceptualize moving beyond it. This blockage occurs because their narratives draw on a shared plot (or what literary critic Peter Brooks calls "the design and intention of narrative, what shapes a story and gives it a certain direction or intent of meaning"[24]) that is principally concerned with promoting Western conceptions of the human rather than centering North Korea as a subject. This familiar global narrative frames depictions of North Korean suffering and conflates fictional and nonfictional representations as they occur throughout literature, film, and journalism, so that "we can still recognize 'the story' even when its medium has been considerably changed."[25] However, as Brooks reminds us, plot is not only about the ordering of events, suturing them together within a narrative, but also about the interpretation of narratives. For this reason, "most viable works of literature tell us something about how they are to be read, [and] guide us toward the conditions of their interpretation."[26] With respect to narratives of North Korea, readers are encouraged to approach them from a historical perspective that favors Western democracy, liberalism, and Global North values. These interpretive constraints emphasize the need for global security and international intervention by offering North Korea as an example of dangerous and heartless authoritarianism.

Part of the provocation of dystopic speculation lies in how, through a process of making and remaking, elements of dystopia and speculative fiction are brought together to produce a genre that guides readers toward very different ideological ends than those promoted by the genres it borrows from. For instance, while North Korea tends to be written in a dystopic mode as a futureless space devoid of happiness and hope, such representations often deviate from the genre of dystopian fiction in terms of where they locate hope. This is a crucial distinction, given that dystopia as a body of writing is marked by a commitment to social change, existing as a literary form that works between "Utopia and Anti-Utopia" and typically features "an alienated character's refusal of the dominant society."[27] But North Koreans are depicted in one-dimensional terms within brutal fantasies—as downtrodden masses, as brutal dictators, and as helpless defectors—that form the impoverished and traumatic backdrop of North Korea; and this fashioning distinguishes them from the rebellious agential figures of dystopic writing. Social transformation is imagined as requiring the aid of non–North Koreans, most often individuals from the West. For Johnson's protagonist, Jun Do, for example, contact with Americans is required before he can grasp the affective dimensions of freedom and consequently imagine "all the lives he might have lived" had Kim Jong-il not existed.[28] In other words, with US guidance, he becomes the kind of individuated subject capable of heroic resistance featured in dystopias.

The genres of utopian and dystopian fiction often blur into speculative fiction, leading to new insights regarding what constitutes ideal and unlivable worlds. For Christopher Patterson, speculative fiction offers valuable critiques of systemic violence as it "focuses not so much on 'what it was' but 'how it remains so.'"[29] To extend this line of thought, we might expect that bringing the genres of utopian, dystopian, and speculative fiction together would open the door to new ways of interrogating past and present violence. However, the genre of dystopic speculation does not demand that its readers interrogate the geopolitics of brutality; nor does it seek to know how its readers' understandings of North Korea are conditioned through liberal conceptions of agency. It is perhaps even uninterested in such investigations. *The Orphan Master's Son*, for instance, reaffirms fundamental beliefs in the superiority of the Global North over the Global South without historicizing these relations in terms of colonialism, imperialism, or the Cold War. The speculative—in the context of North Korean dystopic writing—becomes speculation about the barbarism of North Korea that remains abstract and dehistoricized. While readers of speculative fiction are encouraged to engage with alternate worlds according to the terms of those alternate worlds, so they can learn "to see the world differently (in that Brechtian sense of overcoming alienation by becoming critically estranged and engaged),"[30] Western readers struggle to see speculative work set in North Korea as fictionalized representation. Writing of speculative fiction and speculative finance, Aimee Bahng identifies the negative potential of speculation as its transformation into "a colonizing mechanism when it attempts to capture, profit from, and realize the future."[31] Instead of conceiving of North Korea as part of the world to be changed, dystopic speculative texts cement global hierarchies by positing the West as the change-maker and North Korea as the object to be transformed or even liberated.

The Familiar and the Familial in *The Interview*

Toward the end of 2014, Sony Pictures was the target of a very public cyberattack that saw the release of confidential information that included not only emails between studio executives but also the personal information of employees. A group that identified themselves as Guardians of Peace took responsibility for the attack and demanded at first that the studio not release *The Interview*, a comedic film about a television host and producer who are assigned the task of assassinating Kim Jong Un. Guardians of Peace later demanded that the death scene at the end of the film be revised before they would permit Sony to release the film. This attack resulted in an FBI investigation and even saw US president Barack Obama publicly weighing in on how Sony should respond to these threats. The FBI claimed that the North Korean government was behind the Sony hack, while others disagreed, arguing the language and level of technical sophistication were uncharacteristic of North Korea. An Myong Hun, North Korea's deputy UN ambassador, denied North Korean responsibility for the attack and called for a joint investigation into the hack and for any evidence supporting such claims to be made public. While proof of North Korea's responsibility was never released, these events still upheld public perception of North Korea as a ruthless nation capable of unconscionable acts that violated democratic principles such as the freedom of speech.

The film itself is a satire about Dave Skylark (played by James Franco), an entertainment news reporter, and Aaron Rappaport (Seth Rogen), his producer who has ambitions of producing a serious news show. The pair land an interview with Kim Jong Un who is a big fan of their show. Skylark and Rappaport are thrilled by this rare opportunity as they imagine that it will enable them to pursue more legitimate news stories in the future. The CIA sees a very different opportunity in their interview and tasks them with assassinating Kim Jong Un when they and their news team are in North Korea. This film is a comedy that focuses primarily on the bromance between Seth Rogen and James Franco's characters, and in many respects, North Korea is largely used as a backdrop for the bumbling antics of its American stars. As David Oh notes, the film focuses on white masculinity and cannot be understood as racial or political satire since "North Korea is represented simply as it is understood in the Western imagination. Instead, the satire is the lampooning of the spy genre with the inclusion of two, unlikely White heroes."[32] And while satire can critique its object, it is also a genre that can "reinforce existing hegemonies."[33] It is clear that the DVD release of *The Interview* was aimed at American viewers. The inclusion of a self-reflexively satiric scene in which Rogen and his producing partner Evan

Goldberg address the camera and tell viewers that they are American heroes for watching this movie underscores this intention. And while Americans may be the intended audience for *The Interview*, I want to ask how those of us who constitute its unintended audiences, might engage with this film and critique its representation of North Korea given our particular diasporic and Global South locations and histories.

Early on in the visit to North Korea, Dave Skylark meets Kim Jong Un, and they become fast friends, bonding over shared experiences of fathers who are disappointed in them and a love of American pop music and margaritas. Skylark's producer becomes concerned when Skylark begins to doubt their mission to assassinate Kim Jong Un because he cannot imagine that his new friend is capable of heinous acts of domestic and international terror. In a rather predictable turn of events, Skylark comes to realize the "truth" of Kim Jong Un's inhumanity, and with the help of a North Korean aide named Sooke (played by Diana Bang), Skylark and Rappaport concoct a plan to reveal Kim Jong Un's real self during the interview. It is not the actual death as imagined by the CIA but rather the symbolic death of Kim Jong Un that proves to be the turning point in the film. During the interview, Skylark questions Kim Jong Un about the pressures he experienced from his overbearing father. Skylark's goal in this scene is to reveal that Kim Jong Un is an ordinary human being like all others, as this basic fact would undermine Kim Jong Un's ability to demand absolute respect and reverence from his people. The film satirizes Kim Jong Un by depicting him as being moved to tears when Skylark sings the lyrics to Katy Perry's 2010 pop song "Firework"; Kim Jong Un is so overwhelmed by emotion that he loses bodily control and defecates himself. By making Kim Jong Un cry, the film suggests that he has been emasculated and rendered powerless in the eyes of North Korea and the rest of the world. And, as Oh argues, the film also relies on sexual metaphors in the form of a phallic helicopter tail and a ship explosion to illustrate the domination of North Korea by the United States as the United States reports, "Dave's (cum)shot destroys Kim."[34] The film is quite deliberate in its intention to personalize the critique of the North Korean leadership as it psychoanalyzes Kim and frames his vulnerabilities in terms of gender and sexuality, humanizing him to the point of farce.

The film's mocking portrayal of Kim Jong Un is, of course, not new, as countless jokes have been made about him via memes and other pop culture references; and it is precisely this sense of familiarity for a North American audience that interests me. The ludicrous nature of this scene is heightened by its use of contemporary American pop music—a genre of music better known for its celebrities and catchy but forgettable tunes than for its revolutionary potential—

as the catalyst for Kim Jong Un's tears and the political chaos that follows. The underlying message is that North Korea clearly lacks intelligence and sophistication with regard to art, culture, and political strategy, given that its leader is outsmarted by an entertainment journalist such as Skylark and is unable to resist pop artistry. This dynamic is reinforced throughout the film with depictions of crude North Korean propaganda such as a store that is filled with fake food and child performers that only Skylark is sharp enough to find disconcerting. The climactic dismantling of Kim Jong Un's power is staged as a scene in which Skylark pulls back the curtain and shows North Korea and the rest of the world that there is nothing to fear: Kim is no Wizard but simply an ordinary man. In response, North Korean people are depicted as experiencing genuine shock when they realize that Kim Jong Un is mortal and capable of tears and bodily functions.[35] Within the world of the film, the only plausible reason that revolution has not yet taken place is because the nation holds absolute faith in its leader; other more pragmatic reasons such as economic survival or investments in profitable clandestine businesses are never introduced as explanations for the continued existence of the regime.

While the film is not interested in seriously engaging with North Korea or issues about it (and the film conveys this stance with its liberal use of Asian stereotypes and by having Rogen and Franco mimic Asian accents on more than one occasion), it does pose a moment of self-reflexive critique that I want to address. It occurs while Skylark is interviewing Kim Jong Un and takes place right before Skylark "breaks" Kim by asking him about his father; Skylark asks Kim Jong Un a "tough" question, namely why he doesn't feed his people. In response to the implicit accusation that he is starving North Koreans, Kim Jong Un tells Skylark that he should instead be asking how North Korea has been able to survive given US sanctions. Kim Jong Un also points to the hypocrisy of the United States in monitoring the human rights situation in North Korea given that US rates of incarceration are higher than North Korea's and among the highest in the world. Skylark cannot respond to these criticisms, and as he sits stumped by these points, the film cuts away to Rogen and Bang's characters fighting North Korean guards. When the camera returns to Skylark and Kim, the conversation has progressed, and we hear Kim Jong Un denying the existence of North Korean concentration camps. Significantly, the challenge to US moral authority is never answered by Skylark. Instead, the interview takes the emotional turn that I described earlier that ends with Kim Jong Un weeping. The admittedly small opening to a comparative analysis of prison-industrial complexes and global human rights is bypassed as the film instead returns to racially abstracting North Korea through a storyline that presumes to end the enduring Cold War with mockery and moral indignation. North Korea remains an instrumentalized figure that reinforces liberal ideals rather than a provocation to critique them as part of a global order.

This moment in the film suggests that the complexity of US intervention cannot be unpacked in a short, televised interview, even as it illustrates an American attitude of belligerent unknowing knowingness as Skylark loudly condemns Kim Jong Un in front of international audiences, despite possessing only a superficial understanding of the situation. Skylark exhibits a tendency toward certainty within uncertainty as part of a desire to deny culpability. In his reluctance to address Kim Jong Un's comments about US sanctions and the instrumentalization of human rights, Skylark reveals a fear of knowing "the truth" as it could result in knowing too much about US complicity, imperialism, and culpability. The film merits attention not for putting forth a novel critique of North Korea but rather because it expresses many widely held assumptions about North Korea and gives us an entry point into the Western narrative about North Korea. For instance, while the filmmakers and even US president Obama assumed that North Korea would not like this film, *The Interview* fact plays into the North Korean state's narrative of the West as colonial, racist, and constantly attempting to humiliate rather than enter into dialogue with North Korea on the world stage. Moreover, the film aligns with National Endowment for Democracy–funded radio programming composed of South Korean music, news, and drama that criticizes the North Korean government, its economic system, and its leaders, "all of which converge in their shared desire to destabilize the North Korean government."[36] It does not appear to have occurred to the filmmakers that they may, in fact, have been recreating rather than resisting North Korean state narratives, and that the North Korean characters they created in *The Interview* could, instead of seeing their leader as a "real person," see American journalists attacking and humiliating him and, in turn, the entire nation. This oversight reveals much about the labor performed by the film that, instead of critiquing North Korean domestic politics, reinforces the global order through its racializing fantasies of North Korea.

Reading for Repetition in *The Orphan Master's Son*

Central to the brutal fantasies of North Korea are the stock figures that populate it. Within *The Orphan Master's Son*, the protagonist, Pak Jun Do, is clearly meant to signify a heroic version of the average North Korean. This role is underscored by Pilar, the senator's housekeeper in Texas who comments, upon being introduced to Jun Do, "John Doe? Isn't that the name you give a missing person?"[37] Perhaps unsurprisingly, given Jun Do's narrative function, the novel does not provide an in-depth examination of his background. At this point, the reader has already been informed by the narrator that Jun Do's mother was a beautiful opera singer who was taken to Pyongyang, and his father was the Orphan Master of Long Tomorrows. Broken by the loss of his wife, the Orphan Master was unable to parent his son with kindness or love because Jun Do served as "a daily reminder of the eternal hurt he felt from losing" his wife.[38]

Adamant that this version of his family history is true, Jun Do refuses to entertain the possibility that he might actually be an orphan and that this family history is an elaborate childhood fantasy that he concocted to comfort himself. When Gil, an associate on the kidnapping expeditions, advises him to let go of this narrative and reinvent himself, Jun Do is overwhelmed with anger and bitterness at "the ways it was impossible for people from normal families to conceive of a man in so much hurt that he couldn't acknowledge his own son, that there was nothing worse than a mother leaving her children, though it happened all the time."[39] Jun Do's refusal to accept his orphaned status perplexes Gil who tries to defect during a mission in Japan and asks Jun Do to come with him. While Jun Do counters Gil's proposition by reminding Gil that his parents would get sent to work camps if he escaped, Gil unsentimentally notes that eventually, for everyone in North Korea, "your number comes up."[40]

The novel presents two sides to being an orphan in North Korea; on the one hand, orphans are viewed as expendable and therefore assigned the most dangerous jobs in the country. Without family connections, there is little chance of upward social mobility for them. But on the other hand, as Gil urges Jun Do to consider, the absence of ties means that escaping from North Korea is a much easier task. Readers familiar with defector memoirs know the extent to which defectors go to cover their tracks in order to protect family members who may be held accountable afterward, and defectors often eventually make costly arrangements for their loved ones also to escape. Such readers would also wonder why Jun Do would not take advantage of his family situation, since *The Orphan Master's Son* contrasts the present moment of North Korea and the unknown future outside of the country without exploring Jun Do's attachments to North Korea. The absence of a more detailed understanding of Jun Do's worldview and sense of identity seems glaring given that he is not naive to the dangers of North Korea but nonetheless remains untempted by a future that presents itself in terms of individuality and freedom from social and national ties.

Common to both *The Orphan Master's Son* and *The Interview* is a depiction of North Korean characters as inhuman figures capable only of limited degrees of introspection. The novel draws us into this worldview through its narrative frames and voices. The first section of the novel entitled "The Biography of Jun Do" is told by an omniscient narrator. Later in the novel, we realize that this "biography" has actually been collected under duress by interrogators after Jun Do is imprisoned for helping Sun Moon and her children defect to the United States. In this respect, the novel bears a similarity to Viet Nguyen's *The Sympathizer*, as both texts use the confessional to critique truths, narratives, and biographies. The nameless interrogator who takes Jun Do's story is part of a new generation of interrogators who rely on psychological methods rather than the brute force strategies employed by the old-guard interrogators known as *Pubyok*. These interrogations result in biographies that are bound and shelved in a library but almost never read, for as the interrogator tells us, "Once a book is closed, it never gets opened. . . . We're story takers, not storytellers."[41] Sharing Jun Do's biography in a distanced narrative voice means that the perspective of the interrogator and the conditions under which Jun Do's story has been collected are excluded. Without the consciousnesses of either Jun Do or the interrogator to guide the reader, "The Biography of Jun Do" reads like a conventional thriller in a dystopic setting. The shape of this section is deliberate and produced by the interrogator's deep discomfort with the "I." As he confides in the reader about his attempt to write his own biography, the interrogator expresses his frustration with this genre because it demands he reveal himself: "As an experiment, the biography was a failure—where was the *me* in it, where was *I*?—and of course it was hard to get past the feeling that if I finished it, something bad would happen to me. The real truth was that I couldn't stand the pronoun 'I.' Even at home, in the privacy of my own notepad, I have difficulty writing that word."[42] As a pronoun, "I" produces a deep sense of vulnerability by drawing together accountability and individualism.[43]

"The Confessions of Commander Ga," the second section of the novel, relies on a combination of narrative voices: first person when the interrogator is relaying own story; third person when we learn about Jun Do's story from the narrator who is also the interrogator; and then a different third-person narrative voice that is heard over the loudspeaker. As the official propaganda instrument, one of the functions of the loudspeaker voice is to tell the Best North Korean Story of the year in installments, which, on this occasion, happens to be the official narrative of Commander Ga, a version of Commander Ga (Jun Do) that the rest of the novel tries to debunk. While the interrogator's biography provides details of Jun Do's story that are not recorded in the official state version, it is still an incomplete and partial telling as Jun Do's thoughts or feelings are absent.

The movement between first- and third-person narration to tell the interrogator's and Jun Do's stories produces an odd effect. On the one hand, distance is maintained between the reader and Jun Do, who remains a plot device, while on the other hand, the reader is drawn into more intimate relations with the interrogator. And while the structure of the novel discourages the reader from feeling a significant connection to Jun Do, it permits the interrogator to identify strongly with Jun Do as he recognizes similarities between them (such as being nameless). Eventually, the interrogator has an epiphany as he realizes how deeply intertwined his life has become with Jun Do's and, moreover, that they share a common purpose: "To be given a new life, Ga had to take one away. I proved that theorem every day. After years of failure, I now understood that by writing Commander Ga's biography, maybe I was also writing my own."[44]

The interrogator's alignment with his biographical subject represents a major shift for the interrogator's identity. From his elderly parents who had always been careful to avoid being denounced, he had learned to be a devoted Party follower who was distrustful of stories that veered from the official Party line. Initially, the interrogator sees his work of collecting confessions as a vital part of developing better relations between citizens and the government as biographies teach people that, "instead of keeping things from your government by living a life of secrecy, they're a model of how to share everything. I like to think I'm part of a different tomorrow in that regard."[45] This claim sits uneasily with the interrogator's earlier admission that biographies are bound and shelved in the library but almost never read. But as the interrogator hears more of Jun Do's story, he becomes increasingly aware of how the citizens of North Korea belong to the regime and that this relationship with the state prevents individuals from forming meaningful attachments with each other. Disillusionment for the interrogator occurs when he finally realizes that neither personal truths nor lives are valued by the regime, and therefore that his efforts to preserve the stories of citizens are meaningless.

In an attempt to overcome the distance that characterizes his relationships with his family, friends, and even himself, the interrogator finally shares his own biography with his parents, thereby making them, rather than the state, his intended audience. This is a watershed moment because the telling of this personal story is an event that implicates not only the interrogator but also his audience. Throughout the novel, characters are repeatedly told not to tell secrets as they will inevitably be tortured out of the confidants. Thus, this act of storytelling can occur only between the interrogator and his parents because he has already poisoned them with a can of peaches tainted with botulism—a measure intended to protect them from the torture that would likely be inflicted upon them given his intended actions. Rather than accepting his fate and becoming a member of the *Pubyok*, the old guard interrogators who rely on brutal methods of torture to extract confessions, the interrogator plans to rescue Jun Do by erasing not just his own but also Jun Do's memory. In explaining to his parents how he came to embrace this fearful role as interrogator, the interrogator reclaims his story and reestablishes some semblance of intimacy with his parents before he gives up his identity and their lives end.

The inclusion of the interrogator's story, complete with the details of his birth, the backgrounds of his parents, and his own enlightenment and death (if not in a physical sense), makes it a bildungsroman. The interrogator represents a North Korean reader who is awakened by hearing the true version of Jun Do's story but who cannot live with this knowledge given the conditions of everyday life in North Korea. Fashioning the interrogator's story as a bildungsroman is, however, a move that rewrites the subjectivity of North Koreans in Western terms and artificially separates the literary and historical dimensions contained in a life story from each other. As Gregg Brazinsky points out in his reading of Chinese soldier memoirs of the Korean War in North Korea, we cannot simply impose "distinctions between official discourse and private feeling... onto societies where Western, liberal understandings of selfhood are not prevalent."[46] In turning to these discussions of subjectivity, my point is to underscore how *The Orphan Master's Son* is less useful as a representation of how North Koreans think and feel and more an indication of how Western readers want to imagine North Koreans as extensions of themselves.[47]

Skulduggery, Intrigue, and *The Lovers and the Despot*

Stories of North Korea that emphasize the irrational and arbitrary acts of violence committed by the regime—as illustrated by *The Interview* and *The Orphan Master's Son*—constitute a well-known narrative of North Korea in the West. There are, however, other variations of this narrative in global circulation. For example, within Asia, stories abound that incorporate elements found in *The Interview* and Johnson's novel into plots that dramatize the tension between North Korea and Japan, Hong Kong, South Korea, and other parts of the world. These stories complicate the North Korea–US dynamic that dominates the US imagination by invoking histories that have been forgotten in the West. While Johnson's novel relies on the shock value of North Korean abductions of Japanese citizens undertaken for no apparent purpose, such a reaction is unlikely among readers in Asia who are quite familiar with these events. This section begins by sketching out a context for North Korean kidnappings before focusing on *The Lovers and the Despot* in order to consider how representations of North Korea continue to be written as illiberal threats to liberal freedoms and rights.

During the 1970s and 1980s, North Korea undertook a series of global abductions, including many Japanese victims. The families of the Japanese abductees worked with Japanese activists for years to generate public support for the abduction issue, and they received the attention of Japanese politicians after many years of effort. The kidnappings of Japanese nationals received increased attention after Kim Jong-il admitted, during negotiations with Japanese officials in 2002, that North Korea had ordered the abductions (a topic that I also explore in chapter 2). As Richard J. Samuels notes, after Kim Jong-il's admission, the abduction issue dominated Japan's relations with North Korea to the extent that "one Diet member said that it would be 'political suicide' even to suggest that proliferation of nuclear weapons ought to be of equal or greater concern than the release of the abductees."[48] Missing from most accounts, however, is that Kim Jong-il's apology for the kidnappings was made within the larger context of an attempted reconciliation with Japan, with Prime Minister Koizumi first apologizing for the damages inflicted on Koreans during Japanese colonialism, and Koizumi and Kim then signing the Pyongyang Declaration in 2002.[49] The attempted reconciliation between North Korea and Japan proved to be divisive, with members of the Japanese government blocking the implementation of the agreement. Of the list of missing persons presented to North Korean officials, Kim Jong-il noted that "eight were dead, two they had no record of, and five were alive in North Korea."[50] That same year, five surviving abductees—Chimura Yasushi, Hamamoto Fukuie, Hasuike Kaoru, Okudo Yukiko, and Soga Hitomi—were returned to Japan from North Korea.[51] They were supposed to visit Japan for a couple of weeks and then return to North Korea where they could decide their future plans with their families there. However, Japanese officials reneged on the agreement that Prime Minister Koizumi had signed with Kim Jong-il and refused to send the abductees back to North Korea.[52] While Kim Jong-il attributed the kidnappings to "special mission organizations in the 1970s and 1980s, driven by blindly motivated patriotism and misguided heroism"—in an effort to avoid taking full responsibility for them[53]—his confession nonetheless gave the Japanese government sufficient grounds to repeatedly raise this issue with the UN and other foreign governments.

On multiple occasions, Japanese activists and the government have drawn these events to the attention of international lawmakers as examples of egregious human rights violations. Celeste Arrington traces the development of a human rights agenda in relation to the issue of abductions in Japan by examining "the feedback loop between global discussions of NKHR [North Korean Human Rights] issues and domestic discussions about the abductions (and sometimes *nihonjinzuma* or escapees)."[54] The prevalence of human rights discourses as wielded by the Japanese government, activists, and media meant that North Korea held an additional set of associations for Japan that amplified and sometimes even complicated those significations that circulated within the United States. In Japan, the admission of state-sanctioned kidnappings and the return of five abductees as a result of governmental negotiations were framed in relation to the safety of Japanese citizens and the sovereignty of Japan, thus exaggerating even further the threat posed by North Korea. As Gavan McCormack observes, "Yet, while the specialists saw North Korea as a porcupine, stiffening its quills defensively—or even as a snail, retreating into its shell in fear of any external contact—the Japanese mass media and many politicians painted it as a tiger."[55] These abductions have become a crucial part of a narrative in which North Korea is depicted as a rogue state responsible for many such incidents that include missile launches, unauthorized nuclear tests, spy-ships entering into Japanese waters, counterfeiting, and narcotics trafficking. While the victims of the kidnappings orchestrated by the North Korean government undoubtedly deserve justice, the calls for justice themselves are complicated as they have frequently been incorporated into a right-wing agenda that also includes refuting the accounts of comfort women, cultivating nostalgia in order to bolster Japanese nationalism, and forgetting that "the twentieth century's greatest crimes of abduction had been those committed by Japan, which—more than seven decades later—had still to be satisfactorily resolved."[56] In other words, demands for justice for Japanese kidnapping victims fail to include histories of Korean colonization as part of the conversation and refuse to acknowledge "transwar connectivity,"[57] thus defining justice in narrow and dehistoricized terms that make attempts at reconciliation seem insincere.

Hyun Gu Lynn has shown through careful media analyses that Japanese outlets relied heavily on "the narrative construction of North Korea as evil" as stories of the kidnappings (1977–83) aired in the mid-1990s.[58] The ongoing demonization of North Korea means that it remains a perceived threat and continues Japan's reliance on the United States for military security and strategic purposes. The threat posed by North Korea justifies US military presence in Japan and South Korea, and "paradoxically, to the extent that the US wishes to maintain its East Asian—and global—empire[,] it [the United States] benefits from keeping Kim Jong Il in power."[59] It is perhaps unsurprising then that Japanese depictions negatively characterize North Korea through a "framing [that] centers on emphasizing the condemnation of unruly actions deemed to have been taken against Japan—most ostensibly those of abductions—and upon the heightened risks that the DPRK represents."[60]

While prominent, the Japanese abductions are not the only abductions that have received attention. Others include the kidnappings of South Korean actress Choi Eun-hee and director Shin Sang-ok, who were abducted to further North Korea's plan to become a leader in the film industry, and US soldier Charles Jenkins's forcible confinement within North Korea for years after he inadvertently crossed the DMZ. In addition, the South Korean government alleges that five hundred prisoners of war have been held in the North since the end of the Korean War; that more than a thousand South Korean civilians were kidnapped during the Korean War; and that more than five hundred civilians were kidnapped after the war.⁶¹ In directing attention to these other stories of abduction conducted by the North Korean government, my interest lies not in interrogating these accounts for their truth value, that is, determining the accuracy of these accounts; in fact, many of these stories are disputed by the South Korean government and others who doubt the motivations of the storytellers. Choi Eun-hee, for example, has been accused of willingly defecting to North Korea in order to continue making films after her South Korean career was in decline. My intention here is instead to consider how these real-life events have occasioned new storylines or offered different versions of plots that circulate throughout the West and, moreover, to understand how and why, despite their differences, many of these global stories "so full of skulduggery and intrigue" continue to write North Korea as their villain.⁶²

I dwell on this "skulduggery and intrigue" because it interrupts the selective histories of North Korea as well as the narrow range of dystopic speculative representations that preoccupy the West. Andre Schmid articulates the need for alternative understandings when he observes "one of the grand ironies of North Korean research: that key themes animating our studies are little more than reinventions of propaganda ideas generated in Pyongyang. That we decry the absurdities of the personality cult at the very same time as our own accounts obsess over the Kims evidences a circularity and mutually reinforcing relationship between Pyongyang propaganda and our own writing."⁶³

While these non–North American narratives of abduction also depict North Korea as villainous, they nonetheless introduce new dimensions that permit us to consider how these storylines are mobilized by stakeholders within Japan and benefit the Japanese and American governments. The depiction of North Korea as capable of inhuman acts adheres to colonial narratives of Koreans familiar within Japan, even as they deflect attention from the crimes of imperial Japan. But at the same time, these stories also depict a North Korean awareness of how to flex both soft and hard power within the global sphere. Reading across these depictions of North Korea reminds us that genres, while reliant upon principles of repetition and difference, are malleable entities that "are always in process, and represent shifting categories that result from negotiation within new contexts."[64] Moving between storylines that circulate unevenly throughout the global imagination reminds us that North Korea occasions other plots outside of the West, a crucial insight if we understand "plot as the syntax of a certain way of speaking our understanding of the world."[65] North Korea's role as a figure of alterity to the global order is reflected in the plots that are written about it. In *The Interview*, the climax occurs when Kim Jong Un is revealed to be a sham during his televised interview; and in *The Orphan Master's Son*, Kim Jong-il is depicted in relation to the callous and pointless state-sanctioned abductions of Japanese nationals. In what follows, I consider how these two elements of media and abduction are worked into another set of stories about North Korea that are familiar to audiences in South Korea, Japan, and other parts of the globe but largely forgotten in Canada and the United States.

While *The Interview* depicts North Korea as a backward and incompetent nation that is easily manipulated by the Western media, other accounts construct very different relations between North Korea and the media by emphasizing the government's awareness of how cultural industries and soft power operate. North Korea's familiarity with film and literature as vehicles capable of shaping national consciousness is referenced in Jang Jin-sung's memoir *Dear Leader: My Escape from North Korea*. While describing his role within the Poetry Division of the United Front Department, Jang Jin-sung notes: "The world might damn North Korea as a ruthless regime that kills its own people, claiming that the system is oppressive and run by physical force. But this is only a partial view of how the country is governed. Throughout his life, Kim Jong-il stressed, 'I rule through music and literature.'"[66] One of the distinctions between Kim Il Sung and Kim Jong-il is that the former was committed to literature and relied on it for cultural indoctrination whereas his son directed his energies toward building a North Korean cinema worthy of international attention. Kim Jong-il's own personal collection of films consisted of thousands of films and included many films banned for wider North Korean consumption such as *Friday the 13th* and *Rambo*.[67]

Kim Jong-il's deep passion for film and his strong desire to elevate the North Korean filmmaking industry to reach global standards was made most visible when he ordered the abductions of Choi Eun-hee and Shin Sang-ok with the intention of having them produce films. Kim Jong-il's actions indicate that he understood the value of shaping a cultural imagination through mass culture and reveal the extent to which the state was willing to go in order to develop forms of soft power. Even if Kim Il Sung and Kim Jong-il tended to use culture for the purposes of exerting state control, their deployments nonetheless speak to their understanding of what the arts can do in terms of influencing populations and demand that those of us in the Global North become attuned to the different ways of reading cultural representations produced within North Korea.[68]

Choi Eun-hee and Shin Sang-ok's story has been told a few times recently, once by the documentary *The Lovers and the Despot* (Rob Cannan and Ross Adam, dirs., 2016), by Paul Fischer's book *A Kim Jong-Il Production* (2015), and in a 2020 episode of the podcast *Real Dictators* (Paul McGann). As a British film, *The Lovers and the Despot* is positioned outside the geopolitics that limit US and South Korean access to North Korea. Yet while the filmmakers had access to a capacious archive of material that includes interviews with Choi Eun-hee as well as North and South Korean films, the story within the film is still told in an over-the-top manner with a limited sketching out of the Cold War historical context. At the same time, the UK remains firmly within the US sphere of influence and, like Japan, in a relationship of indebtedness and subordination. To briefly outline the documentary *The Lovers and the Despot*: it opens with an introduction to Shin Sang-ok and Choi Eun-hee, a celebrated director and actress couple who for two decades made many internationally acclaimed films together under the umbrella of Shin Films. By sharing photographs of Shin and Choi as they pose with prominent figures and famous celebrities, fans gazing adoringly at Choi as she receives awards, and the couple with their two young children, the film conveys an impression of a golden existence in which personal lives and film careers were harmoniously wedded together. Eventually, however, infidelity and financial woes lead to the couple divorcing and Shin Films shutting down in 1975, thus ending not only an idyllic period in their lives but also an important era in postwar South Korean filmmaking. Now at a crossroads in her life and saddled with considerable financial debt and the task of raising two small children on her own, Choi agrees to a meeting that a colleague has arranged with a wealthy Hong Kong investor who is interested in her acting school. In a shocking twist of events, the colleague turns out to be a North Korean spy and the meeting a ruse to abduct Choi from Hong Kong and transport her to Nampo Harbor where she is met by Kim Jong-il. After learning about his ex-wife's disappearance, Shin flies to Hong Kong to investigate Choi's disappearance but is then also kidnapped by spies and taken to North Korea. After years of being separately confined in North Korea, the former couple is finally reunited at a birthday party held for Kim Jong-il, and they are suddenly appointed as his film advisers. Choi confides in the camera that while this reunion was occurring, she was thinking, "If this was a film, there'd be lots of tears."⁶⁹ The documentary reveals that Choi and Shin were held hostage for years because Kim Jong-il—a cinephile whose extensive private film collection even contained copies of Shin's films that Shin himself did not own—wanted them to establish North Korean cinema on an international stage and make films capable of competing with those from South Korea. Not only do life and cinema intersect repeatedly throughout *The Lovers and the Despot* as Choi and Shin reflect upon the stakes of their performances—on-screen, behind the camera, and off-screen as they pretend to be enthusiastic allies of Kim Jong-il rather than his captives—but they also begin to blur together as their everyday lives increasingly feel like a high-stakes thriller with a ludicrous storyline.

After being reunited, Shin Sang-ok and Choi Eun-hee begin to think about escaping from North Korea but realize that they require evidence that they had been kidnapped lest the rest of the world believe that they had willingly defected. Worth noting is that unlike the disappearance of Yokota Megumi (a thirteen-year-old girl abducted on her way home from badminton practice) which elicited widespread sympathy in Japan, Choi and Shin never received similar attention from the South Korean public or government, even though South Korea had a longer history of abductions by North Korea than Japan had, dating back to the Korean War (and not just to the 1970s).⁷⁰ Many reasons exist for the differences between how Japan and South Korea handled the abduction issue, one of which being, "unlike Japan, where the abductees were so clearly innocent youths, many of the Korean abductees could not be distinguished easily from defectors."⁷¹ The suspicion with which South Korean abductees were viewed helps to explain why Choi and Shin, after escaping from North Korea in 1986 by seeking refuge at the US Embassy in Vienna, chose to live in the United States until 1999 when they finally returned to South Korea.

Shin Sang-ok and Choi Eun-hee secretly recorded multiple conversations with Kim Jong-il, including one in which he admits to ordering their abductions, and they eventually smuggled one of these cassettes to relatives in South Korea with the aid of Kusakabe Kyushiro and Nishida Tetsuo, two Japanese film critics. While waiting for the right opportunity to escape, Shin and Choi made a number of films for Kim Jong-il, many of which were well-received, and one even earned Choi the award for Best Actress from the Moscow International Film Festival. The couple's success in making internationally acclaimed films made them the recipients of Kim Jong-il's goodwill, and they became his confidants to the extent that Shin began to harbor deep feelings of guilt for plotting to escape as it meant betraying Kim Jong-il. *The Lovers and the Despot* depicts the complexity of feeling with respect to North Korea by demonstrating how individuals are connected to North Korean state secrets, plans for defection, and the dreams of dictators by complicated webs of attachment, suspicion, resentment, fear, and devotion.

Toward the end of *The Lovers and the Despot*, while their ever-present North Korean bodyguards are momentarily distracted, Shin Sang-ok and Choi Eun-hee stealthily escape from their hotel room and into a taxi. The orchestral score begins to build as the bodyguards, having finally noticed the couple's disappearance, pursue them through the streets of Vienna, only to be thwarted when traffic intervenes and the couple's taxi darts off toward the US Embassy.[72] The film splices together this reenacted footage of Shin and Choi's dramatic flight in 1986 with a more recent interview with Choi in which she describes the intense fear she felt at that moment, knowing that being recaptured by her North Korean guards meant certain death. The sequence ends with a shot of Shin's and Choi's legs as they sprint toward the embassy. The expectation that this tension will be resolved with a scene in which Shin and Choi have reached their safe haven is deferred, and the audience is instead shown a snippet of a press conference held by the US government and an interview with a suspicious communications officer who had been posted to the Vienna office of the US Embassy where Shin and Choi sought refuge. Rather than feeling a sense of relief because the couple has successfully escaped from the clutches of the North Korean government, the audience is left feeling unsure about the truth about what happened to Shin and Choi during their years in North Korea and confused by its emotional investments in them. The suspicions surrounding Shin and Choi's time in North Korea are compounded by the fact that they left during one of South Korea's many states of emergencies in which a film law was issued that "introduced censorship of such severity that it rang the death knell of the national cinema of the time."[73] Had Shin and Choi not been in North Korea, it is difficult to imagine how they would have continued making films during this period.

The Lovers and the Despot inspires many competing emotions: incredulity and disbelief that such kidnappings could happen; shock that Kim Jong-il undertook such callous and inhumane actions for the purposes of developing a film industry; and sadness for the many years that Choi Eun-hee and Shin Sang-ok were separated from their children, parents, and siblings. This story of state-directed kidnapping in order to realize the dream of building a North Korean film industry capable of rivaling South Korean cinema is, in many ways, more bizarre than anything the creative team behind Sony's *The Interview* imagined or Johnson created in *The Orphan Master's Son*, even though the novel and film draw on many of the same themes that appear in *The Lover and the Despot*. These commonalities speak to the tendency to imagine North Korea in limited yet sensationalized terms and demonstrate that even outside of the

United States, North Korea is often depicted as villainous. From this, I want to make two observations. The first is to underscore Kim Jong-il's commitment to film that was demonstrated by the lengths to which he was willing to go to abduct Shin and Choi as well as by the number of years he held them captive. As disturbing as these actions are, they still speak to an understanding of how film is able to shape a cultural imagination and a commitment to art as Kim Jong-il gave much latitude to Shin and Choi, encouraging them to produce works that were unlike the narrowly propagandistic films that North Korean cinema had churned out up until then. In this way, North Korea is a site that is more than has been imagined by the West. The second point is that the events featured in *The Lovers and the Despot* give us a way of narrating Cold War legacies that not only focuses on the tensions between Russia and the United States but also takes into account the struggles within the Pacific and between countries that have always been seen as supporting players within Cold War narratives while also taking into consideration the new forms of imperialism that structure global relations within a long Cold War.

As *The Interview*, *The Orphan Master's Son*, and *The Lovers and the Despot* collectively demonstrate, North Korea is often constructed in the United States and throughout the US empire as a banal villain that elicits bewilderment, anxiety, and even amusement, reactions akin to the ugly feelings that Sianne Ngai argues are not resolved by catharsis.[74] Instead, North Korea exists as a constant but minor threat that justifies the need for American protection without prompting scrutiny of the style or duration of US global policing. The kind of dystopic speculative modes by which North Korea is written rely on racialized and imperial practices of knowing that encourage readers to trust Western authors but not the subjects about which they write. This same dynamic makes it possible to focus on North Korea as a singular inhuman figure without also critiquing the violence of Japanese colonialism and US imperialism. The myopia of this brutal fantasy of North Korea helps to maintain a dependency on US security and solidify uneven global investments in the fictions of liberal democracy in a US-dominated post–Cold War era, thereby directing our attention away from the foundational violence upon which the global order rests.

2

The Inhuman Figure of Human Rights

LIFE WRITING, TESTIMONIES, AND

ESCAPE FROM CAMP 14

Legible Subjects

In January 2015, stories circulated throughout the Western media about North Korean defector Shin Dong-hyuk, subject of the bestselling biography *Escape from Camp 14: One Man's Remarkable Odyssey from North Korea to Freedom in the West* (2012), which detailed his life in and escape from the notorious political prison. Public critique focused largely on how Shin had admitted to multiple inaccuracies in his narrative. Faced with this controversy, Shin Dong-hyuk and Blaine Harden (the author who had written and published Shin's story after conducting extensive interviews) claimed that while certain details were altered, the heart of Shin's story remained unchanged. Harden summed up the dilemma as follows: "From a human rights perspective, [Shin] was still brutally tortured, but he moved things around."[1] Yet given that Shin's story of being the only person to have been born into and escaped from Camp 14 had made him a highly visible spokesperson for North Korean survivors of state atrocities, such troubling admissions could not easily be dismissed. The representational value of Shin's story was augmented by his deposition before the United Nations Human Rights Council (UNHRC) in 2013; he was the first witness to appear in the UN's hearings that were part of its Commission of Inquiry (COI) on Human Rights in the Democratic People's Republic of Korea (DPRK). As one of three hundred people whose testimonies contributed to the final report produced by the UN's COI, Shin Dong-hyuk's account (which repeated many of the details that appeared in *Escape from Camp 14*) carried much political weight. One news story notes,

> Shin was something of an activist poster-boy, giving speeches around the world, penning editorials and picking up awards.
>
> The US-based Human Rights Watch described him as the world's "single strongest voice on atrocities taking place in North Korea."
>
> Shin has acknowledged that the damage his retractions have done meant he "may not be able to continue" his activist work.[2]

Critiques of Shin Dong-hyuk's story raise larger questions about the credibility of North Korean testimonials and have significant potential repercussions for other human rights advocates by drawing attention to what has been referred to as "an open secret that some North Korean defectors, and their backers, exaggerate their experiences in North Korea."[3] Because the UN was not given access to either North Korea or the bordering areas of China, its report on the DPRK relied heavily on witness and victim testimony; consequently, at stake for international human rights organizations is not just the authenticity of one individual's story but also the validity of an entire case built against North Korea for its human rights violations.[4] As Ingu Hwang notes in his assessment of Shin's testimony and the impact of his recanting on the COI, much debate ensued about whether his testimony should be admissible because "the ideological agenda of the defector and the political biases of the listener, many argued, made such eyewitness testimony suspect."[5]

I open this chapter with the controversy surrounding Shin Dong-hyuk because it underscores matters of audience, legibility, and recognition that bring to light the limits of human rights and accentuates how the subject of human rights is constructed through these discourses. Without minimizing the potential damage this poses for advocacy groups working on behalf of North Koreans, we must be mindful of how the desire to alter, and even embellish details of, Shin's account speaks to a situation that is not his alone. As Christine Hong argues in her analysis of Kang Chol-hwan's *The Aquariums of Pyongyang* and

Helie Lee's *In the Absence of Sun*, North Korean defector memoirs are often supported by South Korean and US governments and agencies and are "a securitized form of writing whose surface similarity to autobiography and other forms of narrative self-disclosure should not obscure its status as intelligence."[6] It is therefore worth investigating Shin's story for what it reveals about the politics of voice and representation as they are enacted on a global stage via cultural fantasies of North Korea as a place unlike any other in the world. While North Korean refugee narratives accentuate violence, grinding poverty, and difficult circumstances that merit global attention, as Andrei Lankov reminds us, "The real story of the average North Korean refugee is depressing, but hardly dramatic enough for the average media audience."[7] It is in this regard that we can see most clearly how Shin was able to become a human rights star and capture wide audiences with his story. Predictably, *Escape from Camp 14* presents an exceptionalist view of North Korea that is quite extreme in terms of the conditions it depicts. These "extreme" characterizations—which converge on individual inhumanity, familial indifference, and East-versus-West depravity—fashion North Koreans as figures with little, if any, agency as they bring into focus the essentializing impulses that undergird contemporary human rights politics. In order to track the shifting relations of power indexed through Shin's story, this chapter traces the ways in which Shin's text is produced as a "bona fide" defector account through the entanglement of life writing and human rights discourses, and then reshaped as it circulates, finds various audiences, and is remediated as a documentary film.

"Freedom Is Just Another Word for Grilled Meat"

That North Korea is a rogue state guilty of routinely violating the human rights of its citizens as well as those of other countries is a widely accepted belief that circulates throughout much of the world. Images of North Koreans being persecuted by the country's authoritarian government, often in the form of detainment within political prison camps or as individuals subjected to punishment without the benefit of a fair trial, abound within the popular imagination of the international community and are easily accepted as being true, despite often being accompanied by only the scantest supporting evidence. An example of this dynamic of dystopic speculation can be seen in stories that circulated throughout global media outlets (from 2013 to 2014 and then resurfacing in 2020) about how Kim Jong Un's uncle (Jang Song-thaek) had fallen quickly from political favor and had been executed by being fed to a pack of one hundred and twenty hungry dogs. Despite being unverified, the gruesome story of Jang Song-thaek's capital punishment was picked up by the Western press; in fact, one news story claimed that this report "originated with a satirical post on a Chinese social media network, turning a thinly-sourced horror story into an astonishing example of the media echo chamber gone awry."[8] Subsequent reports confirmed Jang Song-thaek's execution but diverged over the method of his execution, with some experts claiming he was put to death by a firing squad and US president Trump alleging that Jang Song-thaek was decapitated.[9] Given that these confirmations appear to be based on speculation and hearsay, it is possible that both, neither, or either version is true. By pointing to these conflicting reports about Jang Song-thaek's demise, my intention is to note the ease with which the global public is persuaded that North Korea is a bad or illiberal subject culpable of even the most outlandish human rights violations and, moreover, maintains such beliefs even as contradictory reports proliferate and claims are debunked. In this way, narrative and law intersect throughout the long Cold War to produce North Korea as a brutal subject of human rights.

The assumption that the North Korean state needs to be carefully monitored, and even policed, is also discernible within the realm of international human rights law; narrative and legal representations of North Korea coalesce to influence specific interventions such as the UNHRC's Commission of Inquiry on Human Rights in the Democratic People's Republic of Korea. Established on March 21, 2013, by the UNHRC and composed of three members—Michael Donald Kirby (Chair, Australia), Marzuki Darusman (Indonesia, Special Rapporteur on the situation of human rights in the DPRK), and Sonja Biserko (Serbia)—the COI was mandated to "investigate the systematic, widespread and grave violations of human rights in the Democratic People's Republic of Korea, with a view to ensuring full accountability, in particular for violations which may amount to crimes against humanity."[10] The COI was given a year to prepare a report that would present recommendations to the Human Rights Council. The process of creating the COI was unusual in that the UNHRC did not first call a vote on the matter. Kirby implies that the serious nature of these alleged violations—which included torture and inhuman treatment, arbitrary arrest and detention, violations associated with prison camps, and violations of the right to food—justified the UN's unilateral decision as he describes how it was with "a measure of the impatience and sense of obligation on the part of the international community that the COI was created without dissent."[11]

While the COI requested cooperation from the DPRK, including access to the country and details about North Korea's human rights situation, these requests were denied by the North Korean government. The North Korean government's refusal to cooperate during the inquiry is hardly surprising given that it had been refusing entry to the Special Rapporteur appointed by the UN Commission on Human Rights since 2004.[12] In 2011, the DPRK had "resolutely and categorically" rejected the mandate of the Special Rapporteur to investigate and report on the human rights situation in the DPRK.[13] According to North Korea, the Special Rapporteur (a position that was renewed annually) and the UN's resolutions were political interventions on the part of the United States, Japan, and their allies rather than genuine efforts to protect human rights.[14] So Se Pyong, the DPRK's ambassador and permanent representative to the UN, drew attention to the circumstances surrounding the adoption of the first resolution as proof for this claim. He argued that back in 2003, human rights dialogue between the DPRK and the EU had been at a good stage and, moreover, that North Korea had neither been consulted nor even given prior notice of the resolution, describing the process as taking "the form of a surprise raid shortly before voting and forcibly adopted through the high-handedness, arbitrariness and behind-the-scenes pressure and trickery of the United States, Japan, and the States members of the European Union."[15] So Se Pyong's response seems to reference events such as the summit with Japan and North Korea and the failed accord, and President Bush's labeling of North Korea as part of the Axis of Evil; it also implicitly acknowledges that the rhetoric of human rights violations was being used globally for "diplomatic denunciation at international fora and theatrical attacks for the sake of media but bombardment, invasion, and occupation" as well as to anticipate the continued efforts of American governmental agencies to intervene in North Korean affairs.[16] It is worth noting that the DPRK's objections to the Special Rapporteur's appointment do not acknowledge that in the previous year, North Korea had admitted to abducting Japanese nationals during the 1970s and 1980s. And it is precisely because the dispute over the appointment of a Special Rapporteur fell into a familiar pattern of accusations, denials, and conflict that continued with the COI that North Korea's critiques of the politics of human rights and the UN's motives for investigating the DPRK's human rights situation demand careful consideration.

North Korea's refusal to cooperate with the COI meant that there was little physical or documentary evidence to support the allegations of human rights violations. As a consequence, the COI relied heavily on witness/victim testimonies and demonstrative evidence (such as satellite imagery provided by expert witnesses). Given the importance of first-hand accounts for corroborating allegations and attesting to the severity of the crimes, the narrative dimensions of these testimonies merit closer scrutiny as do the larger questions that reliance on testimony poses for human rights discourse. Many of the witnesses told their stories previously in public forums to organizations like NK Watch or through collaboratively written memoirs or biographies. Often these stories were then amplified by political organizations such as Amnesty International UK and picked up by major news outlets like the *New York Times*.[17] By including these voices within its investigation, the COI deliberately positioned itself within a larger matrix of stories, listeners, and institutions as indicated by Kirby's suggestion that the committee use Shin Dong-hyuk's published account to supplement his testimony: "We can use the book in elaborating the statements that you make before us today. Is that right? If you then get the time to cover a particular point, the points are covered in the book and you are happy with ways they are covered. Is that right?"[18] This interplay between text and testimony is reinforced through the examples that Shin Dong-hyuk provided for the UN as many of them had already been recounted in *Escape from Camp 14*. For instance, Shin Dong-hyuk's biography describes in detail the relentless hunger he experienced in the camp and how his desire to escape was prompted by the desire to eat delicious food: "Uncle had dared Shin to dream about one day getting out of the camp and eating whatever he wanted. Freedom, in Shin's mind, was just another word for grilled meat."[19] Shin's testimony also states that the stories of food that he heard from his cellmate were a large part of his motivation to escape.[20] Here, Shin's testimony in front of the UN and his published biography are understood to be interchangeable rather than as separate inputs that collectively expand the scope and complexity of his story.

These stories with their layers of mediation must be read, on the one hand, as forms of life writing produced as part of the industry that has emerged around North Korean memoirs and, on the other hand, within the context of human rights discourse, each investing and intending to accrue various forms of capital — political, social, and economic — from North Korean stories. As complementary frameworks, life writing and human rights are part of a larger formation that influences understandings of international justice as it instrumentalizes the stories of North Korean migrants. The COI is a compelling case study because it relies heavily on the testimonies of those who have published their life stories and/or told them in interviews and other forums, thus illustrating a public appetite for stories of suffering that simultaneously entertain and fulfill a political-juridical function. To move beyond these limited terms of engagement requires asking how North Koreans become legible subjects produced through a set of stylistic conventions for particular audiences and, moreover, how their stories generate affects such as empathy, alienation, and pity. Where does the power of such stories lie for human rights audiences and global readers? Can these stories be heard otherwise? What kinds of affects are produced if these stories are read or heard by different and even unintended audiences?

Such questions about the audience for international justice underscore how North Korea was the object of the investigation rather than the intended audience for the report, a distinction that is made clear by how the inquiry maneuvered between the concept of human rights as a universal project and the local and historical circumstances in which human rights are always experienced. In many respects, the transcripts from the COI read like a transitional justice measure intended to repair human rights violations, even though North Korea was not experiencing democratization or even political restructuring. After Kim Jong-il's death in 2011, the leadership of North Korea was handed over to Kim Jong Un, but the country remained a dictatorship. Read from this angle, the COI can be interpreted as an exercise of diplomatic power intended to encourage the international community to press for regime change in North Korea. Or, viewed from yet another angle, the COI appears as the enactment of a fantasy in which the UN returns to 1950 to prevent the Korean War by forcing the DPRK to transition to a democratic government.

The COI's public hearings were held between August and October 2013, beginning in Seoul and then moving to Tokyo and London, before concluding in Washington, DC, with more than eighty victims, witnesses, and experts providing testimonies. Holding inquiries in Asia, the United Kingdom, and the United States emphasized the international stakes of this COI as it was able to highlight human rights violations as experienced by North Korean, South Korean, Japanese, and other national citizens. While many of the testimonies spoke to common experiences of starvation and harsh conditions of imprisonment, there were still clear distinctions between the hearings in terms of national concerns and approaches. For example, the hearing held in Tokyo centered largely on the abductions of Japanese nationals and featured testimonies by the family members of those who had gone missing, whereas the hearing in Washington, DC, featured the testimonies of defectors and several American experts on North Korean human rights, food access, prison camps, and satellite imagery. The focus of each hearing spoke to the particular discourses that had developed within each of the host countries about North Korea as a threat. As noted in the previous chapter, the abduction of individuals from Japan since the 1970s was a long-standing issue that the Japanese government had raised since the early 1990s. During a Japan–North Korea summit in 2002, Kim Jong-il admitted that the DPRK had kidnapped citizens and returned five individuals to Japan; but many families continue to demand justice as they believe their loved ones have not been accounted for or that the DPRK has falsely claimed them as deceased and that they are still being held against their will in North Korea. Of these stories of Japanese abductees, Yokota Megumi, is perhaps the most well-known in Japan; she disappeared in 1977 as a teenager, and her parents, Yokota Sakie and Shigeru, actively campaigned for her return.[21] Megumi's story has been told in her mother's memoir *North Korea Kidnapped My Daughter* (1999), multiple documentaries, and manga. In contrast, the hearings in Washington, DC, were composed of a day of testimonies by North Korean defectors and a subsequent day featuring prominent American scholars based at notable organizations such as the Center for Strategic and International Studies, The Brookings Institution, and Scowcroft Center for Strategy and Security. In the US hearings, the stories of North Korean defectors were put in dialogue with what the COI's agenda calls "DPRK Specialists" who approach North Korea through an area studies lens.

In comparison, the hearings in Seoul were striking for how they incited pity and moral outrage—featuring defectors who spoke about their difficult experiences in North Korea and individuals based in South Korea who worked with North Korea–focused organizations (some of whom were also defectors and others who were not)—to persuade the listener through appeals to emotion rather than by drawing primarily on logical or rational forms of argumentation. In Seoul, Shin Dong-hyuk gave the first testimony of the COI, and Kang Chol-hwan was the last witness to speak; that Shin Dong-hyuk and Kang Chol-hwan bookended the first set of hearings is notable as both individuals published accounts that have garnered considerable international attention. Also, prior to the passage in the United States of the North Korean Human Rights Act of 2004, Kang Chol-hwan had testified before the US Congress in what Dae-Han Song and Christine Hong call an "'axis of evil' moment" in which "defectors like Kang Cheol-hwan and others implicitly made a case for US interventionism, by hard or soft means."[22]

Other witnesses such as Kim Young-soon had also told their stories publicly before.[23] Many of the accounts speak of their experiences with the *bowibu* (North Korean police who handle political criminals) and time spent in political prison camps. The testimonies are quite diverse and illustrate the complexity of North Korean migrant communities with, for instance, the individuals coming from a range of socioeconomic backgrounds, with some individuals like Kang Chol-hwan, Jeong Kwang-il, and Kim Young-soon growing up in privileged households and others such as Kim Eun Cheol, from less affluent families, who left North Korea in search of food. At the same time, the family histories of these witnesses attest to North Korea's shifting place within international communities as well as to transformations occurring within the country. For instance, Kang Chol-hwan's family migrated to North Korea from Japan as

Communists and supporters of the postwar North Korean government; Kim Eun Cheol's family migrated from China in order to escape the persecution of Koreans in China; and Shin Dong-hyuk was born in a prison camp. Kang Chol-hwan escaped from North Korea in 1996, during the Arduous March, a decade before Shin Dong-hyuk, who crossed into China in 2005. Kim Eun Cheol's journey was more circuitous as he first tried to leave North Korea in 1999, but he returned to North Korea to see his father after altercations with authorities in Russia and China. Upon his return to North Korea, Kim Eun Cheol was arrested and sent to Yodok camp. In 2006, Kim Eun Cheol finally arrived in South Korea.

In the decade that separated their departures from North Korea to South Korea, the situation regarding North Korean migrants shifted considerably, with South Korea opening its Hanawon education facility in 1998 and the United States drawing more attention to North Korean human rights concerns by establishing a US Committee for Human Rights in North Korea in 2002, forming a US North Korea Freedom Coalition in 2003, and enacting its North Korean Human Rights Act in 2004.[24] Worth noting is that the 2004 North Korean Human Rights Act, with its twenty-four million dollar annual budget (authorized from 2005 to 2008), has been criticized as "a thinly veiled way in which to pressure or encourage the overthrow of the regime in Pyongyang."[25] But these testimonies were not presented at the hearing in chronological order or even clustered together according to any discernible logic. When hearing these testimonies or reading their transcriptions together, the differences between the witnesses are flattened and made imperceptible. Instead, nuclear issues, food shortages, and the precarity of lives that hinge on the whims of a ruler are concerns that remain dominant within a global public's understanding of North Korea, while more nuanced shifts under the regimes of Kim Jong-il and Kim Jong Un are harder to grasp given how these testimonies are interwoven with each other. Also absent from the COI's framing of the testimonies is a sense of how the South Korean government and wider public's relations to the issue of North Korean defectors has shifted over time, or how the public's perception of North Korean defectors has become an issue within the South-South political landscape that conservative fundamentalist groups have used to press for regime change.[26]

The UN's ahistorical approach to North Korea is consistent with how North Korea tends to be conceptualized by the West. To counter such framings, this chapter historicizes North Korean human rights via two periods, 1948 and the post-1987 era, as key moments in the histories of Korea and human rights discourse. The year 1948 marks both the year that the United Nations General Assembly adopted the Universal Declaration of Human Rights (UDHR) and the year that the Democratic People's Republic of Korea (DPRK) and the Republic of Korea (ROK) were formally established as states. The post-1987 period also holds doubled meaning: from a global perspective, 1987 marks the beginning of a post–Cold War neoliberal era; but viewed from the Korean peninsula, this era marks the South Korean government's transition from military rule to democracy and it marks "an epochal transformation in the political structure and society of South Korea."[27] Historicizing the category of the human and its attendant rights is crucial to understanding why and when the international community mobilized discourses of universal human rights in relation to North Korea. As a genealogy of the inhuman, North Korea offers a very particular set of insights as it draws attention to the simultaneous efforts of countries to undergo decolonization while global militarized infrastructures were being built up. The tensions between North Korea and the UN remind us that the UN participated in the construction of the human and human rights, even as it was a player in the staging of war on the basis of intervention. This chapter then turns to Blaine Harden's influential biography *Escape from Camp 14* for how it depicts Shin Dong-hyuk as an inhuman subject incapable of human attachment and intimacy. This biography is often read for how it promotes a fundamental need for universal human rights; but I argue instead that the terms of such arguments and the practices of reading Shin's story prevent us from attaining such goals. The North Korean is not a subject for human rights advocates to rescue but rather a figure of the minor inhuman that is sacrificed in order to demonstrate to the global community the importance of safeguarding human rights for their own protection.

Postwar Human Rights

On December 10, 1948, the UN General Assembly adopted the Universal Declaration of Human Rights (UHDR). The drafting committee for the document consisted of René Cassin (France), Charles Malik (Lebanon), Peng Chung Chang (China), and John Humphrey (Canada), and it was chaired by Eleanor Roosevelt (United States) who "was recognized as the driving force for the Declaration's adoption."[28] Motivated by the Holocaust and the aftermath of World War II, "the international community vowed never again to allow atrocities like those of that conflict to happen again. World leaders decided to complement the UN Charter with a road map to guarantee the rights of every individual everywhere."[29] Since then, human rights discourse has become familiar and widespread, perhaps even what Joseph Slaughter calls "normative" when he observes that "we are now living in the Age of Human Rights."[30] Yet how are we to read these assertions of international human rights and dignity given that they were made at the same time as the conditions for the Korean War and multiple other wars in Asia were being laid? And how are we to recognize, moreover, that as early as 1951, the United States was seriously contemplating using atomic weapons again, this time to win the Korean War?[31] In what ways are these discourses of human rights unable to imagine either the Asian as a figure or North Korea as a nation-state to be the subject of human rights? Situated adjacent to such discourses, narratives by North Korean defectors exemplify the parameters of the contemporary Western imagination with respect to human rights and demonstrate what Jodi Kim calls "the *protracted afterlife* of the Cold War."[32] Within this context, North Korea functions alternately as a metaphor for the inhuman and as a metonym for Asian incivility.

The UDHR is often referenced as a landmark moment in discussions on human rights. Enshrined in its preamble is a particular vision of human rights that unequivocally asserts a belief in human equality and that declares a firm commitment to human rights defined in terms of four freedoms: freedom of speech, freedom of religion, freedom from persecution, and freedom from want. Such freedoms are not limited to individual subjectivity but are instead universalized as "the foundation of freedom, justice and peace in the world" and "the highest aspiration of the common people."[33] While the document is not legally binding, it articulates the principles and aspirations of the UN General Assembly in 1948. The preamble, as well as the UDHR proper, is marked by a desire to ensure that the previous violations that had occurred in Europe would never be replicated. It is free, however, from any sense of urgency with respect to addressing ongoing violations or conflicts that were being seeded as the document was being drafted. And while the document represents a major moment in human rights discourse, Samuel Moyn argues, the UDHR was never the crucial transformative one that scholars take it to be. Instead, it is "best understood as canonizing political and social rights as part of a consensus that citizens required new and powerful states at home."[34] If we follow Moyn's line of thought, we can read the UDHR as a major moment not because it establishes human rights as a universal mechanism for justice, but rather for how it codifies a global Cold War order. Also weighing in on this tension between justice and order, Randall Williams notes that while human rights discourse provides the West with a lens for viewing political violence in the rest of the world, it is limited in terms of how it can intervene in these violences.[35] And while the West may often be unwilling to recognize these limitations, the Global South is aware that "Western humanitarian intervention is guided by a brute calculus of power, and no amount of mosquito nets or workers will ever cover over this fact."[36]

Costas Douzinas also critiques human rights as an instrument that codifies new forms of imperial power rather than one that defends subjects from domination. In *Human Rights and Empire*, he outlines how human rights is a composite term, with the rights component operating as a legal category and the human "refer[ring] to a more or less concrete sense of morality, which accompanies the institution of legal rights."[37] Noting that after 1945, the sources of human rights shifted from state sites to international and regional conventions, treaties, and case-law, Douzinas argues that this post–World War II turn to human rights discourse

> provided a high moral ground for the new order and the United Nations, its prime institutional expression. But the commitment to morality and rights was schizophrenically accompanied by the principle of non--intervention in the internal affairs of states. The promotion of morality and the defence of sovereignty, two allegedly antagonistic principles, served two separate agendas of the great powers: the need to legitimise the new world order through its commitment to rights, without exposing the victorious states to scrutiny and criticism about their own flagrant violations.[38]

Neda Atanasoski offers a similarly sharp appraisal of human rights and humanitarian discourse as vehicles of power primarily wielded by the United States by arguing that "US militarism—as well as other forms of interventionism—in the present is in fact an instantiation of a *postsocialist imperialism* based in humanitarian ethics."[39] In *Humanitarian Violence*, she traces how US power subjects the world to forms of violence, no longer in order to contain the threat of communism but rather so that all can "enjoy racial and religious freedom, as exemplified by the principles of US liberal democracy."[40] Human rights becomes a means of dividing the world between those who need to be humanized and those morally equipped to humanize, thus marking both a shift as well as a continuation of earlier forms of imperialism.[41] Such assessments reinforce the importance of viewing 1948 not in terms of emancipation but rather in terms of consolidation; for, as Balakrishnan Rajagopal observes, human rights is a discourse whose elements "are directly descended from colonial ideology and practices."[42]

If we extend these critiques of human rights as a discourse that uses its moral power to further Global North interests, it becomes clear how globally unrepresentative the United Nations' Declaration was and that its universal subject entitled to freedoms was not imagined as Korean or even Asian.[43] Instead, we must recognize that "the historical development of human rights reflects Cold War priorities and animosities."[44] While the Korean War (1950–53) is a pertinent example of conflict in Asia that lies outside the UN's understanding of the world in 1948, I emphasize the Korean War as only one moment within a much longer process wherein Asia is separated from the West and its project of human rights. The UN and the United States sought to define and protect human freedoms even as the United States was, as Jodi Kim reminds us,

> install[ing] governments and economic systems favorable to US interests in the name of "democracy" and "collective security." Just as the "civilizing mission" of nineteenth-century European colonialism had provided the ideological cover for conquest, this "democratizing mission" provided the rhetorical justification for the United States in its effort to establish and maintain imperial control over Asia.[45]

As both the first product of the Cold War and its final visible legacy, North Korea represents the limits of human rights as conceptualized by the UDHR. Jodi Kim reminds us that we must be aware of the Cold War "not solely as a historical epoch or event" but also as "a knowledge project or epistemology, which is always also a pedagogy, and [ask] how it continues to generate and teach 'new' knowledge by making sense of the world through the Manichaean logics and grammars of good and evil."[46] Analyzing how North Korea is positioned within human rights discourses requires an understanding of the activities taking place within the nation-state and a consciousness of the Cold War analytics through which we view that space. The year 1948 then is perhaps best understood as a year that has more symbolic than real power for human rights, as well as a year in which the UN codified the marginality of colonized spaces like Korea to humanity.[47]

And yet, scholars such as Jiyoung Song argue that there is a North Korean tradition for thinking about the kinds of values typically understood as human rights in the West. Rather than being a nation devoid of human rights thinking, Song argues that human rights in North Korea are informed by indigenous cultural values as well as by postcolonial and socialist principles. Distinguishing between the adoption of individual versus collective rights as well as between civic and political rights versus socioeconomic rights, she describes how the DPRK has prioritized the latter of each (collective rights and socioeconomic rights) in its project of decolonization and self-determination. This can be seen in the North Korean constitution that binds together economic and political rights and "conflates subsistence rights of the individual with the security and sovereignty of the nation. All rights are converged, and indeed subordinated, to security and sovereignty in the end."[48] As a colonized country outside of the scope of human rights as articulated by the United Nations in 1948, North

Korea's approach to human rights has more in common with the decolonizing and socialist countries that, as Moyn describes, emphasize welfare rights such as the right to housing, food, and education. According to Song, "The main discourse within 'our style' [that is, North Korean style] of human rights includes the right to national survival, dictatorship as the protection of human rights, rights granted by the fatherly and military leader, the primacy of socioeconomic rights, and finally the duty-based language of human rights, both as the offspring of rights and as a correlative term for rights."[49] While welfare rights are included within the UDHR, they are subordinated to political and civic rights. By bringing together Song and Moyn's analyses, it becomes evident that a country like North Korea, which understands its leadership structure as integral to protecting socioeconomic rights and the survival of the nation, is incommensurable with an UN-based program of human rights.

If read in the historically and culturally nuanced terms that Song outlines, North Korea appears as a country in which different conceptions of rights operate rather than as a nation that is incapable of understanding human rights or resistant to the principles. In other words, the conflict between North Korean and UN notions of human rights occurs over different understandings of the role of the nation—which is invoked implicitly for the UN in terms of how human rights are to be implemented and explicitly for North Korea—which undermines the UN's assertions of the universality of human rights. Christine Hong argues that this US-centered version of human rights has been largely unaccountable to the historical and structural conditions of imperial violence and intervention and cites the *We Charge Genocide* petition presented by the Civil Rights Congress to the UN in 1951 as an example of the flawed nature of human rights. This petition brought together the Jim Crow law and US war in Korea in an attempt to position linked racist and imperial histories within the purview of human rights law.[50] As this petition drew the international public's attention to

> the devaluation of nonwhite life—life subjected to collateralization under US sovereignty—this 1951 petition offered analysis along critical human rights lines that neither peddled in a politics of pity and rescue nor reinscribed the inequality of the world system. Instead, it gestured toward a humanism that had yet to assert its fullest political possibility—what Aimé Césaire would in 1955 call "a humanism made to the measure of the world."[51]

Unable to get the UN to investigate the United States on these charges of genocide, the Civil Rights Congress (CRC) was forced to disband after the US government targeted the CRC, which served as "a hint of the 'something rotten' at the heart of the emergent international human rights regime."[52] In addition to illustrating the limits of human rights for colonial and imperial subjects in the postwar period, Hong's argument draws attention to how human rights discourse not only excludes but also actively erases critiques put forward by the Global South by "render[ing] illegible or 'rogue' rights-based interpretations of the structural violence perpetrated by imperial nations."[53] In this way, Hong also underscores how Global South and Global North nations espouse competing understandings of human rights but how only the latter's views are perceived to be legitimate. While Hong's critique is directed primarily toward governments and political institutions such as the UN, a comparable dynamic can be seen in scholarly work that is "caught in an ideological bind, arguing contradictorily that human rights are universal, but that human rights are indigenous only to the West. By so swiftly dismissing other value systems that might successfully be incorporated into an international concept of human rights, such scholars are working against the very universality that they want to achieve."[54]

This project of imagining the subject of human rights in Western terms was further extended by the 1951 UN Convention Concerning the Status of Refugees, a document meant to address the status of refugees and determine the eligibility of asylum for stateless persons, which explicitly limits obligations to vulnerable persons through its temporal and spatial qualifiers. Until the 1967 Protocol was introduced, the scope of the protections afforded to refugees was limited to those affected by events that occurred prior to January 1, 1951. Moreover, signatories were given (and continue to have) the option of limiting their obligations to those persons affected by events that had either taken place only in Europe or that included and extended beyond Europe. These qualifiers underscore the fact that, like the UDHR, the 1951 Convention was produced in response to the events and aftermath of World War II and was initially borne out of a desire to safeguard the Western subject.

The Convention also establishes a distinct narrative of refugee-ism by defining the refugee through his or her relationship to fear. The refugee is explicitly described as a person who,

> owing to well-founded fear of being persecuted for reasons of race, religion, nationality, membership of a particular social group or political opinion, is outside the country of his nationality and is unable or, owing to such fear, is unwilling to avail himself of the protection of that country; or who, not having a nationality and being outside the country of his former habitual residence as a result of such events, is unable or, owing to such fear, is unwilling to return to it.[55]

If we read the Convention in relation to North Korea, the constraints of the language and logic of human rights become visible in two crucial ways. First, the Convention conceives of persecution solely in terms of the state and as occurring for five possible reasons (including race, religion, or political opinion); imagined in these terms, the refugee becomes legible as a minoritized subject that merits protection. In contrast, one kind of fear North Korean escapees often describe is the anxiety that they may be accused of having committed crimes against the state. This constant, low-grade fear is distinct from the kind of deliberate persecution imagined by the UN in 1951, and it cannot easily be translated into the restrictive language of the Convention. Second, human rights discourses position the rational citizen with access to political representation against the fearful figure of the refugee who, "caged within a depoliticized humanitarian space," is made invisible and passive.[56] Located within these relations of power, the refugee is positioned as an irrational figure incapable of being heard by an international community. And while North Korean escapees may not adhere to the UN's rigid definition of the refugee, as the example of Shin Dong-hyuk illustrates, they are still silenced by the discourses of human rights that seek to protect them even as these discourses render invisible the conditions under which they and North Korea emerged. As Pooja Rangan argues in her critique of how humanitarian discourses decontextualize their subjects, we must recognize that "the humanitarian demand for referentiality and immediacy consolidates a particularly apolitical discourse of human rights that is grounded in abstract, essential characteristics of humanity."[57]

The difference between North Korea as a place lived in by its citizens and one imagined by those outside of the DPRK is noted in another memoir, the aforementioned *Dear Leader: My Escape from North Korea*, in which former high-ranking official and North Korean Poet Laureate Jang Jin-sung describes his harrowing experiences of fleeing his country of origin, traveling through China, and finally finding sanctuary in South Korea. Reflecting on his journey, Jang Jin-sung writes in the memoir's epilogue, "As I've written elsewhere: '[Back home] there are two North Koreas: one real and the other a fiction.' After my defection, I recognized the existence of a third North Korea: a theoretical one, one constructed by the outside world."[58] While the state propaganda of North Korea is broadly recognized and forms the basis of what Jang calls a "fiction" of North Korea, what has received less attention is this "third North Korea," a fictional entity "constructed by the outside world." For many, this third North Korea is produced through cultural representations that include commercial or documentary films about North Korea (e.g., Sony's *The Interview* or *Team America: World Police*); memoirs by former citizens such as Jang; and media reports that highlight nuclear threats, egregious human rights violations, and bizarre and even unfathomable acts (such as the friendship between Kim Jong Un and former NBA player Dennis Rodman or the flying of hot air balloons over South Korea with bags of garbage and excrement attached).

Collectively, these representations function as a cultural fantasy of the inhuman, one wherein the brutal and macabre are pitched as the North Korean everyday. These cultural fantasies—which operate in stark contrast to Western notions of quotidian "democratic" existence—serve as the primary backdrop for North Korean life writing and transform a survivor like Shin Dong-hyuk into a human rights star. In its wholesale accounts of unimaginable inhumanity and unending brutality, *Escape from Camp 14* renders urgent the need for human rights intervention; however, such calls for intervention are necessarily decontextualized, as evidenced by the narrative's non-mention of longer colonial histories, complex revolutionary moments, and convoluted global relations. While life writing as a genre is certainly not obligated to tell national or global histories, historical framing becomes imperative vis-à-vis North Korean stories because of the systematic forgetting of such histories by international audiences. Without such framing, Shin Dong-hyuk ran the risk of becoming an ahistorical figure or being reduced to a trope rather than being seen as an individual telling his particular story.

Cultural fantasies about North Korea have not only reinforced how it is a country beyond the reach of human rights law and logic; such dystopic speculative imaginings have also racialized North Korea as an inhuman entity. This becomes visible if we turn to the UNESCO statements on race, a set of documents produced coterminously with the UDHR. Here, it bears noting that UNESCO was also formed in the postwar context; it was "created in order to respond to the firm belief of nations, forged by two world wars in less than a generation, that political and economic agreements are not enough to build a lasting peace. Peace must be established on the basis of humanity's moral and intellectual solidarity."[59] At the core of UNESCO's mission are education, heritage, scientific cooperation, and freedom of expression. With these guiding principles in mind, UNESCO issued a series of statements (1950, 1951, 1964, and 1967) designed to address racial prejudice by debunking the biological determinism attached to race-based difference and emphasizing difference as the product of culture and environment. Reinforcing the unity of humanity through shared potential, the authors of the 1950 statement assert that "the one trait which above all others has been at a premium in the evolution of men's mental characters has been educability, plasticity. This is a trait which all human beings possess. It is indeed, a species character of *homo sapiens*."[60] In emphasizing the plasticity of humans over rigid limitations based on biology, these statements mark a major shift in racial discourses and reflect the global changes underway during the post–World War II period.[61]

Within this modern terrain, North Korea functions as a peculiar anachronism due to its seeming resistance to transformation. By appearing out of time, North Korea resembles other illiberal spaces or "social worlds and modes of governance that do not align with humanitarian and human rights regimes."[62] North Korea remains a space whose state-controlled economy, authoritarian rule, and obedient citizens trigger an outdated logic of biological racialism in the global cultural imagination. If the malleability of individuals is what makes them part of a collective humanity, then the perceived intransigence of North Korea marks it as inhuman. The international perception of North Korea as a historical relic, unwilling to develop economically and unable to change how it treats its citizens, illustrates how this metaphor of the inhuman operates in this context. Both the individual North Korean subject and the nation-state of the DPRK are constructed as inhuman through their inability to follow a progressivist trajectory. But such constructions do not take into account the complexities of North Korean history and its revolutionary ideals as they have been shaped by Cold War politics, colonialism, and imperialism. In other words, while North Korea may not follow a progressivist trajectory to the Western gaze, it has not been a place of stasis. The relative prosperity of North Korea until about the 1970s and its rapid industrialization and the forms of assistance and relations it had developed with nonaligned countries such as Guyana are examples that complicate the narratives of North Korea that depict it as incapable of progress and outside of modernity.[63] The construction of the human and humanity is always a limited and unequal project, one in which systematic exclusion must occur. Pheng Cheah notes that even as the human is a construction, the "humanity effects are concretely real and efficacious and can be progressive and enabling."[64] The case of North Korea illustrates how the effects of the inhuman are also concrete and real.

North Korean Human Rights in a Post–Cold War Era

I want to hold onto these critiques of human rights and ask why human rights becomes an important analytic for understanding North Korea and, moreover, when this approach gains prominence, in order to historicize this yoking together. This is a necessary move, given that North Korea tends to be viewed in ahistorical terms, as illustrated by the COI's hearings and the approach to testimonies delivered. Resituating North Korean stories within a historical perspective makes it possible to reassess what is at stake in these stories and, moreover, to understand why the historical, social, and material dimensions of these stories have been obscured from the global public. While 1948 has been lionized as a key date for universal human rights, we can chart a rise in the prominence of this discourse in conversations about North Korea toward the end of the Cold War and in the post–Cold War era. The increased number of published life writing texts by or about North Koreans in the late 1990s speaks to this growing desire to see North Korea through this lens of universal human rights. To the best of my knowledge, only four North Korean life writing texts were published from the 1960s to the 1980s (and one of those was by a South Korean author who migrated to North Korea),[65] while more than seventy were published between 1990 and 2015. The three texts published between 1968 and 1978 are available only in Korean and the text by the migrant to North Korea is available in Korean and Chinese. In contrast, texts published from about 2005 on were often first published in either Korean or English (but some were also released first in Chinese or French) and often translated into multiple languages. The social status (both within North and South Korea) of North Korean migrants to South Korea also shifted in the mid-1990s, with earlier waves of migrants composed largely of high-ranking officials in the government or military who were welcomed as heroic figures.[66] By contrast, as more North Koreans migrated to South Korea to escape the famine, they were seen less as valuable sources of information or as patriots and more as economic refugees.[67] While the sharp spike in North Korean testimonials can be attributed to a host of factors that drove more people out of North Korea in the last few decades (including the worsening economic conditions that peaked with the Arduous March, the title given by the North Korean government to the famine of the 1990s), it also indicates an increasing level of public interest in these stories of suffering. And often these individuals who migrated after 2000 have become synonymous with North Korean human rights and what the media often refers to as "celebrity defectors."[68]

The timing of this growth is notable as 1987 was the year that, as a result of the pro-democracy movement, the South Korean government capitulated to public demand for constitutional reform and held its first democratic election. As South Korea began to transition away from military rule and toward democracy, human rights discourse became an instrument used more frequently by the South Korean government. Before this, human rights had not been a genuine political issue in South Korea as it was "considered to be an authoritarian country that severely violated human rights during its own era of military rule."[69] Under the regimes of Presidents Park Chung-hee and Chun Doo-hwan, the 1970s and 1980s in South Korea were a time of martial law and frequent human rights violations that included the exploitation of laborers; violent interrogation techniques that included beatings, waterboarding, and sexual abuse of protestors; and the Kwangju massacre of protestors in 1980.[70] Another story of human rights violations committed by the South Korean government is told in *Repatriation* (2003), a South Korean documentary film made by Kim Dong-won. It shares the stories of North Korean spies who had been held in South Korean prisons for decades and who were subjected to physical and psychological forms of torture as part of an effort to make them recant their North Korean beliefs and convert. In 1991, South Korea was admitted to the UN, at which point it ratified most of the conventions on human rights.[71]

From the late 1990s to the mid-2000s, under the more progressive governments of Presidents Kim Dae-jung (1998–2003) and Roh Moo-hyun (2003–2008), South Korea's efforts were directed toward supporting the basic human needs of North Koreans who were suffering during the Arduous March. These years are often referred to as the "lost decade of progressive rule" by conservative critics unhappy with this approach to human rights in North Korea.[72] In 2006, the National Human Rights Commission of Korea (NHRCK) officially adopted the human rights situation in North Korea as one of its mandates.[73] Justified by Article 3 of the ROK's Constitution, which defines the ROK as the entire peninsula, the NHRCK has taken it upon itself to safeguard human rights across the territory. But Jong-Yun Bae and Chung-in Moon note that this need to protect human rights in North Korea has generated a range of interpretations and positions, with conservative factions and liberals taking contrasting approaches. The former emphasize the importance of civil and political rights (CPR) whereas the latter argue that improvements to the economic, social, and cultural rights (ESCR) need to come before civil and political rights can be realized in North Korea. It is worth noting that this division between civil and political rights and economic and social ones continues the "ideological struggles of the cold war" that had characterized liberalism and socialism in the United States.[74] The motivations of the conservative factions, however, seem rather suspect since the "CPR proponents argue that improved human rights in North Korea are virtually inconceivable without regime change."[75]

North Korean human rights have become part of what Paik Nak-chung calls the division system in the peninsula; he argues that "the entrenched establishments on both sides [North and South Korea], despite their belonging to two very different and often mutually hostile societies, have common vested interests in maintaining division, no matter what they might think or say."[76] Interlocked in this system since 1953, the antagonisms between North and South Korea solidified over the decades. Paik Nak-chung notes that dictatorships are inherently unstable forms of government because they lack popular consent. Thus, he observes of the period leading up to 1987 that "the regimes of North and South actually assisted each other in cementing the division system."[77] In the current era, the division continues to exist. Eleana Kim illustrates this point by describing how the New Right in South Korea has attached itself to the DMZ issue and has used the language of nature and peace to reproduce the Cold War bipolar ideological rift in the South and cement its support for US and South Korea relations.[78]

The appointment of the UN Special Rapporteur on the DPRK's human rights situation in 2004 occurred as a number of transformations were taking place on the Korean peninsula.[79] First, South Korea's transition to democracy enabled it to play the role of the model minority (in opposition to North Korea's position as a global bad subject) and actively support the UN's efforts. Second, the effects of the national famine made the North Korean state more vulnerable to outside intervention. Third, the UN's interest in North Korea in the form of the appointment of a Special Rapporteur followed on the heels of former US president George Bush's 2002 State of the Union speech in which he referred to North Korea, Iran, and Iraq as an axis of evil, "arming to threaten the peace of the world."[80] Fourth, 2002 was also the year that Kim Jong-il admitted that North Korea had abducted Japanese citizens during the 1970s and 1980s and returned five individuals. And fifth, the Special Rapporteur's appointment also coincided with the period in which the issue of the comfort women became a special project for the UN.

As Laura Kang notes, a coalition of women's groups penned an open letter to protest the South Korean government's plan to send a representative to Emperor Hirohito's funeral in 1989, given the unresolved issue of the Korean comfort women.[81] Over the next few years, these South Korean women's groups continued to demand an apology for the exploitation of Korean women by the Japanese military during the war; and in 1991, survivor Kim Hak-sun testified publicly about her experiences.[82] Finally, in February 1992, the Korean Council raised the matter of the comfort women at the UN's Commission on Human Rights and requested that an investigation be conducted.[83] In her examination of the comfort women as part of the wider discourse on trafficked Asian women, Kang cites Katherine H. S. Moon and Laura Hein, who ask in their respective essays about the timing with respect to the visibility of comfort women as a matter of international concern, given that earlier movements that had attempted to draw attention to US military-related prostitution in South Korea had been effaced and that the history of comfort women had been public knowledge in Japan for decades.[84] I share their concern about the sudden willingness of the international community to investigate the comfort women, and would add that this shift needs also to be interrogated in relation to the simultaneous interest in the issue of North Korean human rights.

What then can a discourse of human rights do for North Korea, a national entity conceptualized as inhuman and understood as signaling the limits of this discourse? In tracing how North Korea has come to mark the limits of the human, I argue that the inhuman offers a means of interrogating liberal notions of agency and humanitarian aesthetics. The particular kind of inhuman figure that North Korea is imagined to be—one whose capacity to produce fear is intertwined with its seeming incapacity to feel as well as its ability to pose existential danger with its nuclear weapons and alien form of communism—threatens to destroy middle-class American lives and/or lifestyles. In examining how North Korea is produced by a global order as inhuman, this chapter rethinks the guiding logics of human rights and the audiences they speak to and for.

Inhuman Life Writing and *Escape from Camp 14*

In response to an interview question about whether he viewed North Korea as a communist regime, Slavoj Žižek states that "we all know that North Korea is a total *fiasco*."[85] Žižek's blunt statement sums up a general global opinion on North Korea. And while it may be commonly understood that North Korea is an oppressive regime, details about it are few and far between. It is not, however, impossible to find information, as evidenced by Kim Deog-Young's documentary film and book, both titled *Kim Il Sung's Children*, which tell the story of thousands of orphans and a handful of teachers sent from North Korea to Eastern Europe following the Korean War. Over a span of fifteen years, Kim researched these stories by interviewing teachers, husbands, wives, and friends of these North Korean students in Eastern Europe, consulting local historians, finding photographs, letters, and school records, visiting the buildings in which the children were housed, and watching documentary films.[86] By combing through these materials, Kim provides insight into how the shifting conditions within North Korea and the relationships between North Korea and the Soviet Union during the 1950s and 1960s affected the lives of these North Koreans and the friends they made and families they formed in Poland, Hungary, Czechoslovakia, Bulgaria, and Romania.

Another important source of information about North Korea is the memoirs written by former citizens, many of which read like dystopian nonfiction. These memoirs are difficult to discredit, given the levels of secrecy surrounding North Korea. While these first-hand accounts are valuable for their content and satisfy a desire to tell and hear North Korean stories (as illustrated by the COI testimonies), their accuracy is often suspect, and journalists have noted that it is difficult to verify stories before they go to print. Certainly, the controversy over the falsification of details of Shin Dong-hyuk's account speaks to these difficulties. While there may be a real appetite for North Korean stories, there are few mechanisms in place to ensure the truthfulness of the stories that do circulate. As Harden's introduction to Shin's story notes:

> Fact-checking is not possible in North Korea. Outsiders have not visited its political prison camps. Accounts of what goes on inside them cannot be independently verified. Although satellite images have greatly added to outside understanding of the camps, defectors remain the primary sources of information, and their motives and credibility are not spotless. In South Korea and elsewhere, they are often desperate to make a living, willing to confirm the preconceptions of human rights activists, anticommunist missionaries, and right-wing ideologues. Some camp survivors refuse to talk unless they are paid cash upfront. Others repeated juicy anecdotes they had heard but not personally witnessed.[87]

Harden also discusses the process he underwent to verify Shin Dong-hyuk's story before the book went to press. He claims that the story seemed authentic to "survivors of other labor camps, to scholars, to human rights advocates, and to the South Korean government."[88]

The ever-increasing number of North Korean biographies and testimonials written and consumed over the last three decades is significant, given that they are not an unproblematic means of accessing life in North Korea. The popularity of these texts, however, reveals much about the desires and curiosities of a wider reading public as well as about how North Korea is fashioned for global audiences. While Shin Dong-hyuk's text must be classified as a biography or perhaps an oral history rather than a memoir because he is not the author of this story (and in this way, it and much other North Korean life writing resembles more closely "as-told-to" narratives or even collaborative memoirs, given the relationship between the subjects of the texts, authors and/or coauthors, and the controlling narrative voice), I suggest that insights into the genre of memoir can be used productively to analyze the kinds of pleasures and anxieties generated by North Korean life writing. North Korean stories mobilize the power of individual eyewitness and victim testimony while also acknowledging the limits of what we can know in the absence of "hard" and verifiable evidence. They become a weaving together of an international juridical sphere with popular forms of educational outreach and entertainment, as many of these authors are also featured on platforms like TED Talks. The figure of the North Korean as a minor inhuman becomes a macabre global spectacle and a call to moral indignation. In this way, North Korean stories act as an affective mechanism used to uphold the normativity of a post–Cold War global order.

Unlike other life writing published contemporaneously such as Lucia Jang's *Stars Between the Sun and Moon: One Woman's Life in North Korea and Escape to Freedom* (2014), Hyeonseo Lee's *The Girl with Seven Names: A North Korean Defector's Story* (2015), and Jang Jin-sung's *Dear Leader: My Escape from North Korea* (2014) that speak about family ties and witness wide-scale poverty and starvation, *Escape from Camp 14* is unique precisely because of the subject's affective focus, which pivots on the absence of meaningful familial and filial relationships. Shin Dong-hyuk's memoir depicts relationships with family members as emotionally distant and physically violent;[89] of his mother, we are told that while Shin was completely dependent "upon her for all his meals," he nevertheless "[stole] her food," "endur[ed] her beatings," and "saw her as competition for survival."[90] The concept of love was foreign, and Shin claims to have started to feel it for his mother only years after he fled North Korea, while living in the United States, where he "learned that a civilized child should love his mother."[91] While the aforementioned testimonials illustrate the horrors of North Korea and showcase the *regime* as cruel and inhuman, *Escape from Camp 14* presents its *subject* as inhuman. Shin does this by drawing attention to what he describes as his limited range of emotions: "I did not know about sympathy or sadness.... They educated us from birth so that we were not capable of normal human emotions. Now that I am out, I am learning to be emotional. I have learned to cry. I feel like I am becoming human."[92] This passage showcases how the regime damaged his humanity and reinforces the alienness of North Korea. Through his self-characterization, Shin Dong-hyuk—as an individual whose affective capacity to experience his tragedy was curtailed because of profound human rights violations—offers a compelling human rights subjectivity built on his very inhumanness. Unlike the racialized subjects that Xine Yao examines for their refusals to feel for white subjects and as a consequence are illegible as human, Shin Dong-hyuk's perceived lack of interiority is presented as evidence of North Korea's inhumanity. He becomes a figure easy to abstract as a totalizing version of North Korea, with the institution of the prison replacing family as a force that regulates social relations. Shin embodies the racialized subject par excellence who can never be fully recognized as human.

There is a set of highly gendered and culturally specific assumptions at work in the notion that to be human requires the demonstration of affect and the performance of feeling. *Escape from Camp 14*'s definition of the human through affective performance is from the outset framed in terms of failed maternal affection. Here, the Freudian idea that the mother's withheld affection for the male child produces trauma figures keenly; it has been inserted into the geopolitical context of escaping North Korea, producing in the process a narrative in which Shin escapes maternal monstrosity via the embrace, first, of South Korea, and then, of the West. The root of Shin Dong-hyuk's humanity is accordingly traced back to a nonmaternal mother. As a significant counterpoint, the Western democratic nation-state fulfills this "maternal vacuum" as a place of freedom and space of love, contrasting sharply with North Korea's dystopic, unfeeling registers. As theorized through this biography, North Koreanness is an affect rather than a subjectivity. In this sense, North Koreanness is similar to the Chineseness that Lily Wong analyzes through the figure of the sex worker; Wong argues that the sex worker's obligation to perform happiness serves as a reminder of the dominance of happiness as a structure of feeling.[93] She claims that Chineseness offers a means of critiquing happiness, and I extend her logic to argue that North Koreanness can be viewed as critiquing the politicized force of human rights. And rather than disavowing Shin's experiences for failing to conform to Western understandings of familial love and affection, the minor inhumanness of North Korea can instead be seen as "a potential site through which less legitimized *feelings about structures* can take shape" or even as a means of "creat[ing] alternative assemblages around shared discomfort about normalized social structures."[94]

In analyzing Shin Dong-hyuk's testimony vis-à-vis the shape and moralizing tone of human rights discourse, it is difficult to ignore that effective advocacy such as Shin's speaks to the need for human rights, even as it erases individual subjectivities. Shin's story—wherein brutal details of prison camp survival are situated alongside an account involving how he subverted a familial plot (comprising his mother and brother) to escape Camp 14 without him—illustrates the gravity of the North Korean human rights situation. This account, however, does so at the expense of transforming Shin into the figure of the refugee rather than showing him as an individual who fled North Korea. In *Escape from Camp 14*, Shin confesses that he was initially afraid to admit to anyone that he had betrayed family members because he "was terrified of a backlash, of people asking [him], 'Are you even human?'"[95] His reluctance to describe his own role in the execution of his mother and brother demonstrates an understanding of how the human rights victim must inspire sympathy, an imperative that may even trump accuracy if the story is to engage its readers. The ability to affectively move audiences while instantiating empathy for the North Korean subject, whether a UN Commission or a reader of a testimonial, simultaneously demonstrates the power and limits of human rights discourse. *Escape from Camp 14* presents its subject through the lens of emergency and as falling into "the humanitarian mandate" that "demands action over thinking, ethics over aesthetics, and immediacy over analysis."[96] In assuming refugeeness, Shin's self-characterization relies on a world outside North Korea as a means of establishing a contradictory site of asylum; such human rights counterpoints influence Shin's testimony, which draws on audience expectations about North Korea through received notions of authoritarianism, totalitarianism, and violation and limit how Shin can tell his story.

One way of reading *Escape from Camp 14* is as the story of an inhuman North Korean subject as he fled the state and attempted to become human. By extending Joseph Slaughter's practice of reading human rights law and the bildungsroman as intertwined modes of writing the Western subject, we can see Shin Dong-hyuk's story as an extreme version of the bildungsroman: more than the story of an individual maturing into an adult, Shin was on a journey to becoming human, one that he did not complete by the end of the text. The incomplete journey of Shin toward humanity is crucial since, as Slaughter's work on human rights narrative demonstrates, there are multiple correspondences between the norms and forms of international human rights law and the literary form of the bildungsroman.[97] In the instance of North Korea, the failure to become the ideal subject of either the bildungsroman or international human rights means that North Korea functions as the limit of these forms. Here we can see how the logics of race and the limitations of the nation-state work to position North Korea in discourses of human rights in highly circumscribed ways.

The bulk of the narrative tracks Shin Dong-hyuk's life in Camp 14, his flight from the prison camp and then North Korea, and finally his travels through China. It is replete with lurid details, such as the electrocution of the prison mate who tried to escape with Shin, Shin's use of his friend's dead body "as a kind of insulating pad" to protect him from the electric currents as he crawled over the live fence, and the burning smell of his friend's corpse.[98] These sensationalistic descriptions make the text memorable, and it is perhaps unsurprising that relatively little of the story is devoted to Shin's life after his arrival in South Korea or after he migrated to the United States. The story does not subject either of these two countries to the same degree of scrutiny that it uses to examine life in North Korea. *Escape from Camp 14* narrates the shocking tale of the inhuman subject's flight away from the repressive mechanisms and conditions of a dystopic state and toward the freedoms of capitalism and democracy symbolized by the United States, and it is this act that has captured the attention of countless readers and human rights advocates.

This body of life writing resonates with readers and audiences in ways similar to the genre of the memoir. In her overview of memoir as it has been produced for and consumed by a Western audience, Julie Rak highlights the changing market orientation of these texts. While memoirs were being written earlier in Europe, a major shift occurred during the eighteenth century when prostitutes, libertines, and former courtesans anonymously published their stories. The popularity of these "scandalous memoirs" lay in the salacious details they provided.[99] The anonymity of these authors suggests that, even as their stories found readers willing to buy copies, the market was for tales of vices and shocking appetites rather than for the stories of individuals' experiences. Much like narratives of North Korean refugees, these early memoirs could reach a wide audience by erasing the individual subjectivities of their authors and creating an almost interchangeable generic subject.

And yet, I want to also suggest that Shin Dong-hyuk's story manages to be more than that of the generic North Korean subject of human rights. While these platforms of UN testimony and biography released by a major US publishing house are restrictive, Shin has told his story in other venues, one of which is in the documentary *Camp 14: Total Control Zone*. The film intersperses scenes in which Shin talks about his experiences as a child in the prison camp with interviews with former North Korean prison camp guards and footage of Shin after giving speeches around the world. Many of the stories that Shin tells in the film also appear in *Escape from Camp 14* and in his testimony before the COI, but some are supplemented in the documentary with sketches that depict the scenes. For example, when Shin is asked to recount his earliest memory, he describes the first time he witnessed a public execution as a child. The camera shows us the drawing that accompanies this story and zooms in, letting us see the overwhelmed and scared expression on his face. While *Escape from Camp 14* also includes images that depict key scenes, they are drawn in a less nuanced style than the ones in the film, with less shading and detail. The film also expands the viewer's relation to Shin's story by showing us the impact that these experiences continue to have on him. In the opening scene, we meet Shin in his apartment, and he describes his nightly nightmares, the deep exhaustion he constantly feels, and how he must field continual requests to tell his story. These first few minutes of the film convey the physical and mental toll that being a survivor and, moreover, having to perform this role, take. This becomes a reframing that makes the audience acutely aware of the larger framings that operate within human rights discourse, with the execution of Shin's brother and mother falling into the category of "anachronistic" violence that is typically considered to be "out of the frame of historical progress" and unlike the morally justifiable killings committed by the West that are understood as "necessary to advance liberal reform and rights."[100]

Shin Dong-hyuk speaks in the film about his relation to North Korea and how he still sees it as his home. Absent from Harden's biography of Shin or from Shin's UN testimony, here Shin speaks about how, if the border ever disappeared, he would want to return to North Korea and, more specifically, to the prison camp he grew up in. While his desire to return to a place in which he experienced so much pain is unexpected, he explains it through a critique of South Korea that he says is a place in which people are consumed by thoughts of money. While the prison camp in North Korea was exhausting and often inflicted punishment, it was still a place in which his heart remained pure. The prison camp was also the site in which Shin remembers experiencing support and affection from another person, as a cellmate had taken care of Shin when he was badly injured from beatings by guards. This memory provides a more nuanced lens through which to understand the affective landscape of the North Korean prison camp, and it contrasts with *Escape from Camp 14*'s emphasis on the lack of feeling Shin Dong-hyuk had for his mother. A similar analysis is offered by another North Korean defector named Song-yi who is featured in the documentary film *The Children Gone to Poland* (Chu Sang-mi, dir., 2018). Reflecting on her earlier beliefs about South Koreans as needing North Korean aid and also what she has learned about the dominant mentality in South Korea since defecting from North Korea, Song-yi states that she is concerned about the possibility of reunification because South Koreans are accustomed to always asking how something will benefit them, and reunification may make them feel that someone is invading their home. Like Shin Dong-hyuk, the entrance into a capitalist democracy has been an unkind experience for Songi-yi as it has revealed the cruelties of racial capitalist systems and mindsets.

By giving Shin Dong-hyuk the space to explore North Korea in more complex terms, the film gives him more control over his story and is unlike *Escape from Camp 14* that, in contrast, feels very much like Harden's voice. Here, it is useful to think of Sidonie Smith and Julia Watson's definition of oral history as "a mediated form of personal narrative that depends on an interviewer" and their observation that "in oral history the one who speaks is not the one who writes, and the one who writes is often an absent presence in the text who nonetheless controls its narrative."[101] In his critique of the dehumanizing effects of South Korean capitalism, Shin idealizes his former life in North Korea to a degree and provides a very different narrative from that desired by Western readers or international human rights advocates.

The Double Bind of Human Rights

The typicality of the North Korean subject is thus what makes North Korean life writing coherent as a genre and why it can reach millions of readers without necessarily changing perceptions of North Korea in any of its readers. Like Georg Lukács's typicality of the nineteenth-century novel,[102] the subject in North Korean testimonials stands in for a collective in order to telescope experience into one body or consciousness. The failure of the inhuman subject to realize the dream of being human is reenacted in each of these texts as the individual flees North Korea and, in many ways, this limitation serves as the condition of possibility for this genre. It is the hope that the promise of humanity for the inhuman subject will eventually be realized that drives the reader to read multiple texts in this genre. As Rak observes of genre more generally, "Genre provides the conditions for understanding in everyday life because its operations... [rely on] the recognition of elements that are similar to ones that have appeared before. The temporality of these elements generates similar, but not the same, relations."[103] She cites the expectation that the same characters will appear when one reads one of the novels in the *Twilight* series or even the expectation that fruit purchased weekly at the same market will be of the same quality to illustrate how the principle of similarity operates in genre. And while the genre of North Korean life writing and the industry's material and symbolic investments in it pose the risk of instrumentalizing stories and making them interchangeable in their sameness in order to emphasize the gravity of the human rights situation in North Korea, they also offer much potential for those advocating for North Korean human rights, given the size of the audience it can reach. At the same time, the seeming sameness of North Korean life writing for non–North Korean reading publics reminds us that we need to develop sharper critical eyes to see the individual subjectivities of these writers and supplement our readings of these texts with other versions of North Korean stories.

In recognizing this double bind, I ask whether we can hold onto the frame of human rights discourse while enacting ruptures within it, ones that insert more complex understandings of what constitutes the human, which subjects consequently are entitled to these rights, and how those rights are made accessible to only a few. Seen from this vantage point, the story of North Korean escape is not just a simple flight outward to freedom, but also one that depicts a complex knot of family, obligations, national loyalty, and poverty. To return one final time to Shin's struggle to feel a range of emotions after betraying his mother and brother: this moment draws attention to the traumas inflicted by the North Korean state that dehumanized Shin Dong-hyuk. An alternative way of reading that scene is that it reveals that Shin was never human, at least not in the way that the category of the human has operated within human rights discourse. What *Escape from Camp 14* does not critique is the specificity of the emotions that define the human, and why sympathy and sadness—rather than other emotions, such as self-loathing, or qualities such as resilience—are viewed as the hallmarks of the human. We can begin to engage productively with the limits of how the human is conceptualized within human rights discourse and the global order more broadly by interrogating the historical frame that has been implicitly employed as well as the cultural specificity of how the universal subject has been imagined. In unpacking the human/inhuman binary that has shaped human rights discourse and operated along national and racialized lines, we can begin to interrogate not just the cultural fantasies of North Korean inhumanity but also those that imagine the Western subject as universal and the fears and anxieties that underpin both.

3

Imperial Diasporas

SOUTH KOREAN DIASPORIC
EXCEPTIONALISM, NORTH KOREAN TERROR, AND
HOW I BECAME A NORTH KOREAN

My father grew up in North Korea. From the time of his birth until the end of the Second World War, the country was occupied by the Japanese. Soon after the Second World War, the Korean Civil War broke out. During that time, he and his family walked south, across the mountainous Korean peninsula, with thousands of others in search of freedom. My mother grew up in an orphanage in war-torn South Korea, raising her younger brother from the age of five. After graduating from high school, she worked as a secretary for the government, at which time she met my father. They arrived in Canada in 1975 with two hundred dollars, three kids, and a lot of hope. My father worked at my uncle's convenience store by day and went to ESL classes by night, while my mother took care of me and my two older sisters.

After a performance of *Kim's Convenience* at the 2011 Toronto Fringe Festival, my parents came up to me, hugged me, and said, "We are very proud of you. Thank you."

Kim's Convenience is my love letter to my parents and to all first-generation immigrants who call Canada their home. —INS CHOI, *Kim's Convenience* (2016)

With the unfurling, viruslike, explosive mass of the terrorist network, tentacles ever regenerating despite efforts to truncate them, the terrorist is concurrently an unfathomable, unknowable, and hysterical monstrosity, and yet one that only the exceptional capacities of U.S. intelligence and security systems can quell. This unknowable monstrosity is not a casual bystander or parasite; the nation assimilates this effusive discomfort with the unknowability of these bodies, thus affectively producing new normativities and exceptionalisms through the cataloguing of unknowables. —JASBIR PUAR, *Terrorist Assemblages* (2007)

The Canadian Broadcasting Corporation's (CBC) TV series *Kim's Convenience* is based on the play of the same name written by Toronto-based playwright Ins Choi. The play debuted at the Toronto Fringe Festival in 2011, was remounted by Soulpepper Theatre, and subsequently toured throughout Canada. The play differs significantly from the television series in many ways. The play (on which I focus primarily in this chapter), centers on a Korean Canadian family of four, living in Toronto: a father, mother, a younger child named Janet, and her older sibling, Jung, who is estranged from his father. The father imagines passing the convenience store on to his daughter, but she is uninterested in such a future as her intention is to become a photographer. As the play unfolds, we watch the family interact with customers, and eventually Jung and his father mend their rifts. The staging of this play was a landmark moment for many Korean Canadians as it was one of the few plays (to my knowledge) to cast direct light onto this community, and it elicited a profound sense of recognition in many of its Korean audience members. At the same time, for those of us who grew up as part of this Toronto community of corner store owners, dry cleaners, and fruit and vegetable vendors, it is difficult to ignore that *Kim's Convenience* feels like a snapshot of a specific era in a community that no longer exists (and in this respect, the play and the television series are similar, even as Kevin White, cocreator and executive producer of the TV series, notes that in the play, Umma and Appa are imagined as having migrated from South Korea to Canada in the late 1960s, whereas the TV series presents them as having migrated in the 1980s).[1] Moreover, this immigrant community is depicted in the television series through the celebratory lens of multiculturalism that is very different from the stinging racism that many community members remember experiencing firsthand. More recent migrants from South Korea, including those who migrate temporarily to Canada as international students or are sponsored by their employers as well as those who migrate permanently under more affluent circumstances are examples of the kinds of Koreans and Korean Canadians excluded from the play's landscape. The play instead looks nostalgically at a hard-working family that strives to attain the vague but ever-present promise of a better life for their children.

In other words, the play provides us with a portrait of a model minority family that reinforces notions of diasporic exceptionalism.

This is, of course, a narrative with which scholars of Asian American and Asian Canadian studies are intimately familiar; it is a cornerstone of the diasporic experience, as are the accompanying sentiments of guilt and melancholia. The play *Kim's Convenience* expands this narrative by depicting how the younger generation is drawn into the population of exploited labor. While Janet refuses her father's offer to "make Kim's Convenience dynasty"[2] and opts out of the family legacy, her brother is unable to follow suit. He is instead overcome with happiness at the prospect of running the store. The difference in their futures underscores not only how birth in North America does not guarantee freedom but also how younger generations continue to be trapped within the rhetoric of diasporic exceptionalism and practices of devalued labor as they intersect in discourses of Canadian multiculturalism. The impossibility of pure freedom is perhaps best illustrated by the fact that while it is possible to escape difficult economic situations through lucrative careers, such paths of upward mobility are accompanied by their own forms of professional and psychic disciplining.

I return to this well-worn narrative of the model minority with the intention of disturbing it, more specifically, by rereading the figure of the Korean migrant not only in relation to the assimilatory discourses of the Canadian nation-state and North America more generally but also within the context of the global histories of Korean migration. To this end, I ask where North Korea and North Korean migrants might fit into a Korean diasporic imaginary dominated by model minority concerns. I take the author's note that precedes the play and that functions as my first epigraph for this chapter as an invitation to the play's readers to complicate their understanding of migration and multicultural framing given how Choi's note gestures to the Korean War and the Cold War and repositions the Canadian nation-state as part of those formations. Choi traces his own family history back to bleak beginnings in Korea, namely to North Korea via his father and to a South Korean orphanage through his mother. His parents are then described as having undertaken the journey to Canada in 1975, "with two hundred dollars, three kids, and a lot of hope," a quintessential framing that sutures the specific story of Choi's family to the wider narrative of upward migrant mobility and that works to validate the constant sacrifices of migrants who remain oriented toward the future. Like many other Korean migrants to Canada and the United States, Choi's father's journey involves being displaced first from North Korea to South Korea. But the majority of the play's subsequent references to Korea are to South Korea, with the author's note and a mention of North Korea's appearance in the 1966 World Cup quarter finals during one of Appa's many lectures and tests (which are intended for the play's audience as much as for Jung and Janet) on Korean history and identity. This mention constitutes one of the only invocations of North Korea.

Choi's play is representative of how North Korea is sidelined within understandings of the Korean diaspora in Canada and the United States, reduced primarily to signifying the traumas of the Korean War rather than understood in terms of the complex and often messy social, political, familial, and historic relations that continue to connect diasporans to North and South Korea within the long Cold War. I draw attention to the limited terms in which the Korean diaspora in North America engages with North Korea in order to resituate this "potted history of the war"—a phrase that Daniel Kim borrows from Susan Choi's *The Foreign Student* and that he defines as "a selective *translation* of Korean events that serve a colonial purpose."³ As Daniel Kim observes, the Korean War is told through a process of selective telling that decontextualizes historical moments in order to embed them within other narratives that uphold US imperialism. One consequence of this practice of writing Korean histories for how they further understandings of the benevolence of American empire as welcoming new immigrants is that other kinds of narratives of Korean displacement and movement are pushed out of our intellectual purview. As Ji-Yeon Yuh argues, unlike the migrants who are understood as moving abroad for better educational and economic opportunities, those leaving Korea after 1950 can be understood as "refuge migrants [who] are motivated by a deep psychological need to leave behind chaos, and insecurity, and trauma, and ... seek out emotional/mental peace and a stable environment that doesn't feel like it's always threatening to explode."⁴ Figures coded as model minorities such as Appa, and perhaps even Ins Choi himself, can be read in terms of what Crystal Baik calls "militarized migrations" to describe how "subjects seemingly removed from war are always already touched by militarized violence."⁵ It is with this doubled positioning in mind that I rethink representations of North Korea in conjunction with the Korean diaspora in order to provide an alternate analysis of how Cold War politics gives shape to the Korean diaspora and also to make space for the crucial yet unwieldy dimensions of familial and migratory histories. But in addition to recognizing how the discourses of liberal multiculturalism and Cold War that produce the figures of the model minority and the radical Communist, respectively, are intertwined within a North American imagination, this chapter also attends to Korean migration outside of Canada and the United States, migrations that took place *before* the Korean War, in order to extend Yuh's and Baik's efforts to consider the "complexities of *refuge* migrations."⁶

I open this chapter, which will focus on the melancholia and terror invoked by North Korea for the Korean diaspora, with this foray into *Kim's Convenience* before moving on to a reading of Krys Lee's *How I Became a North Korean* in order to illustrate the tightly intertwined relations between the nation-state and what Jasbir Puar calls the exceptionalisms of diasporas and terrorist bodies. While Puar investigates this tension within the context of queer South Asian diasporas, her insights into the classification of racialized bodies either as exceptional or as terrorist can be extended to other marginalized groups, with "the deferred death of one population reced[ing] as the securitization and valorization of the life of another population triumphs in its shadow."[7] Within Puar's schema, the diasporic subject allies themself with the project of whiteness in the hope of permanently benefiting from the power and privileges whiteness can bestow,[8] whereas the queer terrorist cannot be assimilated into the nation because they are both "failed and perverse."[9] A comparable tension can be identified within postwar Korean migrants who are disciplined as model minority subjects even as many struggle with the complex associations with North Korea that include discomfort and even shame and anger with respect to the US-led critiques of the North Korean state; sadness over the separation from family members; and pity for those in North Korea who have experienced deep famine and other challenges that, given the dearth of direct communication, they can only imagine. But at the same time, the examples of Jung and Appa remind us that migrant subjects often strive for diasporic exceptionality in order to protect themselves and their families from the crushing oppressiveness of everyday life, figured most often for them as racism and poverty. In such cases, their goals are not necessarily to reap privilege but rather to survive the structures of racial capitalism. While Choi's father and countless others left the northern part of Korea, parting with family members, property, and social relations among other things, as they walked southward during the Korean War before eventually migrating from Korea, succeeding generations continue to frame North Korea as the place they might have been born into if their parents had not migrated. For diasporic Koreans, including myself, North Korea is often understood as a fantasy of the past and a present that almost was for us, one that simultaneously invokes melancholia and terror. In other words, North Korea functions as the inhuman bad subject that contrasts sharply with the South Korean good subject, and these national tensions complicate diaspora's relations to multiple nation-states.

North Korean Specters

While a familiar conception, this brutal fantasy of the North Korean present that might have been is not the only representation of North Korea that appears within the stories of migration as told by diasporic cultural producers. Many fictionalized and (auto)biographical stories of migration to Canada and the United States contain connections to North Korea, with some narrating journeys from Korea in terms similar to Choi's, while others describe alternate circuits through North Korea, and still others depict migration *to* North Korea. For instance, in R. O. Kwon's *The Incendiaries*, the protagonist, Phoebe, becomes involved with a religious group led by John Leal, a Korean American activist-turned-minister who was imprisoned for helping North Koreans escape from China to South Korea. While Leal's stories about his experiences in a North Korean prison camp fascinate Phoebe and many other listeners, Will, Phoebe's boyfriend and the narrator of the novel, is highly suspicious of Leal's accounts and observes the transformations that occur between Leal's various versions and his "shifting harlequin cast. The penitent assassin. The ex-trapezist, who escaped. The spy, the kingpin. He even invented a hanged child to fill out this troupe plucked from a fortune-teller's pack of obvious lies."[10] Susan Choi's *The Foreign Student* moves between flashbacks to Korea during the Korean War and mid-1950s Tennessee—the present moment in the novel—by focusing on the experiences of a Korean foreign student named Chang. During the war, one of Chang's closest friends joins the Communist forces and goes to North Korea, which Chang thinks of as "what was now the other country."[11] And "Drifting House," the short story in Krys Lee's eponymous collection, writes of three young children who trek toward the Tumen River in the hope of crossing into China and finding their mother. Their journey takes place in the dead of winter, after their father perishes in an accident and their mother abandons them when she runs out of ways to feed the children and herself. Rather than ending on a happy note, the story concludes with the oldest son, Choecheol, being unable to run away from an armed soldier because he is weighed down by the memories of his four-year old sister who froze to death during their attempted escape. Instead, Choecheol watches as his terrified younger brother, Woncheol, runs across the frozen river alone. And we are left hoping that Woncheol survives and will someday be able to heal from these tragic events. "At the Edge of the World," another story from K. Lee's *Drifting House*, tells the story of a family now living in Los Angeles. Everyday occurrences transpire, with nine-year old Myeongseok falling in love with a girl who rents part of the duplex his father manages, and his parents arguing over the *kut* Myeongseok's father holds for his brother. While ostensibly arguing over the expense of a shaman to conduct this ritual, the real cause of the parents' friction is the father's longing for his family in North Korea and the mother's refusal to "let her son be infected by his [the father's] inability to live in the present."[12] In the latter half of this chapter, I turn to K. Lee's novel, *How I Became a North Korean*, which features a character who traces his family history in China via his grandparents' migration from North Korea. He tells his North Korean friends, "My *eomma* was born across the river in Hamgyong-do, actually. We crossed back into China early,"[13] a story that illustrates the gradual hardening of the border that separates China and North Korea during the twentieth century.

These kinds of stories of migration throughout the twentieth and twenty-first centuries draw our attention to the many imagined and historical connections to the region that became the Democratic People's Republic of Korea (DPRK) in 1948 and that morphed into the brutal fantasy of North Korea in the succeeding decades. However, they are not often cited within discussions of the Korean diaspora. I historicize the transformation of this diasporic gap in order to underscore the simple but often overlooked fact that the northern part of Korea was not always North Korea. In her examination of the social and economic transformations in North Korea in the 1990s, Hazel Smith contextualizes the particular dimensions of the brutal fantasy of North Korea, or what she calls the caricatures of North Korea, such as its military aggressiveness, starving populations, corrupt government, and brainwashed people. In doing so, Smith reminds us that these representations are marked by a historicity that current readings of North Korea fail to recognize.

North Korea's exclusion from a Korean American and Korean Canadian diasporic imaginary raises many questions about the structures of class, citizenship, and feeling that shape the Korean diaspora as a cultural formation, such as how has the Korean diaspora come to be imagined primarily as the experiences of South Korean migrants to the United States and Canada? By utilizing both North Korea and South Korea as entry points into conversations about the histories of Korean migration throughout the twentieth and twenty-first centuries, I ask how we can take into account the transnational dimensions of diasporas instead of using diaspora as a metaphor for select global migrants. Situating North Korea within the Korean diaspora is a means of querying the terms of diasporic legibility and is, more specifically, a means of querying how certain forms of relationality are rendered illegible while others are centered. This approach follows on the influential thinking of Laura Kang's "compositional subjects," as she urges us to be conscious of the figuration of Asian American women;[14] and Kandice Chuh's prompts toward a "subjectless discourse" that would mean giving up on the task of "looking to complete the category 'Asian American,' [and instead] to actualize it by such methods as enumerating various components of differences (gender, class, sexuality, religion, and so on)."[15] Chuh argues that such an approach would permit us "to critique the effects of the various configurations of power and knowledge through which the term comes to have meaning."[16] To conceptualize the relation between North Korea and the Korean diaspora in this manner is to realize that the Korean American and Korean Canadian exclusion of North Korea from their diasporic imaginary emphasizes the always-incomplete nature of representation. At the same time, the absence of North Korea is also necessary for diaspora as a cosmopolitan formation to resonate with Koreans in the West and to exist as part of the Global North.

Both Kang and Chuh direct us toward the question of how subjects become legible through particular kinds of reading practices; and asking this through an analysis of *Kim's Convenience* makes us cognizant of how diaspora holds meaning for nation-states. By comparing the various versions of *Kim's Convenience* to each other, I recognize how more recent processes of Asian racialization often rely on instilling feelings of gratitude and a desire for respectability into postwar Korean migrants. If the US empire's "gift of freedom" to Southeast Asian refugees "is no untruth," Mimi Nguyen explains, "but instead coexists with violence, or because of violence that appears as something else, then the concept of the gift of freedom must encompass all those forces that promise new subjects as well as new forms of action, new events, a new order—such as a grateful refugee or enduring war."[17] For postwar Korean migrants, the US functions as a signifier of imperialism; but it is an imperialism that has positioned itself in opposition to the inhuman tyranny of North Korea and Communism. The political disciplining of South Korean subjects through this anticommunism and pro-American rhetoric "was so indelible in the minds of South Koreans that historian Sŏ Chungsŏk noted in the late 1980s that older Koreans simply could not utter slogans such as 'Yankee, go home' and 'Antiwar, antinuke,' even if they agreed with the slogans."[18] Diasporic guilt over the relations left behind in North Korea and gratitude for the United States' gift of freedom inform the racialization of Koreans within national and global contexts. And yet, if we consider the television and play versions of *Kim's Convenience*, we become conscious of how even homogenizing discourses of the model minority are rarely simple; because they are, to return to Chuh, likely "grounded in difference."[19] If we historicize diaspora as a formation, on the one hand, by tracing the connections between North Korea and the Korean diaspora and, on the other hand, by contextualizing these investigations within longer histories of Korean migration and movement, we can illuminate the workings of colonialism and imperialism as well as the neoliberal dimensions of diasporic aspirations. To read North Korea as part of the Korean diaspora, then, is a decolonial method that both centers difference within diaspora and engages with the many transnational life worlds that precede entry into Canada and the United States.

Ethnic Nationalism, Colonial Migrations, and Post-1948 Diaspora

Seen often in relation to the disruptions and traumas of the Korean War, North Korea is part of a melancholic narrative that centers on the Korean diaspora's desire for a reunified Korea. Such emotions are central to documentary films such as Deann Borshay Liem and Ramsay Liem's *Memory of a Forgotten War*, a film about four diasporic Koreans whose lives were devastated by the overnight imposition of the demilitarized zone (DMZ) and the events of the Korean War, as well as to Jason Lee's *Letters from Pyongyang*, a documentary short film that records Lee's journey from Montreal to Pyongyang with his father in an effort to be reunited with their lost-lost family. Similar collective memories also fuel, to a certain degree, the concerted efforts of humanitarian organizations like Liberty in North Korea (LiNK) and HanVoice that work with refugees and strive to "change the narrative" of North Korea.[20] Like the films made by the Liems, LiNK and HanVoice provide space for the stories of ordinary North Koreans and families separated by the DMZ within global conversations that are dominated by a morbid fascination with North Korean tyranny and the skeptical yet anxious responses to the threats to global security posed by North Korean nuclear missiles. For diasporic Koreans, the DMZ becomes the signifier of *han* and reinforces the weight of the legacies of the Korean War. Operated by Korean Americans and Korean Canadians who are separated from the Korean War by geographical as well as by temporal distance, these grassroots organizations have produced material benefits for numerous people even as they inadvertently raise complex questions of what North Korea means to diasporic Koreans.

The labor of activists and humanitarian organizations on behalf of North Koreans has yielded significant, even life-altering benefits and, without intending to minimize these, I point out that such interventions emerge out of a diasporic structure that relies on US-centric memory work. Even as discourses of diaspora lay claim to globality and historicity, they are in practice primarily fashioned upon a very specific postwar migrant subject within whom imperial and diasporic guilt often intersect. This is evidenced in much diasporic scholarship, including my own work that interrogates the traumas experienced during Japanese colonialism, the Korean War, and in the shadow of US imperialism.

I note this scholarly trend in order to diagnose the critical moment and to understand the limited space available for conversations about Asian diasporas. My intention is not to critique these conversations for their oversights; to do so would be to impose the kinds of impossible model minority expectations that I critique in this chapter. I instead want to make us conscious of the parameters that shape contemporary Korean diasporic conversations and point out the centering of US concerns. For instance, Grace Cho engages with the sexual labor of Korean women from 1945 until the 1990s in order to consider militarized prostitution, war brides, and comfort women as part of the story of Korean and US relations. Cho's *Haunting the Diaspora* argues that the conditions for the wave of Korean migration to the US in the post-1965 period were laid during the Korean War and that the sexual labor of Korean women played a crucial role in the migration of thousands of Koreans. By drawing together academic and personal narratives of war and migration, Cho outlines the connections between the sex trade that took place in camp towns and the military brides produced by the war, many of whom then sponsored their families to come join them in the United States. The repression of these stories about the origins of diaspora in dominant narratives of diaspora means that "the Korean diaspora in the United States has been haunted by the traumatic effects of what we are not allowed to know."[21] Haunting constitutes the diaspora for Cho as she argues, "If the historical condition of possibility for Korean diaspora is the Forgotten War, the psychic condition is that of enforced forgetting."[22] Cho's book represents a major intervention within Asian American studies and diaspora studies with its analysis of the shame and secrecy attached to the sexual labor of Korean women, and while her argument is astute and compelling, its premise that the Korean War marks the beginning of the diaspora is only true for a particular generation.

Elided from this discussion are the many people who migrated in the decades or even the century prior to the Korean War in order to escape Japanese colonialism and Chinese domination and who went to destinations other than the United States, Canada, or Europe, instead electing to migrate to Manchuria, Russia, and Japan. For these people, their different migratory journeys mean that they may not share Grace Cho's psychic condition of enforced forgetting or in a collective desire to dismantle the DMZ and see reunification, a fantasy that sutures Koreans in the United States and Canada to those in the peninsula; it is, however, a narrative that appears to be more powerful for those located in the diaspora than for those on the peninsula.[23] Tracing migration and empire as material histories delinks the Korean diaspora from national frameworks, including those that inevitably privilege the Korean War. In recognizing the affective hold of nationalisms on the diaspora, we can begin to interrogate how these ideologies are often manipulated throughout global histories to further racialize and oppress Koreans.

For diasporans in the West, the Korean War era structures their relation to Korea and Korean identity. Key dates within this history (a topic discussed in more detail in chapter 2) include the separation of Korea into two nations in 1948 and the 1953 ceasefire; the nostalgia of the US-based Korean diaspora ensures that these pasts are not forgotten. To return briefly to *Kim's Convenience*, Appa often quizzes younger Koreans with what he calls his "proud moment Korea history test" that checks knowledge of Korean inventions, sports, and the Korean naming of geographical sites such as the East Sea (Sea of Japan) to ensure that a sense of national identity is deeply ingrained within them.[24] But this particular attachment to Korea via the Korean War obscures other, earlier waves of colonial migration from Korea that were often undertaken to Japan and China. Illegible within a US-centric diasporic formation, the labor migrations of Koreans to China and Japan throughout the twentieth century represent a different set of imperial relationships that call for a rewriting of the narrative of diasporic haunting by grounding it in fuller historical accounts.

In *Two Dreams in One Bed*, Hyun Ok Park writes the entangled histories of Korean migrants, Chinese nationalism, and Japanese imperialism in Manchuria from the late nineteenth century until 1945, as "bedfellows who share a capitalist dream."[25] Park traces in detail how peasant Korean farm workers were caught between the competing ambitions of China and Japan. For example, in China since the late nineteenth century, naturalization was offered to Koreans as a prerequisite to owning land; it was part of the Qing government's strategy for preventing Japan from interfering in the territorial disputes between China and Korea.[26] Those Koreans who refused to naturalize were allowed to work as laborers and short-term tenants and continued to develop Chinese land. The ability of Korean farmers to turn desolate land into farmland capable of growing rice was valued by China and Japan who both "chased after Koreans to claim sovereignty and ownership over the areas they had settled."[27] When these migrants were pushed off the land they had made arable, Japan would offer them loans to enable them to migrate from Kando (which is now known as the Yanbian Korean Autonomous Prefecture) to other parts of Manchuria.[28] And if these Korean migrants defaulted on their loans, Japan took over their mortgaged land.[29] By outlining this process, Park demonstrates how,

> when Koreans were driven from their lands, their repetitive displacement set into motion the social metabolism of the osmotic expansion of the Jap-

anese empire. This osmotic expansion progressed because Koreans envisioned a better life in a new place and invested their labor in wasteland to transform it into productive rice fields. The dreams of the Japanese and Chinese powers were embedded in the dreams of the Korean migrants themselves. Each instance of migration signifies a new relation with the spatio-temporality of colonialism, nationalism, and capitalism. The social practices of Korean migrants were therefore double edged: while Koreans pursued their dreams of landownership, their participation in the market was a process through which their surplus value was expropriated with each loan payment and every time they were displaced.[30]

The pressures to naturalize as Chinese or to function as agents of Japanese imperialism trapped farmworkers in a cycle of hard labor and displacement, transforming these migrant workers into a means of "territorial osmosis" into China for Japan.[31]

Central to the dominant narrative of post-1948 diaspora is the pairing of Korean subjects who have endured colonial and imperial violence over the past century with ethnic nationalist discourses that imagine liberation from such subjugation. These stories of oppressed Korean subjects are present within the Korean diasporic imaginary in the United States and Canada and also, as the histories of migrant farmworkers in Manchuria demonstrate, in other parts of the world such as Japan and China. And while they are powerful and even seductive constructions, Jin-kyung Lee argues that these current essentialist conceptions of Korean ethnicity must be historicized as modern inventions produced through transnational forces. She underscores the influence of Japanese colonialism on Korean identity by pointing out that while premodern Korea was not grounded in an ideology of ethnicity, early twentieth-century Korean nationalism "was built on the resistive assertion of ethnic purity that performatively helped create unity and solidarity around a single ethnicity. Put another way, Korean ethnic nationalism was a reaction to the Japanese empire's production of Koreans as an ethnicized or racialized collective."[32] Hyun Ok Park offers a similar observation by noting:

> The distinction of Korean (Japanese) nationals and their "others" was never complete in Manchuria, although the diaspora literature portrays a binary distinction: nationals as localized, national, fixed, stable, and bounded by the national state; and nonnationals as global, cosmopolitan, floating, moving, hybrid, and deterritorialized. The indeterminable spatial and temporal experiences of the Korean diaspora in the early twentieth century arose not merely from their multiple national identities. They

also resulted from the dual position of Koreans as both the colonized and the bedfellows of Japanese imperialism.[33]

By outlining the process by which Korean nationalism was constructed, Jin-kyung Lee and Park counter the essentialism of these identities and direct our attention to how they have been mobilized. This narrative of Korean identity, for instance, binds together more affluent overseas Koreans with those in Korea and reinforces complex imperial ties and movements. Given that many Koreans migrated to the United States in the postwar period, diaspora becomes one of the many intimacies that tie South Korea to the US empire. But since then, many other peoples from formerly colonized parts of Asia have migrated to South Korea as laborers and toil under exploitative conditions for low or even no wages, many suffering injury and even dying. For these reasons, Jin-kyung Lee describes South Korea as a site that simultaneously invokes postcolonial, neocolonial, and sub-imperial relations and now performs "a series of surrogate labors for the empire."[34]

The postwar histories of ethnic Koreans in Japan, or Zainichi, reveal that ethnic nationalist conceptions of Korean identity are not only fictitious but also potentially dangerous. In *Exodus to North Korea*, Tessa Morris-Suzuki pieces together the complex history behind the "repatriation" of Koreans in Japan to North Korea, an act designed as a covert solution to the problem of Koreans who remained in postwar Japan. To summarize Morris-Suzuki's research: In 1945, when Japan surrendered to the Allied forces, over two million Koreans were living in Japan. In the period immediately following the end of World War II, over one million Koreans left Japan for South Korea, and a few hundred of these Koreans went instead to North Korea before repatriation to the North was outlawed due to growing Cold War tensions. This left six hundred thousand Koreans who remained in Japan, many of whom had originally been from the southern end of the peninsula, and this number increased as Koreans continued to migrate from Korea to Japan. Some of these new Korean migrants hoped to be reunited with family, others were leaving behind the economic and political turmoil of the newly divided Korean peninsula, and still others were refugees displaced by the massacre on Jeju Island. As the Japanese empire was dissolved, new national borders were erected. And as the Allied forces that occupied Japan did not want an unregulated flow of Koreans to and from Japan, they closed the border between Korea and Japan. When the Korean War broke out, General McArthur refused to let Koreans enter Japan as refugees.

During the postwar period, Zainichi faced extreme discrimination and economic hardship in Japan,[35] which worsened after they lost their Japanese nationality in 1952, when the occupation of Japan ended. As Morris-Suzuki makes clear, the stripping of Japanese citizenship from Koreans was done to facilitate their "repatriation" to North Korea (as they could not be repatriated if they were Japanese citizens). But as many of these Zainichi had been in Japan for a long time, even for generations, their family ties were to neither North nor South Korea but rather to Japan or to pre-division Korea. Their southern or northern origins, moreover, did not necessarily map neatly onto their political ideologies. Yet within the group that aligned themselves with North Korea, some advocated for the option to "return" to North Korea. Such a story is shared in Yang Yonghi's documentary *Dear Pyongyang* in which Yang reflects on her father's decision to repatriate her three older brothers from Japan to North Korea in 1971. Yang's father, a leading Chongryun (the North Korean–affiliated community association in Japan) figure whose ancestral home was Jeju, sent his sons in part out of loyalty to North Korea and in part so they could avoid the deep discrimination that Koreans in Japan faced. Since Yang was only six years old when her brothers relocated to North Korea, she remained with her parents in Japan. *Dear Pyongyang* shows Yang and her parents visiting her brothers and their families regularly and sending care packages of school supplies, clothing, and other items to support their lifestyles. After the documentary was released, Yang was no longer able to enter North Korea.[36]

More than ninety thousand Zainichi migrated to North Korea between 1959 and 1984; and many of them were eventually purged by the North Korean government. Despite the fact that the majority of the "returnees" were originally from what had become South Korea, this mass migration was framed as a repatriation scheme. Morris-Suzuki counters this narrative of ethnic Koreans being overwhelmed by patriotism and wanting to rejoin North Korea by suggesting other motivations and forces on the part of the Japanese government and Japanese Red Cross that influenced this movement. Citing a book by a former Chongryun official, she provides a bold alternate reading of this repatriation scheme, arguing, "The central message of Chang Myeong-Su's book was simple and startling. The repatriation, he claimed, had been an act of ethnic cleansing carried out on behalf of a racist Japanese establishment by none other than that supposed standard-bearer of humanitarianism, the Japanese Red Cross."[37] While official accounts claim that the mass repatriation movement was originated by the Korean community in Japan in 1958 and that the Japanese government and Red Cross simply facilitated this migration, the "problem" of Koreans in Japan had actually been raised in 1955 by the Japan Red Cross Society and the idea of sending Koreans to North Korea had been formulated by Japanese officials in 1956.[38] The narrative of Korean diasporans longing to return home was used to facilitate the mass exodus of ethnic Koreans—who were seen by Japan as both an ethnic taint and an economic burden—while avoiding international condemnation.

In Japan's repatriation scheme, the collective nostalgia for an imagined homeland was used to further the ethnic cleansing of a Korean minority from Japanese society under humanitarian pretenses. While ethnic nationalism promises to overcome colonial histories, the impossibility of such a scenario becomes evident when we look more closely at the relations between the Korean diaspora and North Korea. On the one hand, as a signifier of the partition, the war that has not ended, and the ongoing domination of the Koreas by other powers, North Korea enables a kind of memory work for the diaspora and speaks to economies of mourning, melancholia, and nostalgia. At the same time, North Korea is also a complex site of disavowal, operating as a source of embarrassment and perplexity for some. But North Korea also functions as a site of rescue for others, as evidenced by human rights groups that help defectors escape; offers of support in the form of US dollars as well as CDs and DVDs that contain news, films, and information about the world outside of North Korea; and Christian groups dedicated to North Korean spiritual salvation. From this angle, North Korea is an odd and anachronistic formation whose inhuman subjects feel decidedly and disturbingly not modern. As a point of common identification and disidentification, North Korea gives the Korean diaspora in North America a certain cohesiveness, something that is shared even as it is disavowed by some. In other words, North Korea gives scholars and diasporans a means of becoming conscious of how colonial legacies and the current global order slide into each other and produce various kinds of minor imperial subjects. In this way, we can begin to understand the complex and contradictory investments—affective, political, economic, and social—in remembering and forgetting how the Korean diaspora is produced in large part through Japanese colonial and US imperial forces and legacies. Reading postwar migration to the United States and Canada as one of many waves of Korean migration forces us to ask what distinguishes a US-centric diaspora from other migrations, and what is at stake in maintaining this difference.

"Poor and Politically Suspicious" Relations: Krys Lee's *How I Became a North Korean*

To begin to work through the relations of power that suture a post-1948 diaspora together with colonial migrations within a post–Cold War landscape, I turn to Krys Lee's novel *How I Became a North Korean* (2016). Lee's novel gives us the stories of three youths: Jangmi, Yongju, and Danny. Jangmi and Yongju are defectors from North Korea who come from very different socioeconomic backgrounds. When the novel begins, Jangmi is a poor North Korean who is in her early to mid-twenties. She is pregnant with the child of a North Korean cadre who protected Jangmi's smuggling enterprise in exchange for sexual favors. She is now fleeing through China after having been sold into marriage to a Chinese groom. In contrast, Yongju is in his late teens or early twenties and had been raised as part of an elite Pyongyang family before his father was suddenly shot and killed by Kim Jong-il at a dinner party. After successfully crossing the border into China, his mother and sister were taken by Chinese brokers, and Yongju was left behind. The third main character, Danny, is a sixteen-year-old ethnic Korean from China, or a Joseonjok, who has been living in the United States for the last six years. These three individuals meet in 2009 in northeastern China as Jangmi and Yongju, along with a group of other North Korean youths, try to find their way to a safe haven after having crossed the border into China. I analyze K. Lee's novel in order to understand the relations between diasporic structures of feelings and discourses of citizenship and humanitarianism.

Danny's story is quite different from those of Jangmi and Yongju, who fear imprisonment or execution if they are returned to North Korea. In contrast, Danny has returned to China to live with his mother after experiencing difficulties adjusting socially to life in the United States, but he flees his mother's apartment after he realizes that she is having an affair with a church deacon. While living on the streets, Danny is robbed of everything except for a little bit of money that he had hidden on his body. Even though his passport has been stolen, Danny's status as a US permanent resident and his Chinese citizenship offers him a safety net that his North Korean companions lack, a fact that he never shares with them. Even though Danny does not need his friends to survive, he remains with them because he craves human companionship and has fallen in love with Yongju. Unlike all the other relationships in his life in which he feels alienated, Danny sees in Yongju the possibility of being part of "those mysterious friendships that I'd watched from the sidelines back in America."[39]

In order to be part of these intimate friendships, Danny passes as an orphan with nowhere else to go, and he offers his language and survival skills to the group so that they will let him live with them in their cave. Danny is aware that there are serious ethical problems with this situation, namely, that he prolongs the group's stay in China for selfish reasons even though their lives are at stake. Danny reflects upon this conflict between desire and duty when he thinks, "Maybe my life would have spun out differently if Yongju hadn't crouched on the floor and put his arm around my shoulders and one around Cheolmin's.

But he pulled me into his musk and amber, drew me into the secret fraternity of men, until I was drowning in the oceanic span of his long arms, finally lost."[40] At the same time, he feels a very real connection with Yongju and the other boys, and Danny is responsible for getting them to a Christian safe house run by Missionary Kwon. And when it becomes apparent that Kwon's intention is to teach the youths about the Bible and then return them to North Korea to proselytize rather than to get them to South Korea,[41] Danny calls his mother who arranges for brokers to get the teenagers to safety. But before the brokers arrive, the youths, frustrated and afraid after waiting months in the safe house, erupt in violence and injure Kwon quite badly.

Years later, Danny returns to the former site of this Christian safe house in an effort to come to terms with these memories. While he claims his role as witness to these events,[42] this is also a partial coming to terms with his participation in the violence inflicted on Kwon. Danny's reluctance to intervene and arrange rescue for his friends earlier means that his witnessing was not innocent but produced by an emotionally parasitic arrangement. He could have intervened but chose to wait because his companionship with the North Korean youths made him feel part of a collective. When he walks into this former safe house from which he can see North Korea and the Tumen River, Danny expects that "images would come rushing back to [him] as soon as [he] face[d] the building, like in a movie, but nothing of the sort happens. Shredded, weather-worn Bubble Wrap hangs from the windows, the building's walls are streaked green with water stains, and the stairwell is rusted orange to the point of looking dangerous. In the building's shadows, the ice is still hard and stubborn."[43] In this light, Danny is unable to see the building through sentimental or nostalgic eyes. Instead, the space as part of a desolate landscape affirms the brutal truth that the youths trapped within the house had no choice but to resist in order to survive.

By the end of the novel, Danny has returned to his life in the United States and has nearly finished his sociology degree at Harvard. He has lost touch with Yongju and Jangmi, and it is telling that neither has made an attempt to find him. Yongju and Jangmi, however, reunite in Pusan after losing touch when their stays at the Hanawon resettlement center (in South Korea) come to an end; they choose to meet again, despite the complications and painful memories they evoke in each other, because Yongju and Jangmi represent each other's "real life."[44] By this point in their lives, Yongju resembles other real-life North Korean defectors whose stories have been made public, often through human rights testimonies or the publication of their life stories. Yongju reflects on the value of his story when he notes, "I work part-time for the South Korean government as a source of information on the North. . . . I am a model North Korean refugee;

I testify in front of churches, to the National Assembly, to anyone who will listen."⁴⁵ Similarly, it is difficult to overlook the strong resemblance between Jangmi's story and those of North Korean women such Yeonmi Park, who describe experiences of being trafficked while trying to reach South Korea. Jangmi's story includes difficult experiences such as being forced to perform sexual acts in Chinese cyber chat rooms, miscarrying after being beaten by gang members who run the online sex operation, and being raped by Missionary Kwon. To be each other's real life suggests that Jangmi and Yongju are able to exist outside of these narratives of North Korea and beyond the terms set by human rights discourse and human trafficking debates, choosing to claim each other and lifeworlds that are inaccessible and even undesirable to most people in South Korea.

At the same time, the promises of reunification and the overcoming of trauma that underwrite narratives of diaspora in North America never materialize. Instead, we are left with an insurmountable chasm between Danny and Yongju and Jangmi as well as with the realization that freedom translates in very different ways for each of them. While Danny is left feeling confident that he will live a happy life as he has a new boyfriend, is applying to graduate programs, and has developed better relations with his parents,⁴⁶ the future looks less certain for Yongju and Jangmi who struggle with feelings of loneliness and emptiness.⁴⁷ Despite Danny's desperate desire to believe that he could become North Korean through his relationships to Yongju and Jangmi, the protections afforded by US permanent residency prevent this transformation from taking place fully.

This reading of Danny as a figure who speaks to the privileges of American legal status and a US Ivy League education is initially how I entered this novel. It is also an interpretation that relies on the understanding of the Asian American as a model minority and as a subject formed by the Cold War. Within such a frame, Yongju and Jangmi are characters whose oscillations between hope and hopelessness reinforce the triangulated relations between South Korea/North Korea/the United States as they reinforce our turns to human rights and humanitarian aid. And one of the privileges of Danny's US permanent residency and Chinese nationality is that it lets him bypass the scenario that instrumentalizes Yongju and Jangmi's stories, even as he temporarily identifies with them. Danny's identification with these North Koreans represents a spin on what Rey Chow critiques as the problem of first-world scholars who "choose to see in others' powerlessness an idealized image of themselves and refuse to hear in the dissonance between the content and manner of their speech their own complicity with violence."⁴⁸ Unlike the diasporic intellectuals Chow targets, Danny is aware of the differences in power and positionality that separate him from his North

Korean friends, but he chooses to sustain the fantasy of sameness for as long as he is able. But to end the analysis of this novel here would be a mistake because this critique of the United States, while it recognizes the uneven terrain of global power and human rights, focuses primarily on the role that America plays and renders invisible other histories. For this reason, it is important to query the transnational histories embedded within the novel. More specifically, I focus on the novel's decision to make Danny a Joseonjok instead of simply a Korean American or a Chinese American, and I consider how the category of Joseonjok generates other ways of thinking about diasporic identifications. More specifically, to focus on the Joseonjok is to direct our attention to migrations that took place before the Cold War and to diasporas situated outside of North America.

As mentioned earlier, one of the key moments in the novel occurs when Danny is robbed of his backpack that contains his passport. In my initial reading, my impulse was to approach this scene as a critique of US privilege and post–Cold War relations of power. This is an interpretive frame enabled by our introduction to Danny earlier in the novel as a suburban American teenager, albeit one who is ostracized and cruelly bullied by his peers. But if I rethink my first reading of Danny, his particular narrative of immigration and assimilation does not fit seamlessly into Asian American discourses of citizenship, migration, and racialization as they typically pertain to Korean Americans and Chinese Americans. The uneasy fit between Danny and Asian American critique is flagged for us as the home that Danny longs for is not Korea or even just China but rather a very specific location and community of about two million people, namely the Yanbian Korean Autonomous Prefecture in China that his family migrated from when he was about nine years old.[49] He describes his hometown in Yanji as being unimportant to China but comfortable for him as it lay "wedged in a forgotten corner of China [that] felt like it belonged to another self. After six years away, its buildings seemed to me as plain as the people, worn out like saggy granny panties."[50] Danny's complex relations to US and Chinese racial and ethnic formations as a Joseonjok, his relative comfort within China's statist project, and his ambivalent relation to Korean American communities underscore the divergences and overlaps between the Chinese and US projects of ethnic governance and liberal multiculturalism.[51]

To center the category of Joseonjok instead of folding it into more familiar forms of Korean or Chinese diasporic critique is to begin with a different set of questions about law, identification, and migrant subjects in relation to China, North Korea, the United States, and South Korea. To return to the scene in which Danny's papers are stolen, he thinks to himself:

> I had lost my passport, my identification cards, my tools, everything except the cash tucked into my underwear and the inner lining of my pants. Daniel Daehan Lee, a citizen of the People's Republic of China and a permanent resident of the United States of America, was now paperless, undocumented, as if I had never existed. I rubbed where the cold knife had pressed against my skin, feeling strangely free.[52]

I emphasize here that Danny's immediate reaction to the loss of his passport and ID cards is to feel free rather than to feel like a Joseonjok with Chinese citizenship. In a sense, this works to deepen a sensation of disorientation that Danny expresses as he leaves California for China: "I couldn't even remember why I had wanted to go to Harvard."[53] The loss of the passport and ID makes Danny feel both free and lost, which is perhaps how he has felt all along, even when he had an American identity and documents that linked him to two powerful nations, China and the United States.

One of the points that the novel makes is that while the question of what it means to be Joseonjok is complicated and ambiguous in many respects, it is unwavering in its belief that at least part of what it means to be Joseonjok is to *not* be North Korean. This is conveyed clearly by Jangmi's mother-in-law, who angrily denounces Jangmi by shouting, "You're not his wife. You're a North Korean," before chasing Jangmi out of the apartment, leaving her vulnerable to being captured by Chinese police who routinely patrol the streets for North Koreans.[54] The differences between North Koreans and Joseonjok are many, but paramount here are Chinese citizenship and social status. We also see this distinction made when Danny recounts his family's history and sketches out his maternal grandparents' migration from North Korea to China, emphasizing how random their move was at that time and, in the process, reminding us that the border between North Korea and China was much looser then. The novel then tells us that Danny's mother was born in North Korea and the family recrossed:

> My family was Joseon-*jok*, ethnic Koreans who'd lived alongside the Han Chinese in northeastern China. That is, except during the madness of China's Cultural Revolution when my grandfather crossed into North Korea, where my mom was born. If my mom and her family hadn't recrossed while they still could, I might have been born in North Korea. As it was, I still had relatives on both sides of the river, and having grown up in northeastern China until I was nine, I could pass for a North Korean from the Hamgyong region when I spoke Korean, like many in the Chinese border towns.[55]

Danny's very brief story of family migration returns our attention toward those long histories of movement of Koreans across the Yalu and Tumen Rivers into China. A more recent chapter of this migratory history that Danny's story alludes to is the migration to Manchuria during Japanese colonialism.

Chih-ming Wang argues that by bringing together the stories of North Korean refugees and Asian American returnees, Lee's novel offers an opportunity to consider "the ethics of co-presence that undergirds Asian American studies" which includes "the linkage between Asian America and Asia."[56] Foregrounded in his reading of *How I Became a North Korean* are the migrant networks, directions, and desires of Korean movements prior to the establishment of the Republic of Korea and the Democratic People's Republic of Korea in 1948. By taking 1948 as a historical marker of the Korean peninsula, Wang shows that the establishment of South Korea and North Korea as nation-states also involved a delegitimization of migrations from earlier eras:

> The *Joseonjok* is a shadow presence of what it means to be "Korean" and "Chinese" today, and a nebulous third space for connecting the global Korean diaspora through rooted claims of Korean lineage on Chinese territory. In contradistinction to the model minority image of Korean Americans in the global family of Korea, the *Joseonjok* is a related yet differentiated diaspora, poor and politically suspicious. It conjures up conflicted specters of (Japanese and American) colonialism, (Korean and Chinese) nationalism, as well as wartime collaborations (between Japanese and Koreans to rule Korea and between Chinese and Koreans to fight Japanese and American imperialisms), all tossed into the treacherous settings of human trafficking, political defection, and sexual exploitation across the border.[57]

And yet, Danny is a provocative figure because, as an American permanent resident, Chinese citizen, and ethnic Korean, he embodies multiple forms of Korean migration and diaspora. Danny's loss of his papers, in effect, folds in half the spectrum of Korean migrant and diasporic representations and makes us aware that he is simultaneously the model minority Korean American and the poor and politically suspicious Joseonjok within a global cultural imagination.

The privileging of the West within discourses of diaspora has had very real consequences for ethnic Koreans in China, whether they are North Korean refugees or Joseonjok, in terms of their claims to citizenship and the legality of their labor in South Korea. This complicated and counterintuitive chain of relations can be seen as coming together, for instance, through South Korea's

Overseas Korean Act (OKA). This is a piece of legislation that returns citizenship status to those who once possessed South Korean nationality or gives it to those who are the offspring of former South Korean nationals. But because South Korea as a nation-state was not legally defined until 1948, the original version of the OKA did not extend citizenship rights to those Koreans who left during the Japanese colonial period or before. As cultural anthropologist Jung-Sun Park and sociologist Paul Chang point out, Northeast Asian geopolitics played a major role in this decision, given China's "concern for real and potential ethnic independence movements by a few major ethnic groups, including the *Chosonjok* (Korean Chinese), [which] seems to have impacted its strong stance against the inclusion of Korean Chinese in the OKA."[58] But regardless of the specific motivations for adopting this post-1948 qualifier, its effect is to turn the OKA into a document that privileges what have become the more affluent parts of the diaspora and that erases from view most Joseonjok and Koryo Saram (ethnic Koreans in Russia and former Soviet countries such as Kazakhstan and Uzbekistan), thereby translating into legal terms diasporic differences.

The selective recognition at work within the OKA is tied to the production of an ethnic Korean migrant labor population in South Korea. For instance, Joseonjok and Koryo Saram are hirable in South Korea because they are ethnically Korean and may be fluent in the language. At the same time, they are not citizens and can therefore be deported when their stays become illegal. The construction of Joseonjok as a pool of cheap and flexible migrant labor for South Korea demonstrates the negative ways in which ethnic nationalism can be mobilized. And for the Joseonjok, "the OKA's insider/outsider boundaries are not merely a matter of ethnic/national membership but also of economic membership."[59] According to June Hee Kwon, among the reasons the South Korean government excluded Korean Chinese from the OKA was a fear that they would provide too much cheap labor and also that they "were associated with the aftereffects of the Cold War.... It was feared that overseas Koreans with socialist affiliations could be a threat if they were granted unlimited free entry."[60] The restriction of mobility for Joseonjok contrasts quite sharply with the South Korean government's practice of recruiting English-speaking professionals from other parts of the world. And to return us to *How I Became a North Korean*, it bears mentioning that the novel is set in 2009, immediately after the economic crisis of 2008. While the OKA has undergone many revisions since it was initially adopted in 1999 to address, among other issues, the large numbers of Joseonjok who were in South Korea illegally, the economic crisis in 2008 led to a tightening of immigration policies and "a strong social discourse... emerged against taking in immigrants" in South Korea.[61] In other words, the novel directs our attention to a time of heightened precarity for Joseonjok in South Korea, and it underscores the kinds of consequences that policy fine-tuning has for more vulnerable global populations. It is worth noting that the demand for Joseonjok in South Korea as flexible labor is also highly femininized. Many workers are hired as domestic labor as South Korean women enter the paid workforce and look for others to take over the labor of domestic work, childcare, and caregiving for aging parents. The willingness of Joseonjok women to migrate to South Korea to take on this employment produces a ripple effect: "If the ethnic Korean women from China filled the gap for 'female' jobs avoided by women in South Korea, it was the North Korean women with illegal statuses working for a lower wage and enduring all sorts of injustices who filled the gap in China."[62]

In contrast with a Cold War reading of *How I Became a North Korean* that focuses on what happens after the Korean partition, a Joseonjok-centered reading focuses on pre-1948 migration and gives us different contexts for understanding the significance of 1948 as a key date. Such an approach also enables us to revisit melancholia as a structure of feeling for the Korean diaspora in the West and the kinds of effects that it has (i.e., a desire to save North Korea via humanitarian efforts; guilt and sadness over the continued separation of families that are positioned within North and South Korea; ethnic nationalism and patriotism). By taking into account colonial migrations to non-Western countries, I argue that other forms of historical and contemporary violences become visible and the Korean War no longer functions as the sole analytic for understanding Korean diasporic experiences and identities. We can see this in Danny's nostalgia for his childhood in Yanbian, and this sentiment makes us uncomfortably aware of how different his status (with or without physical documents) is from many of the Joseonjok who aspire to migrate to South Korea for employment purposes. This is conveyed most visibly in that Danny is not trying to enter South Korea to earn *won* to send home but is instead in China to avoid his parents and to come to terms with his disillusionment with the church by seeking intimacy with a group of North Korean refugees.

This positioning of North Korean refugee, Joseonjok, and Korean American subjects highlights how economic and political power is distributed within East Asia and the United States and the way that diasporic affect forestalls a recognition of that geopolitical design. As Wang writes,

> This inter-Asian condition where Cold War and neoliberal logics persist creates a spectre of comparison where the *Joseonjok* are juxtaposed to Korean Americans and North Korea defectors/refugees. Whereas the defectors/refugees are seen as the proof that Communism is bad and

passé, the *Joseonjok* is viewed as a national subaltern that South Korea is reluctant to accept even as it opens its arms to its North American brethren.⁶³

While Danny's Chinese citizenship, US permanent residency, and family history of North Korean migration position him within multiple ethnic minority formations in various national contexts and as part of pre– and post–Cold War migrations, his desire is to focus on the idealized ethnic ties that bind him to the North Korean boys he encounters and to avoid recognizing the material differences between them. We see this when, to earn their trust, Danny pulls out his mother's migratory history and tells the boys that his mother had been born on the North Korean side of the river before his grandparents returned to China without mentioning that his family eventually migrated to the United States.⁶⁴ This emphasis on shared ethnicity and romanticized connections to North Korea lets Danny fantasize for brief moments that he might eventually belong with these boys, and it reminds us of the dangers that ethnic nationalism has posed for the Korean diaspora.

These feelings of ethnic nationalism also further other political projects by normalizing them. As Hyun Ok Park points out, while discourses of reunification continue to dominate conversations about the Korean peninsula, they almost always emphasize physical reunification. She argues that this neglects all the ways in which the North and South have already been reunified through, for instance, economic forms such as joint projects between North and South Korea or the labor migration of Korean Chinese to South Korea and North Koreans to China.⁶⁵ With her analysis, Hyun Ok Park reframes the relations between ethnic Koreans across the globe from fantasies of diaspora to the lived realities of capitalist ordering, noting that "a hierarchical transnational community is anomalous with the ethnic principle of citizenship and the dichotomy of home and diaspora."⁶⁶ Alyssa M. Park also examines the disparity between the experiences of Korean migrants to China and Russia during the nineteenth and twentieth centuries and the tendency to portray Koreans in China or in Russia as bound to Korea.⁶⁷ Given the "world of encounter and fluidity" created by frequent border crossings in and out of these countries,⁶⁸ it is perhaps not surprising that by the mid-twentieth century, at least 12 percent of all Koreans lived outside of Korea.⁶⁹ The widespread migration practices of Koreans in the century before the Korean War throw into question the motives of reunification discourses that center 1948.

Joseonjok Aspirations

I end this chapter by turning to two other characters in this novel, one who is also Joseonjok and another who aspires to be Joseonjok, in order to push this examination of the marginalization of Joseonjok or other ethnic Korean populations in sites such as Russia and Japan within the Korean diaspora in a slightly different direction. To return to the question of how Joseonjok is imagined in the novel, I position my reading of Danny in relation to Seongsik, Jangmi's Joseonjok husband, with the intention of generating a very different set of meanings.

When we first encounter Seongsik, it is through Jangmi's eyes as she is meeting with men whom a marriage broker had found. There is a sense of urgency here because Jangmi is desperate to leave the country as she is both pregnant and unwed. The crossing and wedding occur quickly and are given brief descriptions within the novel. We are, however, given more detail about how Jangmi exerts considerable effort to become Joseonjok. While she is upfront with the reader about how she never intends for this arrangement with Seongsik to be permanent, she still values the relative safety that marriage to him offers her, and she wants to remain with him for a period of time, at least until her child is born. Unlike Danny, for whom being Joseonjok is largely constructed in nostalgic terms, for Jangmi, being Joseonjok offers her a way to survive until the future arrives.

Seongsik is not depicted in great detail, but we are told that in the past he had traveled to South Korea to work. Speaking of his missing leg, he tells Jangmi, "I lost it in a factory. In South Korea. I went there to make money—all the healthy Joseon-*jok* in China leave to make money if they can—but I came back with debts and one leg."[70] While Seongsik implies that he is unique in returning to China in worsened physical and financial condition than when he left, this is far from true. Many migrant laborers from China and other parts of Asia are injured while working in hazardous conditions for low wages that they do not always manage to collect. The South Korean government is aware of the inhumane working conditions for migrant laborers as it is "through various legal provisions, and also by refusing to provide regulations or refusing to enforce them, [that] the South Korean state sanctions and underwrites a racialized and racist labor exploitation of the migrant population; racism and state power are welded to each other."[71] Presumably, the financial pressures and hopes for economic security were at least part of the reason that Seongsik's first wife left him and their daughter, Byeol. As a result, Seongsik is lonely and afraid that Jangmi will also leave him, so he tries to romance her and convince her that they can have a happy life together. But when he realizes that she is already pregnant with another man's child, he is unable to trust her as he no longer believes that she entered into this arrangement with sincere intentions. Yet even before their brief marriage begins to fall apart, we become acutely conscious of the precarious ground upon which their relationship is perched. Jangmi herself is aware that she is not "exactly married" as she, like all the other North Korean women "who entered China, and all the children created from these marriages, didn't officially exist."[72] Thus while she lives in an apartment with Seongsik and Byeol that has running water and a washing machine, she knows that she is still unfree and dependent on the goodwill of those around her. Later in the novel, Seongsik tells Jangmi about his work leading Christian groups through the Yanbian province and mentions the North Koreans he encounters: "'You know, I try to get the tourists to help your people at their hideouts. Some live for years in underground caves like moles.' There [is] sympathy in his voice but also a vein of satisfaction in telling [her] this."[73] In addition to reasserting the power dynamics within their relationship, Seongsik's comment undermines any kind of diasporic romanticism by making it clear that he, much like his mother, does not see North Koreans as 'his people' but rather as inhuman others.

While ethnic nationalism may not unite Jangmi and Seongsik, I propose that what does link them is, to borrow a term from geographers HaeRan Shin and Soyoung Park, a kind of "translegality" that draws attention to the "constantly changing legality of transnational migrants."[74] H. Shin and Park's approach to Joseonjok working in South Korea turns away from a focus on the differences between being documented and undocumented and toward a language of liminal legality or semilegality.[75] Translegality gives us a means of comparing North Koreans in China, Joseonjok in South Korea, and migrants in North America while also recognizing the diasporic hierarchies that continue to inform how these subjects migrate, live, and are imagined.

Such an approach makes us conscious of the political and economic structures — as well as structures of melancholic feeling — and ideologies within a global order that influence our subject positions and reading practices; but it fails to engage with individual stories independent of how they illustrate the limitations of discourses and frames. Jangmi, for instance, is a character who is noteworthy for her refusal to apologize for her attempts to survive, for her inability to conform to the ideal subject demanded by discourses of humanitarian aid and human rights, and for her antagonistic relationship with Danny. Her illegibility within our most familiar frames for understanding North Koreans challenges our desire to romanticize her story or instrumentalize her as a laboring body. Taking inspiration from Saidiya Hartman's return to the archives to write enslaved women as more than the violences inflicted upon them, I read

Jangmi as an attempt to imagine North Korean women differently. Such projects of describing the illegible let us engage with, to borrow Hartman's words, "the detritus of lives with which we have yet to attend."[76] Hartman's words point us toward a North Korean studies to come, one that sees beyond the victimization of the individual without losing sight of the victimization. By questioning North Korean representation and the othering of these lives by Koreans in South Korea and within the Korean diaspora—in relation to the humanitarian self, and in other formations—we can begin to understand the complexity of North Korean subjectivity. And I suggest that Lee's novel points us toward what representations of North Korea might look like beyond the Cold War coordinates that have long defined it. From such new spaces, we can start to look past cartoonish post–Cold War images of an inhuman North Korea and toward the lives impacted by them.

Epilogue

SITUATING NORTH KOREA WITHIN
SOCIALIST LIFEWORLDS

Over the past decade, a number of documentary films have been released that explore North Korean history. Many have been made by South Korean filmmakers, including Cho Sung-Hyung's *Verliebt, Verlobt, Verloren* (2016), Chu Sang-mi's *The Children Gone to Poland* (2018), and Kim Deog-Young's *Kim Il Sung's Children* (film 2020; book 2023). These films sketch out the migrations from North Korea to Eastern Europe by orphans, workers, and students during the Cold War and explore the heartbreak experienced by family and friends when the North Koreans were called back. For many of us situated in Canada and the United States, these are unfamiliar episodes of migration history, so these films function as invaluable resources for reconceptualizing the Korean diaspora. Other films such as Kim Soyoung's Exile Trilogy (*Heart of Snow, Heart of Blood* [2014]; *Sound of Nomad, Arirang* [2016]; and *Goodbye My Love, North Korea* [2017]) also expand our knowledge of Korean migration within other geographies. Kim Soyoung's films direct our attention toward the stories of ethnic

Koreans in Central Asia and their historic and current travels between Korea and Central Asia.¹ While Stalin's mass deportation of Koreans from Russia to Uzbekistan and Kyrgyzstan in 1937 is "an undercurrent" in Kim Soyoung's films, it is not one that "rob[s] the ongoing victories-in-process in the survival of the people, of their culture, and their beliefs in an access to the future."² Korean American filmmakers have also made thoughtful contributions to this socialist archive. For example, Joseph Juhn's *Jeronimo* (2019) traces the migration of Koreans under Japanese colonialism to Mexico and then Cuba in order to contextualize the life of Korean Cuban revolutionary and later government official Jeronimo Lim Kim. Moving in a slightly different direction, *People Are the Sky* (2015) follows Korean American filmmaker Dai Sil Kim-Gibson as she is given permission to visit North Korea seventy years after her birth there. The film weaves together Kim-Gibson's autobiographical narrative and North Korean history. Each of these films poses challenging questions about how to locate subjects within collective histories while holding onto their multiple, competing, and shifting ideological commitments. By carefully mapping out a network of socialist lifeworlds, these films give us access to a broader sphere within which we can situate North Korea.

In working through this archive of films, I am struck by the kinds of questions posed by these filmmakers as they route us through unfamiliar histories and engage with North Korea without intending to reproduce Cold War binaries and tensions. Their work contextualizes North Korea as an actor among others within a shared set of historical forces, querying the pressures North Korea exerted and examining how it responded to others rather than dismissing it as an inhuman figure, anomalous, irrational and always unknowable. In these concluding pages, I engage with these lesser-known histories of migration by focusing on a few South Korean films that orient us toward North Korea in new ways. These films fulfill a doubled function by modeling new modes of inquiry as they also offer unfamiliar parts of the archive of North Korean representations, thereby generating new forms of knowledge production. By extending this discussion of migration into socialist worlds, my intention is to bring this examination of North Korea full circle, back to the goals I outlined in the preface, namely, to engage with North Korea in terms of relationality rather than in terms of absolute difference. Here I ask: How can we understand Korean migrations and diasporas through the socialist world? What other ways exist to understand the complex lifeworlds that involve North Korea? And is it possible to deconstruct the binary of East and West by nuancing the complexity of both as well as their intertwined relations?³

To examine one small piece of this history, I return to the stories of North Korean orphans sent to socialist countries in the 1950s. Chungmoo Choi provides an overview of this history, noting that in 1951, Kim Il Sung had asked Warsaw Pact countries to take in the children who had been left orphaned. According to her research, 25,000 North Korean children were sent to socialist countries in Europe, 20,000 to China, and 250 to Mongolia. In 1959, those who were in Eastern Europe were repatriated with little warning. Choi notes that while the official reason given by the North Korean government was that the children were needed to help rebuild the country now that the war was over, another reason may have been that Kim Il Sung did not want the orphans to be exposed to the liberalization movements that were breaking out in Hungary and Poland, as they "might start a Korean version of the Poznań protest."[4] Once in North Korea, "the repatriated orphans—now in their late teens to early twenties—were subjected to a forty-day ideological 'head cleansing' program to wash out any liberal ideals or disinfect what was referred as the 'revisionist virus' that the orphans might have contracted while growing up in Europe."[5]

Notable is an embracing of slowness on the part of *The Children Gone to Poland* and *Kim Il Sung's Children*; this is unlike the humanitarian aesthetics that rely on a logic of "emergency thinking" in which "saving endangered human lives takes precedence over all other considerations, including the aesthetics and politics of representation."[6] The absence of urgency also marks these films as being outside of the state of emergency that characterized South Korea for two decades and that continues to exist as a lingering aftereffect, for "while the political and legal states of emergency have now been lifted, an *affective* state of emergency continues to be mobilized intensely in South Korea as a way of processing the new phase of capitalism we are facing today."[7] Panic and urgency are absent as driving forces, for not only have the orphans been repatriated to North Korea for more than sixty years now, but also these films have taken considerable time to make. In the case of *Kim Il Sung's Children*, we learn that it took Kim Deog-Young fifteen years to trace these histories before he was even able to begin making his documentary.[8]

As I watch these films, I cannot help but be aware of the layers of mediation that separate us from their subjects. When, for example, I question why some subjects who initially expressed reluctance to be on camera later changed their minds and gave interviews, I become conscious of the complex negotiations that must be ongoing outside of the frame. In the book version of *Kim Il Sung's Children*, Kim Deog-Young describes speaking with Miran Cho, the daughter of Georgeta Mircioiu and Cho Chung Ho, after she suddenly and unexpectedly consented to an interview. The conversation they have is brief as Miran Cho has agreed only to ten minutes, and the discussion raises almost more questions about her father, Cho Chung Ho, than it answers for Kim Deog-Young. At the same time, this exchange underscores the artificial circumstances in which we come to know documentary subjects, as filmmakers frame and edit their stories. And by extension, it prompts me to wonder how, even as they set out to query official histories and move us outside those framings, these films continue to be informed by global forces and imperialist logics.

Documentary Subjects, Audiences, and Filmmakers

Many of these independent films seek new ways of telling stories by forming different kinds of relations between subjects who are on and off screen. To explore this problem, I want to take a brief detour through the documentary film practice of Kim Dong-won, a prominent South Korean filmmaker. In his essay on Kim Dong-won's *Another World We Are Making* and *Sanggyedong Olympics*, Chris Berry addresses the activist dimensions of Kim's documentary filmmaking practice, noting that a central goal of these films is to support the struggles of local communities. Unlike conventional documentaries, Kim Dong-won's films do not clearly distinguish between subjects and audiences, as oftentimes the subjects are also the primary audience when they come together as a community to discuss the documentary:[9] "For example, if we understand the primary audience to be the residents themselves and other residents, when they are interviewed about what they are doing and why, it appears that the purpose of the documentary making is not only—or even firstly—to convey this information to later viewers like ourselves, today. Rather, it is to provoke self-reflection and exchange amongst the residents themselves."[10] Taking Berry's essay as a model for reading documentaries about North Korea, I ask: Who is the audience for these films? And how do they nuance our understanding of global, transnational, and even national publics?

If, following Jin Cheon, we extend Berry's reading of Kim Dong-won's work to include *Repatriation* (2003), another film that blurs conventional distinctions, we can see community being created as lifeworlds are complicated and transnational identifications become ways of refusing national disciplinings. In *Repatriation*, Kim Dong-won records the stories of men who had been imprisoned by the South Korean government during the 1970s and 1980s as spies sent from North Korea. Tortured in the prisons in an effort to make them convert to South Korean ideologies (some for four decades), many of these men refused to acquiesce. Some prisoners, we learn, were still being held even as this film was completed. But *Repatriation* is not a film in which the audience is able to sit comfortably with a sense of moral outrage at these human rights violations. Our naivete is dispelled as the filmmaker brings us on his journey of growing self-consciousness and makes us aware of how the camera frames our understandings of the men.

Initially, Kim Dong-won wants to hide the presence of his camera so that his subjects will talk, undertaking a kind of documentary filmmaking that "provoke[s] people into uttering the 'truth' that they would not otherwise unveil in ordinary situations."[11] But there is a gradual shift in his technique and relations to his subjects as well as to his viewers. In one scene, a few of the men are reunited after having not seen each other for years. Instead of happiness, we feel an acute awareness of just how intrusive Kim Dong-won's camera is. Not only does it interrupt the free flow of conversation between former prisoners who have been separated for years and are aching to heal from their experiences within and out of prison, but it also places the men under surveillance, vacillating between silencing and spying on them. Kim Dong-won's film is filled with running commentary that provides insight into his reactions and thoughts, beginning from the moment he contemplates whether to pick up the newly released prisoners to his judgments of them, to his feelings of provincialism as well as his fear when he hears them sing openly in praise of Kim Il Sung at an outdoor gathering. Far from being an invisible presence, we are constantly aware of how his camera and voiceovers mediate our experiences. As a viewer, I am caught within a dilemma as I resent Kim Dong-won for intruding even as I realize that without his presence, I would not have access to these stories.

I also realize that Kim Dong-won is aware of this bind, particularly after the men have been repatriated to North Korea and he longs to see them again, especially one named Mr. Cho. Kim Dong-won asks a friend who is going to a festival in Pyongyang to deliver his greetings and is rewarded with a videotaped message from Mr. Cho talking about how he had come to care for Kim Dong-won as a son. When watching this tape, Kim Dong-won expresses his regret for not being able to have done more for Mr. Cho, much as any filial son separated from his father would. This scene marks a transformation in Kim Dong-won's world as well as in his sense of self. He is no longer distanced from the men and worried about being put in danger through association with them; nor is he concerned about getting interviews from them about their stories. This shift begins earlier in the film, after Kim Dong-won is investigated by the South Korean police for his film project about the North Korean prisoners. After experiencing this police coercion, Kim Dong-won feels closer to their cause, even as he remains more skeptical of North Korea than they do.[12]

Repatriation not only records the men as they struggle to maintain their beliefs and dignity within an unfamiliar and often cruel South Korean landscape; it also witnesses the filmmaker's evolving relationship to these men and the Cold War histories that have formed North and South Korea. Jin Cheon examines how similar questions are taken up more broadly by independent documentary films made in East Asia. Arguing that these films illustrate Heonik Kwon's conceptualization of the Cold War as one that is in the process of decomposition, Cheon notes that these films "reveal the continued persistence of *lived* Cold War structures in *discursively* post–Cold War East Asia."[13] By turning to three films about the lives of everyday people in order to trace a shift in the filmmaker's relationship to her subjects, Cheon asserts that independent documentary films made in East Asia after the mid-1990s focus on relationality rather than pursuing truth and authenticity:

> Erased from the official historical record and excluded from public commemoration, the alternate history of pain traced by these documentaries resubmits the Cold War to examination from deep inside its most private wounds. In the process, the filmmakers encounter not only the memories of the earlier generation that lived through the most violent episodes of the Cold War, but also come to question their own history and identities within the process of the Cold War's decomposition.[14]

Making these films allows the filmmakers not only to learn about minor Cold War stories but also to turn their gazes inward and critique their own relations to history.

For Cheon, "The trend toward the use of the first-person perspective or the autobiographical form through which the filmmaker reveals his presence within the work suggests that the documentary itself refuses independence from the self-transforming work of being with the subject."[15] A similar kind of style of participatory documentary filmmaking in which the filmmaker brings in their story and explains their interest in the subject is employed by *The Children Gone to Poland*. We are told that Chu Sang-mi's interest in this subject was directly related to her experiences as a new mother suffering from severe postpartum depression and doubtful of her abilities to care for her young son. During this time, she encountered an image of a malnourished young North Korean woman foraging for food, and her first thought was to wonder where the girl's mother was. This was a transformative moment that solidified her newfound identity as a mother. Chungmoo Choi reads this encounter in terms of compassion, and as "the moment of Chu's emotional commitment to the suffering 'clover girl' or to the reality of the *kkotchebi* woman's suffering that the image represents."[16] The maternal becomes the dominant lens through which Chu Sang-mi approaches and engages with the story of the North Korean orphans in Poland and how she bonds with Songyi, the young North Korean actress who was cast in a feature film called *The Stumps* she was making. Indeed, toward the end of the film, Chu Sang-mi expresses gratitude on behalf of all the North and South Korean parents who could not care for their children, cementing her position as a parent in this story despite being younger than the now-grown children would be.

Throughout the film, Chu Sang-mi annotates her reading process by continually sharing how her motivations shaped the making of the film, explaining how she came to the story, commenting on which are the saddest parts of it, and sharing other insights. We watch, for instance, as she and Professor Jung Hong Boo view a Polish documentary on the North Korean orphans. Chu Sang-mi is overcome by curiosity as she sees the former teachers weeping, and she wonders, "Just what kinds of relationship and bond did the teachers have with the children?"[17] Later in the film, Chu Sang-mi tries to find out about what happened to Songyi during her time in China (after escaping North Korea and as she was trying to cross over to South Korea), but Songyi refuses to satisfy her curiosity. Noting that Songyi stopped talking about her own experiences after this particular conversation, Chu sang-mi observes that Songyi does not trust her.[18] This silence is notable in a film in which other North Korean youths share their traumatic stories, and thus Songyi's refusal "to share the story of her years as *sans papiers* in China [...] makes it all the more appalling."[19] And yet, the film itself seems to question whether Songyi's inability to fully trust Chu Sang-mi is legitimate or misplaced. Chu Sang-mi's feelings toward the girl seem sincere as they bond while exploring Poland, listen to the stories of the former teachers as they remember the orphans, and as Songyi struggles with sorrowful memories. In one scene, the camera shoots the women as they stand on a beach, bluish-gray sky and water behind them, and Chu Sang-mi's face luminous with empathy as she holds Songyi who sobs uncontrollably as she calls out to her younger brother Huk in North Korea. It is a heartbreaking scene, aesthetically beautiful, and one that frames Songyi's grief like a sea with unimaginable depths.

But neither filmmaker nor audience can ever forget that these moments of bonding further the investigative elements of the documentary and that all these actions, even if motivated by good intentions and genuine emotions, benefit the film. These concerns are raised when Chu Sang-mi reflects on Songyi's reluctance to share her story. Instead of becoming angry, Chu Sang-mi contextualizes Songyi's distrust within the landscape of South Korean society by acknowledging that "South Korean society often exploits North Korean defector's pain for political purposes."[20] She extends this point about exploitation by asking,

"What's the difference, even for the sake of art?"[21] As viewers, we are left wondering whether a documentary film can ever be freed from all tendencies to instrumentalize North Korean stories. This is a problem that came up earlier in *The Children Gone to Poland*, when Chu Sang-mi, Kang Dong Wan, and Lee Hae Kyoung were casting their feature film. Lee Hae Kyoung stressed that the particular challenge facing them was that they had to "reflect their [the North Korean youths'] reality well in this project without making their emotional trauma worse."[22] A sense of trepidation that such an outcome might still occur always looms over this film. For instance, when Chu Sang-mi invites Songyi to Poland, we cannot help but worry that this journey might be traumatizing. And after Chu Sang-mi queries the similarities between South Korean politics and art as they exploit North Korean pain, I become acutely aware that the camera is capturing the pain it sees. And consequently, I am left wondering whether the filmmaker can ever fully shed the South Korean mentality that Songyi identifies, one always preoccupied by the question, "What's in it for me?" And by extension, can the viewer?

Shared Structures of Feeling

Throughout *The Children Gone to Poland*, we are made aware of the growing friendship between Songyi and Chu Sang-mi as well as its limits. The differences between the women, as North and South Koreans, appear, for example, in the image of Chu Sang-mi's healthy and happy son who is shown at the beginning of the film. This contrasts with the story of Songyi's baby brother who is described as rarely having more than two potatoes to eat at a time and who must carry his schoolbooks in his hands because his backpack is too tattered to use. The film conveys an awareness of the structures that continue to separate worlds and shape subjectivities in one of its final scenes as it films the women walking on either side of the wall that separated East and West Germany, and as they are reunited when the wall comes to an end. In this way, they symbolize a collective on the cusp of becoming.

While the film struggles with the divisions that separate North and South Korea, it also works to make legible the shared histories of Poland and North Korea. While the teachers and students were from different continents and initially did not speak each other's languages, they had all experienced the devastating effects of war and the deep pain of losing loved ones. Chungmoo Choi notes that the Polish teachers, who were often not much older than the students, understood the terrors of bombing and loss of family members, as Poland had experienced the war in horrific ways with the loss of nearly five million citizens by Germany and the deportation of 1.7 million Polish citizens to labor camps in Siberia and Kazakhstan by the Soviet Union.²³ For instance, Józef Borowiec, the director at Plakowice, had fought for Poland since he was fourteen years old. By the time he was directing the orphanage, he was only in his twenties. Similarly, the other staff members at Plakowice had also experienced the devastating effects of the war: "Many had lost family members and friends and had seen their homes and communities reduced to rubble and lives shattered. Some testified that they had had to step over bodies lying on the streets while walking to school. Still others were Holocaust survivors. All of them had experienced poverty and devastation at the war front without a government to protect the nation."²⁴ In their interviews, the teachers speak about how they asked the children to call them mother and father instead of teacher. It is clear that they fully embraced the children without concern for how much pain they would feel if the children left. After the children were repatriated to North Korea, the teachers worried for their safety and well-being and were distressed for decades that they had not been able to keep these children in Poland.

In the process of caring for their North Korean students, the Polish teachers became not humanitarian saviors but rather "wounded healers";²⁵ the children and their caregivers "journeyed together as a community of sufferers toward hope. They needed each other to heal."²⁶ Remapping the Cold War era via these remnants of memory and feeling enables us to rethink much of what we know about shared histories. When filmmakers such as Chu Sang-mi and Kim Deog-Young "open up ethico-historical issues surrounding collective memory and shared structures of feeling,"²⁷ we are able to see that these collectives also include peoples without any attachments to the Korean peninsula. In *The Children Gone to Poland* and *Kim Il Sung's Children*, the wartime experiences of the Polish teachers and North Korean students become wounded openings that connect them together. The viewer is left wondering whether the intimacies between the Polish teachers and the North Korean children might be deeper and longer lasting than those between Songyi and Chu Sang-mi. And if the connections that bind together socialist and former socialist countries could be stronger than those that cohere North and South Korea.

I have assembled this archive of films in the hope that contextualizing North Korea within a socialist landscape will complicate our understandings of it. I offer these preliminary thoughts about the relations between North Korea and Eastern bloc countries in the 1950s in order to sketch out the beginnings of a space in which we can read North Korea outside of the terms set by the West.

Throughout *Brutal Fantasies*, I have sought an understanding of how the West uses North Korea as an inhuman figure to fashion its version of the Cold War and, moreover, what such framings have produced. By shifting our gaze now toward North Korea's relations to socialist countries, I gesture toward future conversations that might be had about the long Cold War and toward potential research about Korean diasporas and migrations outside of the West.

Notes

PREFACE

1. Saunders, "Fugitive Dreams," 5; see also Hartman, *Lose Your Mother*; Sharpe, *In the Wake*; Troeung, *Refugee Lifeworlds*.

INTRODUCTION

1. George W. Bush, "President Delivers State of the Union Address," January 29, 2002, https://georgewbush-whitehouse.archives.gov/news/releases/2002/01/20020129-11.html.

2. Bruce Cumings provides context for President Bush's grouping together of these countries as an axis of evil by noting that "Osama Bin Laden and friends" disrupted "the Cold War doctrine of containment [that] was still in place" formally and informally in much of the world (Cumings, *North Korea*, 96). He critiques the logic behind President Bush's decision to categorize "a group of nations that could easily be contained and deterred, namely, Iraq, Iran, and North Korea, with the diabolical and uncontrollable Al Qaeda. Thus emerged the 'axis of evil.' These evil-doers were not suicidal and had return addresses, but no matter: they might give or sell their weapons to terrorists" (96).

3. See J. Kim, *Ends of Empire*, for an extended analysis of North Korea and *The Manchurian Candidate*.

4. Many other scholars have also noted the tendency to fashion North Korea in inhuman terms. Historian Suzy Kim's study of the North Korean everyday opens with a description of a satellite image of North Korea that Secretary of Defense Donald Rumsfeld interpreted as an illustration of North Korean tragedy. Kim notes, however, that this is "not an image that speaks for itself, as Rumsfeld would have us believe" but is instead a composite of images that have been carefully crafted together (Suzy Kim, *Everyday Life*, 1). Similarly, International Relations scholar Hazel Smith begins her book on economic change in North Korea by challenging the widely held belief that North Korea is "mad, bad, and sad," arguing instead that North Korea is, like many other countries, undergoing the transformation from socialism to capitalism (H. Smith, *North Korea*, 1). Immanuel

Kim's study of North Korean comedy films also starts by observing a global tendency to belittle North Koreans, this time as the target of jokes told in China, shared via US-made YouTube videos, and performed on South Korean comedy shows (I. Kim, *Laughing North Koreans*).

5. Harootunian, "Shadowing History," 192.

6. In Daniel Vukovich's analysis, illiberalism is a means by which China scholars and media experts frame China's difference from Western norms. He notes that illiberalism is often used by Western nations to critique the intolerance of authoritarian governments and to advocate for the core tenets of liberalism that include individualism, normative universalism, and free markets (Vukovich, *Illiberal China*, 7). While mapping a genealogy of liberalism, Vukovich points out, by way of Raymond Williams's keywords, that in the sixteenth century, *liberal* was a term that referred to class, not to political ideology. This layer of meaning in which illiberalism signifies "vulgarity, ignobility, intolerance, and—still—servility" is crucial to understanding the affective threat that illiberal figures such as North Korea and China pose for the liberal world and, moreover, how "illiberalism can then index not just ugly people and classes but ugly, unfree, non-liberal regimes and nations" (21). But it is worth noting that even for Vukovich, North Korea remains a limit point for how far illiberalism can be stretched as he argues for an understanding of China as a legitimate economic regime rather than dismissing it as "North Korea Lite" (229).

7. Tadiar, *Fantasy Production*, 29, 31.
8. Bow, *Racist Love*, 18.
9. Cheah, *Inhuman Conditions*, 3.
10. Cheah, *Inhuman Conditions*, 4.
11. Cheah, *Inhuman Conditions*, 4.
12. White, *Figural Realism*, 8.
13. "North Korea Sends."
14. Aristotle, *Poetics*, chap. 5.
15. White, *Figural Realism*, 9.
16. Ngai, *Ugly Feelings*, 6.
17. Slaughter, *Human Rights, Inc.*, 11.
18. H. Kwon, *Other Cold War*, 58.
19. H. Kwon, *Other Cold War*, 1.
20. H. Kwon, *Other Cold War*, 34.
21. Klein, *Cold War Orientalism*, 11.
22. Man, "Anti-Asian Violence," 28.
23. Singh, "Culture/Wars," 510.
24. H. Kwon, *Other Cold War*, 37–38.
25. See "Eun-Joung Lee—Video Excerpt," Legacies of the Korean War, 2015, https://legaciesofthekoreanwar.org/story/eun-joung-lee/.
26. As Namhee Lee observes, the discourse of anticommunism, fear of North Korea, and anxiety about being labelled a Communist was not restricted to South Korea: "The reunification movement in South Korea and among Korean diasporic communities was also particularly hard hit by the division between those who were rumored to have ties

with North Korea—and were therefore 'impure'—and those without such ties. The overseas Korean communities, particularly foreign students' communities in the United States and the former West Germany, were extremely cautious about any unintended link with North Korea" (N. Lee, *Making of Minjung*, 107).

27. Jason Lee, *Letters from Pyongyang*, 12:47.

28. Ju Hui Judy Han provides valuable historical insight into one set of relations between South Korean Protestant churches and anti–North Korean sentiments by tracing the migration of middle-class Christians from the northern part of Korea after the land reforms of 1946: "Newly dispossessed and displaced, Christian landowners from the North fled to the South in large numbers, carrying with them intense bitterness and personal animosity against North Korea and Communism" (Han, "Shifting Geographies," 200). This is not to say that all South Korean Christians are as conservative as these anti–North Korean and anticommunist Protestants as there are also more progressive Christians in South Korea (201). As Ingu Hwang notes, Christian organizations such as the World Council of Churches played a crucial role in developing pro-democracy and human rights campaigns in South Korea (Hwang, *Human Rights*, 34).

29. Yoneyama, *Cold War Ruins*, 49.

30. Yoneyama, *Cold War Ruins*, 49.

31. Xiang, *Tonal Intelligence*, 3.

32. Williams, *Divided World*, xx.

33. Yoneyama, *Cold War Ruins*, 49.

34. Xiang, *Tonal Intelligence*, 3.

35. Cheng, *Melancholy of Race*, 6.

36. Cheng, *Melancholy of Race*, xi.

37. Weheliye, *Habeas Viscus*, 4.

38. See Yoneyama, *Cold War Ruins*; J. Kim, *Ends of Empire*; Kang, *Traffic*; and Troeung, *Refugee Lifeworlds*.

39. Harootunian and Sakai, "Japan Studies," 596–97.

40. Shih, "Racializing Area Studies," 35.

41. Tadiar, "Ground Zero," 173.

42. Shih, "Racializing Area Studies," 36.

43. Shih, "Racializing Area Studies," 37.

44. Said, *Orientalism*, 22.

45. Said, *Orientalism*, 21.

46. Amin, *Disturbing Attachments*, 8.

47. See J. Kim, *Ends of Empire*; Daniel Kim, *Intimacies of Conflict*; Baik, *Reencounters*.

48. Ryang, *Reading North Korea*, 3–4.

49. Cumings, *Parallax Visions*, 1.

50. Saunders, "Fugitive Dreams."

51. Weheliye, *Habeas Viscus*, 20.

52. Weheliye, *Habeas Viscus*, 3.

53. Wynter, "Unsettling," 261. Elsewhere, Wynter further underscores the effects of this hierarchy of the human and subhuman in her response to the police brutality experienced by Rodney King and the ensuing civil and criminal trials, arguing that the no hu-

mans involved (NHI) category often used by the Los Angeles judicial system to refer to young Black men is a direct outcome of this logic (Wynter, "No Humans Involved," 42).

54. Wynter, "Unsettling," 264.
55. Wynter, "Unsettling," 282.
56. Wynter, "Unsettling," 301.
57. Jane Park, *Yellow Future*, 25.
58. Jane Park, *Yellow Future*, 5, 24.
59. Bow, *Racist Love*, 4.
60. Bow, *Racist Love*, 7.
61. Bow, *Racist Love*, 111.
62. Roh, Huang, and Niu, *Techno-Orientalism*, 15.
63. Bow, *Racist Love*, 12.
64. C. Kim, *Minor Intimacies*, 8; Jane Park, *Yellow Future*, 1.
65. Yapp, *Minor China*, 5.
66. Hong, "Reframing," 514–15.
67. Hong, "Reframing," 515.
68. Williams, *Divided World*, xx.
69. Moyn, *Not Enough*, 7.
70. Moyn, *Not Enough*, 6.
71. Monica Kim, *Interrogation Rooms*, 4.
72. Hong, "Reframing," 513.
73. For more thorough accounts of the Korean War, see Monica Kim, *Interrogation Rooms*; Cumings, *North Korea*; Cumings, *Korea's Place*; Cumings, *Parallax Visions*; H. Smith, *North Korea*; and Lankov, *Real North Korea*.
74. In South Korea, a different set of struggles exists over how to narrate the war. Jae-Jung Suh sketches out the war as "a site of contestation where different epistemological projects clash" (J. Suh, "Truth and Reconciliation," 504). The hegemonic narrative writes the Korean War as "6/25," the officially sanctioned date of when the war began with the North firing the first shot. But other versions of the war exist and approach it as a war that began before the Korean division in 1945, as a war in which the South Korean state committed acts of violence against civilians before 6/25 and long after, and as an international war with disproportionate US intervention (504). Suh also observes that efforts to create an independent and modern nation-state were underway before and after 1945, but these were contested given the uneven effects of colonialism. Thus "the Korean War could break out only when the discrepant post-colonialities were straight-jacketed into two antagonistic nation-state building projects that were at once hegemonic in aspirations and constrained in capacities" (505). See also United Nations Command, *Armistice Agreement*.
75. Monica Kim, *Interrogation Rooms*, 45.
76. For example, the annual Ulchi Freedom Guardian exercise involves ROK and US troops and demonstrates their readiness for battle. According to the US Department of Defense, the "exercises also highlight the longstanding military partnership, commitment, and enduring friendship between the two nations, help to ensure peace and security on the peninsula, and reaffirm US commitment to the Alliance" (US Department of

Defense, "Exercise Ulchi," August 18, 2017, https://www.defense.gov/News/Releases/Release/Article/1282786/exercise-ulchi-freedom-guardian-2017/). Perhaps unsurprisingly, the DPRK tends to interpret these military exercises as offensive rather than defensive in nature and responds by testing its own weapons; see Choe and Ramzy, "South Korea and U.S. Begin Drills." A lower stakes illustration of the warring relationship between South and North Korea is the blaring of K-pop, propaganda music, and speeches at each other across the DMZ. The broadcasts have been condemned by An Myong-hung, North Korea's UN representative, as "psychological warfare" and "in essence an open act of war" (as quoted in Choe, "North and South Korea").

77. Monica Kim, *Interrogation Rooms*, 5.

78. Responsibility for the Korean War has been assigned to various parties and is often contingent upon who is telling the story. According to Heonik Kwon, responsibility for the war depends on when its origins are dated. If one locates the origin of the war in 1950, then the North's attack on the South, backed by China and the USSR, was the instigating event. However, if one traces the origins of the war back earlier, then the South is equally responsible as it provoked border skirmishes and suppressed nationalist forces. And if one links the origin of the Korean War to the end of the Pacific War in 1945, then the United States and the USSR must be held responsible as they partitioned and occupied Korea (H. Kwon, *Other Cold War*, 2).

79. Sonia Ryang and Daniel Kim are two of many critics who make this point; see Ryang, *Reading North Korea*, 6; Daniel Kim, "Bled In," 550.

80. Daniel Kim ("Bled In," 553–57) discusses this term at length. He adopts it from Susan Choi's 1998 novel, *The Foreign Student*.

81. H. Smith, *North Korea*, 2.

82. In Bruce Cumings's words, the aftermath of Japanese colonialism can be seen in how "postwar South Korea, far from being an anti-colonial entity, often contained virtual replicas of Japanese forms in industry, state policies toward the economy, education, police, military affairs, the physiognomy of its cities, and its civic culture (such as it was). Newspapers were identical in form, if not in content, to Japan's; South Korean schools were museums of colonial practice until the early 1980s—down to the black uniforms, pressed collars, and peaked hats that every male student wore" (Cumings, *Parallax Visions*, 77).

83. Cumings, *Korea's Place*, 193–94.

84. Lankov, *Real North Korea*, 29.

85. Cumings, *Korea's Place*, 232.

86. Lee Min Yong and Chun Sun Tae's experiences in South Korea are sadly not unique, since "under the system of punishing family members and relatives of those accused of a major crime such as *lèse-majesté* (*yŏnjwaje*), the family members and relatives of an alleged leftist were barred from employment as public servants, attending military academy, and travel abroad, which prevented them from obtaining jobs in corporations" (N. Lee, *Making of Minjung*, 78).

87. Crystal Baik's examination of the oral histories contained in *Memory of Forgotten War* (Borshay Liem and Liem, dirs.) and in the digital archive Legacies of the Korean War illuminates the process by which Korean migrants displaced by war were remade as

American immigrants. An important point is made through Baik's reading of Eun-Joung Lee's description of her father's silence regarding his wartime experiences, even when speaking to his children. Baik argues that Lee Min Yong's "hesitation to speak and share is not a symptom of forgetting but a mode of fragmented communication that resonates loudly and painfully within the domestic confines of their family" (Baik, *Reencounters*, 59). See also the archive website, Legacies of the Korean War, 2015, https://legaciesofthekoreanwar.org/.

88. E. Kim, *Making Peace*, 35.

89. While North Korea made a concerted effort to decolonize its policies and politics, "in its haste to deny everything Japanese, it created mirror-image institutions, beginning with the emperor-like leader principle, the corporate political system, the leader's ubiquitous *chuch'e* ideology, and the establishment of the leader/emperor's birthday as a national holiday" (Cumings, *Parallax Visions*, 77).

90. Baik, *Reencounters*, 62.

91. Sung-Hyung Cho's documentary *Verliebt, Verlobt, Verloren*, for example, examines the stories of the North Korean men who were studying in East Germany during the 1950s, the German women they married, and their children. In the 1960s, North Korea recalled these students, and they were forced to leave their families behind in Germany. Kim Deog-Young's *Kim Il Sung's Children* traces the migration of North Korean orphans and teachers to Hungary, Poland, Romania, Bulgaria, and Czechoslovakia during the Korean War and their return to North Korea in the late 1950s. Like Cho's film, Kim pays close attention to the friends and families with whom these North Koreans had to cut ties.

92. Waxman, "You Can Send Your Child."

93. H. Lee, "Life as a North Korean Refugee."

94. Vicki Kwon's *Mass Games: Nation-Building Spectacles in Postcolonial Guyana and North Korea*, an exhibit of artistic materials produced during cultural exchanges between North Korea and Guyana from 1980 to 1992 also traces the ideological, cultural, and material flows between the countries via the mass games staged in each country.

95. Eldridge Cleaver, foreword to Li, *Juche!*, xii.

96. Eldridge Cleaver, foreword to Li, *Juche!*, ix.

97. B. Suh, "Controversies," 25.

98. Cumings, *Parallax Visions*, 127.

99. Cumings, *Parallax Visions*, 149.

100. Hall, "Constituting an Archive," 91–92.

101. Walker and Sakai, "End of Area," 3.

102. Nguyen, "Mẹ-Search," 469.

CHAPTER 1. DYSTOPIC SPECULATION

See also Christopher P. Hanscom's *Impossible Speech: The Politics of Representation in Contemporary Korean Literature and Film* (New York Columbia University Press, 2024). I regret that I did not have the opportunity to more fully engage his writing as I only discovered this book very late in the publication process of my book.

1. Adam Johnson's imagining of a North Korean spy vessel disguised as a fishing boat

seems to draw loosely on the detainment of South Korean fishermen whose human rights violations have been investigated by the South Korean Truth and Reconciliation Commission. As described by Choi Moon Soon, governor of Gangwon-do, "The lives and human rights of those who were illegally detained and harshly interrogated despite being kidnapped and detained by North Korea while squid fishing were ignored in the name of national security" (Truth and Reconciliation Commission, Republic of Korea, 6). The abduction and interrogation of these squid fishermen were not the only instance, as the first Truth and Reconciliation Commission reported having investigated seventeen cases of abducted fishermen (23). In *The Orphan Master's Son*, Jun Do's fishing vessel is depicted as a threatening entity for its ability both to cross international boundaries and to plausibly deny ulterior motives; but the historical context of North and South Korean tensions is not provided. The authoritarian practices of Cold War South Korea are thus written onto North Korea to fashion it as an inhuman figure.

2. Lies, "Fictional Everyman," R10.

3. For example, even as journalists describe how North Korean officials eluded the attempts of US pundits and policymakers in 2020 to know when it would hold its military parade, therefore demonstrating the unknowability of North Korea, they freely speculate about how Kim Jong Un's public apology to his people for being unable to tend to all of their difficulties "is likely to have elicited hollow laughter" from North Koreans who had endured severe beatings and starvation ("Not So Splendid Isolation"). The narrative tone here is one of certainty as the report confirms the brutal fantasy that the Global North believes North Korea to be, with familiarity determining what seems sufficiently plausible and self-evident enough as to render corroboration or even historicization unnecessary.

4. Jameson, *Political Unconscious*, ix–x.

5. Bahng, *Migrant Futures*, 2, quoting Donna Haraway.

6. Yapp, *Minor China*, 23, 8.

7. Lies, "Fictional Everyman," R10.

8. Cussen, "Korea" 477.

9. Cussen, "Korea," 479.

10. This conflict can also be seen in other reviews of the novel. Michiko Kakutani, for instance, notes that "the hardships of real life in North Korea, described by defectors, can be Kafkaesque in their surreal horror" (Kakutani, "North Korean"). An anonymous reviewer describes North Korea as "the land of Kim Jong Il, the unhappy Potemkin Village land of North Korea, where even Josef Stalin would have looked around and thought the whole business excessive" ("The Orphan Master's Son," *Kirkus Reviews*, December 18, 2011, https://www.kirkusreviews.com/book-reviews/adam-johnson/orphan-masters-son/). Collectively, these reviews fashion the country in imaginary terms legible to the West under the pretext of making readers feel sympathy toward real North Koreans.

11. Kang, *Compositional Subjects*, 3.

12. Cussen, "On the Call," 140.

13. For more details regarding the controversy surrounding Shin Dong-hyuk and Harden, please see chapter 2, which examines North Korean memoirs and human rights discourse. Park's story has also been critiqued for the discrepancies between her published memoir, speeches, and interviews. Mary Ann Jolley, for instance, outlines many

of these differences and suggests that these inaccuracies pose dire consequences for other defectors by causing "the world [to] start to doubt their stories" (Jolley, "Strange Tale"). Park's collaborator, Maryanne Vollers, explains these inconsistencies as the product of language barriers, her desire to keep certain details of her experience private, and trauma (Vollers, "Woman Who Faces").

14. Brooks, *Reading for the Plot*, 7.
15. Huang, *Contesting Genres*, 12.
16. Dimock, "Introduction," 1380.
17. Huang, *Contesting Genres*, 6.
18. Huang, *Contesting Genres*, 6.
19. Shine Choi, *Re-Imagining North Korea*, 1.
20. Shine Choi, *Re-Imagining North Korea*, 2.
21. Shine Choi, *Re-Imagining North Korea*, 4.
22. See, for example, Subramanian, "These Are North Korea's"; Quinn, "Unicorn Lair"; Nuwer, "North Korea"; Zurcher, "Did Kim Jong Un?"
23. Bonner, *Made in North Korea*, 39.
24. Brooks, *Reading for the Plot*, xi.
25. Brooks, *Reading for the Plot*, 4.
26. Brooks, *Reading for the Plot*, xii.
27. Moylan, *Scraps*, 147.
28. Johnson, *Orphan Master's Son*, 438.
29. Patterson, *Transitive Cultures*, 179.
30. Moylan, *Scraps*, 5.
31. Bahng, *Migrant Futures*, 169.
32. Oh, *Whitewashing the Movies*, 83.
33. Oh, *Whitewashing the Movies*, 83.
34. Oh, *Whitewashing the Movies*, 86.
35. This is a sentiment that many defectors have noted. For example, in his memoir, Jang Jin-sung describes his discomfort with watching Kim Jong-il cry. However, his discomfort is produced not by the realization of Kim Jong-il's biology but because Jang realizes that "those were not the tears of a compassionate divinity but, rather, of a desperate man" (Jang Jin-sung, *Dear Leader*, xxii).
36. D. Song and Hong, "Toward 'The Day After,'" 53.
37. Johnson, *Orphan Master's Son*, 140.
38. Johnson, *Orphan Master's Son*, 7–8.
39. Johnson, *Orphan Master's Son*, 29.
40. Johnson, *Orphan Master's Son*, 36.
41. Johnson, *Orphan Master's Son*, 187.
42. Johnson, *Orphan Master's Son*, 188.
43. Throughout the novel, repeated references are made to the value of story and the meanings it carries in North Korea and in the US, and these reflections complicate how we are to read both the interrogator's commitment to preserving stories and reluctance to be tied to his own story. Earlier in the novel, a character notes the dissonance between individuals and their stories:

"Where we are from," he said, "stories are factual. If a farmer is declared a music virtuoso by the state, everyone had better start calling him maestro. And secretly, he'd be wise to start practicing the piano. For us, the story is more important than the person. If a man and his story are in conflict, it is the man who must change.... But in America, people's stories change all the time. In America, it is the man who matters. Perhaps they will believe your story and perhaps not, but you, Jun Do, they will believe *you*. (Johnson, *Orphan Master's Son*, 121–22)

44. Johnson, *Orphan Master's Son*, 308.
45. Johnson, *Orphan Master's Son*, 188.
46. Brazinsky, "Remembering Ŏmŏni," 265.
47. If we take seriously the differences between North Korean and North American lifeworlds, then the cultural imperialist tendencies of Johnson's novel also become apparent in other ways such as the erasure of memories that occurs toward the conclusion. Such a fate invokes the image of brainwashing that appears in many Cold War representations of Communist countries, with *The Manchurian Candidate* being perhaps the example par excellence. And yet, as Andre Schmid writes in his introduction to the special issue that contains Brazinsky's essay, we must consider carefully Brazinsky's question about "the power of official discourse in shaping the worldviews of the population in ways more subtle than the Cold War clichés of 'brainwashing' while also showing the ways the population actively participated as authors of this discourse and used it to their own ends" (Schmid, introduction, 176). As Schmid and Brazinsky remind us, the trope of brainwashing oversimplifies the ideological conflicts of the Cold War by reading only for coercion and psychological pressure. Such a reading discounts the capacity of individuals to critique their realities and sets aside the terms through which they find meaning in their lives. As Brazinsky observes of Chinese soldiers fighting during the Korean War, far from being "brainwashed," these soldiers believed deeply in the causes they were fighting for and saw the official narrative as "part of a coherent and rewarding view of life that guided them in their interactions" (Brazinsky, "Remembering Ŏmŏni," 256). In contrast, Johnson's novel represents brainwashing as an uncomplicated forgetting, with Jun Do and the interrogator forgetting what they know in order to be reborn as content residents "in a rural village, green and peaceful" (Johnson, *Orphan Master's Son*, 412), a space somehow far from the reaches of North Korean politics and power. The utopia imagined at the end of the novel is an imperialist fantasy of a North Korea that exists outside of history and that is populated by individuals who possess limited forms of agency.
48. Samuels, "Kidnapping Politics," 370.
49. McCormack, *Client State*, 97.
50. Lynn, "Vicarious Traumas," 490.
51. Lynn, "Vicarious Traumas," 491.
52. McCormack, *Client State*, 97.
53. Quoted in Funabashi, *Peninsula Question*, 5.
54. Arrington, "Mutual Constitution," 497.
55. McCormack, *Client State*, 94.
56. McCormack, *Client State*, 16, 113.
57. Yoneyama, *Cold War Ruins*, 49.

58. Lynn, "Vicarious Traumas," 494.
59. McCormack, *Client State*, 120.
60. Mason, *Japan's Relations*, 6.
61. Bae and Moon, "South Korea's Engagement Policy," 19.
62. Boynton, *Invitation-Only Zone*, 164.
63. Schmid, introduction to "Reconsidering North Korea," 179.
64. Patterson, *Transitive Cultures*, 151.
65. Brooks, *Reading for the Plot*, 7.
66. Jang Jin-sung, *Dear Leader*, 3.
67. Boynton, *Invitation-Only Zone*, 67.
68. Minsun Kim offers guidance for how to read North Korean literature by reminding us, "North Korean literature chooses a safe narrative and format in an effort to avoid any possible conflict and danger. Therefore, North Korean literature usually appears to be propaganda literature with the same repetitive content. It reveals different sides, however, when one understands the hidden tensions and strategies that contributed to its production" (Minsun Kim, "Inside North Korean Literature," 303). Thus, North Korean authors produce literature that is shaped by the state but that nonetheless contains meaning beyond the literal: "The imperative is that of 'literature for the people,' and its significance is twofold. It is a directive to aesthetically reflect the realities of socialist society in the text as well as to produce texts that are compliant with the direction of state leadership. The literary works of North Korea, whether or not their aesthetic expressions are successful, are inevitably confronted with this dual imperative" (300).
69. Cannan and Adam, *Lovers and the Despot* (51:04–51:11).
70. Samuels, "Kidnapping Politics," 378.
71. Samuels, "Kidnapping Politics," 381.
72. Choi Eun-hee and Shin Sang-ok sought refuge at the US embassy in Austria. They had been permitted to travel there after earning Kim Jong-il's trust by producing critically successful films by international standards for North Korea and under the pretext that they were securing a coproduction deal to finance a film on Genghis Khan. Paul Fischer's account of Choi and Shin's escape in *A Kim Jong-Il Production* differs by offering details absent from the depiction in *The Lovers and the Despot*. In Fischer's version, Shin had a contingency plan as he had informed an employee at the hotel that they were seeking asylum and asked him to alert the Austrian police. The next day, they meet with a Japanese journalist named Akira Enoki who helps them navigate their taxi to the US embassy (Fischer, *A Kim Jong-Il Production*, 296–301). Enoki's presence in the cab is never directly mentioned in *The Lovers and the Despot*, but he is visually acknowledged as an Asian man is standing next to the taxi that Shin and Choi take when they flee the hotel. Fischer's version also counters allegations that Shin Sang-ok and Choi Eun-hee were working with the US government because it points out that the hotel in Vienna in which they were staying had relationships with the embassy and would have helped them reach safety instead of having them undertake their perilous escape.
73. Kim Soyoung, *Korean Cinema*, 43.
74. Ngai, *Ugly Feelings*, 6.

CHAPTER 2. THE INHUMAN FIGURE OF HUMAN RIGHTS

An earlier version of part of this chapter was published as "Figuring North Korean Lives: Reading at the Limits of Human Rights," in *The Subject(s) of Human Rights: Crises, Violations, and Asian/American Critique*, ed. Cathy J. Schlund-Vials, Guy Beauregard, and Hsiu-Chuan Lee (Philadelphia: Temple University Press, 2020), 217–32.

1. Quoted in Shoichet and Park, "North Korean Prison Camp."
2. "UN Dismisses North Korea's Claim."
3. Onishi, "Campaigning for Human Rights."
4. See Hong, "Manufacturing Dissidence." Hong notes that this heavy reliance on human intelligence is one of the "primary post-9/11 modes of *knowing* North Korea within both Washington, DC, policy and US-based human rights advocacy circles" (746). The specific importance of Shin's testimony to the UN's investigation into North Korea is expressed by Marzuki Darusman when he thanks Shin Dong-hyuk for speaking and tells Shin that "you are now the single strongest voice that speaks to the atrocities that have taken place" (United Nations Human Rights Council, "Commission of Inquiry" [transcript], 36).
5. Hwang, *Human Rights*, 263.
6. Hong, "Manufacturing Dissidence," 747.
7. Lankov, "After the Shin Dong-hyuk Affair." Lankov's article continues with a description of the plight of North Koreans vis-à-vis other victims of poverty and violence that bears repeating for how it sketches out the struggles around being heard by international audiences:

> The story of the average North Korean refugee does not appear to be that remarkably different from the life stories of the countless millions of people from Africa and South Asia. Sadly, malnourishment, daily violence and for many women, thinly disguised institutionalized rape are ubiquitous in many parts of the poor world.... So, North Korean refugees—and their assistants—have to compete with the poorer elements of the rest of the world. This creates an incentive for them to deliver more dramatic and, if necessary, embellished stories in order to win some attention in a rather crowded media market.

8. Kaiman, "Story about Kim Jong-un's Uncle."
9. See Simpson, "Kim Jong-un's Uncle"; Associated Press, "Kim Jong Un Showed off."
10. United Nations Human Rights Council, "Commission of Inquiry on Human Rights in the Democratic People's Republic of Korea," accessed May 25, 2024, https://www.ohchr.org/en/hrbodies/hrc/coidprk/pages/commissioninquiryonhrindprk.aspx.
11. Kirby, "Report of the UN Commission," 2.
12. United Nations Special Rapporteur, *Situation of Human Rights in the Democratic People's Republic of Korea*, 61st Session, 5.
13. United Nations Special Rapporteur, *Situation of Human Rights in the Democratic People's Republic of Korea*, 66th session, 3. The responses to the UN on these two occasions are part of a longer pattern of interactions. As Bo-hyuk Suh notes, "North Korea has continued to ignore what is known as the 'Resolution on North Korean Human Rights' passed by the UN Human Rights Committee (1997–1998), the UN Commission on Human Rights (2003–2005), and the UN General Assembly (2006). North Korea

refers to passage of such resolutions as a direct form of political oppression and nothing short of a violation of North Korea's sovereignty" (Bo-hyuk Suh, "Controversies," 25).

14. So, "Note Verbale," 1.

15. So, "Note Verbale," 2.

16. Douzinas, *Human Rights and Empire*, 32. One such example is the National Endowment for Democracy (NED). Dae-Han Song and Christine Hong note that since 1998, the NED, a "quasi-private, grant-making organization funded almost entirely by the US Congress via the US State Department, has been, directly or indirectly through its four core institutes, supporting right-wing, neoconservative South Korean human rights and defector groups. In addition to technical assistance, this support has included $6.7 to $11.9 million from 1999 to 2010, with an additional $3 million starting January 2009 directly disbursed to many of these groups by the State Department under then newly elected Barack Obama" (D. Song and Hong, "Toward 'The Day After,'" 39). This funding continues to be allocated, and $4.9 million was set aside for 2021; see National Endowment for Democracy, "North Korea 2021," February 14, 2022, https://www.ned.org/region/asia/north-korea-2021/.

17. "North Korea: Is Change Really Around the Corner"; Choe, "Escapee."

18. United Nations Human Rights Council, "Commission of Inquiry" (transcript), 5.

19. Harden, *Escape from Camp 14*, 101.

20. United Nations Human Rights Council, "Commission of Inquiry" (transcript), 24. During his testimony, Shin Dong-hyuk noted, "Through [a] new inmate, I have heard about the outside world and I was especially interested in the food that people ate. And I heard from this new inmate that the people outside could eat the same food as the guards, freely. So, just that alone (the food) was the incentive for me to escape."

21. Yokota Megumi was abducted when she was thirteen years old in 1977. In 1986, she married a Korean man, had a child the following year, and according to North Korean officials, Yokota committed suicide in 1993 or 1994. In 2004, Kim Chol Jun, Yokota's former husband, gave her cremated remains to Japanese officials. Upon DNA testing, Japanese officials concluded that these were not Yokota Megumi's remains and that North Korea had deceived them (McCormack, *Client State*, 101). But as McCormack explains, the situation involving Yokota Megumi's remains was far from straightforward. First, he notes that Kim Chol Jun was likely a South Korean man, previously known as Kim Young Nam, who disappeared from South Korea, possibly as an abductee, at the age of 17. Second, the analysis of Yokota Megumi's remains was not definitive. They were initially sent to Japan's National Research Institute of Police Science, where the remains were deemed to be too far degraded to be analyzed. The remains were then sent to Teikyo University to be analyzed, but those results were later critiqued in an international journal on multiple grounds: that the professor who conducted the tests had no prior experience in analyzing cremated remains, that the samples could easily have been contaminated, and that the results could not be verified because the tests had used up all of the sample. Third, shortly after his critique of the forensic testing was published, Dr. Yoshii Tomio "was promoted to the prestigious position of head of the forensic medical department of the Tokyo metropolitan police department—making him unavailable for media comment" (103). And fourth, North Korea responded to these allegations by suggesting

that the remains be taken to a third country for independent verification, but Japan did not respond to this suggestion.

22. D. Song and Hong, "Toward 'The Day After,'" 42.

23. Along with other North Korean prison camp survivors, Kim Young-soon testified before the House Foreign Affairs Subcommittee on Human Rights in 2011. "Human Rights in North Korea," C-SPAN, September 20, 2011, https://www.c-span.org/video/?301652-1/human-rights-north-korea.

24. I. Lee, "North Korean Human Rights," 180; Wang, "Refugee, Returnee."

25. B. Suh, "Controversies," 37.

26. Bae and Moon, "South Korea's Engagement Policy," 18.

27. Lynn, *Bipolar Orders*, 26.

28. United Nations, "History of the Declaration," accessed October 5, 2024, https://www.un.org/en/about-us/udhr/history-of-the-declaration.

29. United Nations, "History of the Declaration."

30. Slaughter, *Human Rights, Inc.*, 5, 2.

31. Bruce Cumings details General MacArthur's requests for atomic and cobalt bombs. Truman's decision to remove MacArthur from command was not because he was opposed to the idea of using these weapons but rather that "he wanted a reliable commander on the scene should Washington decide to use nuclear weapons; that is, Truman traded MacArthur for his atomic policies" (Cumings, *North Korea*, 23).

32. J. Kim, *Ends of Empire*, 4.

33. United Nations General Assembly, *Universal Declaration of Human Rights*.

34. Moyn, *Not Enough*, 7.

35. Williams, *Divided World*, 67.

36. Williams, *Divided World*, 68.

37. Douzinas, *Human Rights and Empire*, 9.

38. Douzinas, *Human Rights and Empire*, 24. After the signing of the UDHR and the executions of seven people who had been found guilty at the Tokyo war crime tribunals, "the allies started reoccupying their old colonies in an endgame before decolonisation. The trials were used to introduce legal principles that could outlaw the coming anti-colonial struggles" (25).

39. Atanasoski, *Humanitarian Violence*, 3.

40. Atanasoski, *Humanitarian Violence*, 3.

41. Atanasoski, *Humanitarian Violence*, 14, 17.

42. Rajagopal, *International Law from Below*, 176.

43. As Cheah reminds us, the post–World War II institutionalization of human rights discourse was motivated by a desire to recognize the crimes committed by the Nazi regime as violations of not just individuals but of humanity as a whole (Cheah, *Inhuman Conditions*, 145). Within this concept of crimes against humanity, the human becomes a metaphor that stands in for the Western subject and the citizen. I want to suggest that the timing of the adoption of the Universal Declaration of Human Rights in 1948 makes it clear that outside of those parameters lie the overlapping circles of North Korea and the figure of the Asian. This is perhaps unsurprising since, as Mignolo points out, "In the eighteenth century, the 'rights of man and of the citizen' was formulated instead

within the planetary consciousness of a cosmo-polis analogous to the law of nature, with Europe—the Europe of nations, specifically—as the frame of reference. There was a change but within the system, or, better yet, within the imaginary of the modern/colonial world system" (Mignolo, "Many Faces," 731).

44. Coombe, "Honing a Critical Cultural Study," 236.

45. J. Kim, *Ends of Empire*, 19.

46. J. Kim, *Ends of Empire*, 8.

47. The limitations of human rights discourse become abundantly clear if we also look at the history of South Korea. While activists sought to mobilize human rights alongside their efforts to democratize South Korea in the 1970s, international organizations such as Amnesty International rebuffed their efforts, preferring to maintain the political neutrality of human rights. More recently, human rights scholars have critiqued such desires for political neutrality as impossible to realize in practice while also noting that the "underlying binaries—apolitical versus political, timely versus prolonged, exception versus norm—are riddled with internal contradictions" (Rangan, *Immediations*, 70). For South Korea—as a country that had struggled with colonialism, imperialism, civil war, military rule, and the exploitation of labor—it was impossible to conceptualize human rights in apolitical terms without rendering them completely useless. Like many others in the Global South, South Korean protestors were "frustrated by the repeated failure of world powers to recognize their concerns about national self-determination, economic unfairness, and human rights," and reacted by bringing these discourses together and making "domestic pro-democracy disputes into transnational contestations on human rights issues in South Korea" (Hwang, *Human Rights*, 2).

48. J. Song, *Human Rights Discourse*, 30.

49. J. Song, *Human Rights Discourse*, 12.

50. Hong, "Reframing," 512.

51. Hong, "Reframing," 512.

52. Hong, "Reframing," 513.

53. Hong, "Reframing," 515.

54. J. Song, *Human Rights Discourse*, 32.

55. United Nations High Commissioner for Refugees, "Convention," 14.

56. Nyers, *Rethinking Refugees*, xiii.

57. Rangan, *Immediations*, 11.

58. Jang Jin-sung, *Dear Leader*, 311.

59. UNESCO, "Building Peace in the Minds of Men and Women," as archived September 9, 2015, by Internet Archive's *Wayback Machine*, https://web.archive.org/web/20161026121124/https://en.unesco.org/70years/building_peace.

60. Montagu, "Statement on Race," 32.

61. Banton's reflections on the changes that had taken place since the UNESCO statements in the early 1950s speak to the changing international social and political conditions: "Educational campaigns were mounted. More important, probably, most colonial nations won their independence and were admitted to the United Nations" (Banton, "Social Aspects," 19). While this was a major shift, it did not necessarily lead to a lessening of racial conflict:

New population movements occurred which brought previously separated peoples into closer contact and increased the points at which the sparks of hostility could be struck. African, West Indian, Indian and Pakistani workers migrated to their former metropolitan countries, the United Kingdom and France in search of work. Indonesians who had never previously left the land of their birth, but were Dutch citizens, took ship to the Netherlands. Negro farm workers in the Southern region of the United States were driven from the land as tractors and mechanical harvesters were adopted; they, and their families, travelled north and to the cities. In South Africa the government intensified its efforts to enforce a pattern of separation. Over much of the globe it seemed as if racial friction was growing more frequent and more intense. (19)

62. Atanasoski, *Humanitarian Violence*, 4.
63. Taylor, "'One Hand Can't Clap,'" 41.
64. Cheah, "Humanity in the Field," 1556.
65. Memoirs published by North Korean defectors between 1968 and 1978 are Ŭigŏdan Myŏlgong and Kwisun Yongsahoe's *Sasŏn ŭl nŏmŏsŏ* (available in Korean; 1968); Kim Sin-jo's *Na nun minjok ui choein iotta: Kim Sin-jo sugi* (Korean; 1968); and Kim Yong-gyu's *Sihyo in'gan* (Korean; 1978). The fourth publication, Kim T'ae-jin's *Chiok t'alch'ulgi* (available in Korean and Mandarin; 1987), is by a South Korean who migrated to North Korea.
66. B. Chung, "Between Defector and Migrant," 8.
67. B. Chung, "Between Defector and Migrant," 9. Eunyoung Christina Choi notes the gendered dimensions of these migrations. She points out that most North Korean migrants crossing into China until the mid-1990s were men. However, the majority of North Korean migrants fleeing since the 1990s, during the period of political and economic decline, were women (Eunyoung Christina Choi, "Introduction," 3).
68. John Lee, "North Korean Defector."
69. Bae and Moon, "South Korea's Engagement Policy," 16. In many ways, South Korea's authoritarian government acted as a continuation of the Japanese colonial one that had not been substantially altered under US occupation. In regard to the postcolonial era, Ian Neary traces the way that colonial law was largely adapted (rather than abandoned) after 1945 by the US military government and subsequent administration under Rhee Syngman after the creation of South Korea in 1948. He notes that the US "decided to retain and strengthen those who had served the security interests of the colonial regime—the police, judges, prosecutors and military officers. So, although virtually all Japanese people left Korea, the systems of security, arrest, imprisonment, torture and legal process that had been created by the colonial regime were retained and even strengthened after 1945" (Neary, *Human Rights in Japan*, 70–71).
70. Hwang, *Human Rights*, 20.
71. Neary, *Human Rights in Japan*, 89.
72. Bae and Moon, "South Korea's Engagement Policy," 25.
73. Bae and Moon, "South Korea's Engagement Policy," 17.
74. Douzinas, *Human Rights and Empire*, 30.
75. Bae and Moon, "South Korea's Engagement Policy," 18.

76. Paik Nak-chung, "South Korean Democracy," 160.
77. Paik Nak-chung, "South Korean Democracy," 161.
78. E. Kim, *Making Peace with Nature*, 36–37.
79. United Nations Office of the High Commissioner for Human Rights, "Special Rapporteur on the Situation of Human Rights in the Democratic People's Republic of Korea," accessed July 22, 2021, https://www.ohchr.org/EN/HRBodies/SP/Countries Mandates/KP/Pages/SRDPRKorea.aspx.
80. George W. Bush, "President Delivers State of the Union Address," January 29, 2002, https://georgewbush-whitehouse.archives.gov/news/releases/2002/01/20020129 -11.html.
81. Kang, *Traffic*, 3.
82. Kang, *Traffic*, 3.
83. Kang, *Traffic*, 3, 11.
84. Kang, *Traffic*, 15.
85. Žižek, *Demanding the Impossible*, 48.
86. "Kim Il Sung's Children," *FilmFreeway*, accessed October 15, 2023, https://filmfreeway.com/kimilsungschildren.
87. Harden, *Escape from Camp 14*, 10.
88. Harden, *Escape from Camp 14*, 46.
89. During his testimony, Shin Dong-hyuk also referenced the emotional distance that separated him from his family: "Well in fact, I'm not sure whether other children share the same feeling or share the same idea but there was no concept of family in the cell where we lived. We called our parents Mom and Dad, but that was just the way we addressed them. My Mom was an inmate and my Dad was an inmate. We were all inmates and there was nothing that I could do to them, for her as a son. And, they had nothing they can do as parents, so I guess I did not feel any attachment or feeling for my parents. I try even now, but I have a hard time doing that" (United Nations Human Rights Council, "Commission of Inquiry" [transcript], 15).
90. Harden, *Escape from Camp 14*, 16.
91. Harden, *Escape from Camp 14*, 16.
92. Harden, *Escape from Camp 14*, 190.
93. Wong, *Transpacific Attachments*, 3.
94. Wong, *Transpacific Attachments*, 3.
95. Harden, *Escape from Camp 14*, 47.
96. Rangan, *Immediations*, 3.
97. Slaughter, "Enabling Fictions," 1407.
98. Harden, *Escape from Camp 14*, 115.
99. Rak, *Boom!*, 5.
100. Atanasoski, *Humanitarian Violence*, 14.
101. Smith and Watson, *Reading Autobiography*, 275.
102. See Lukács, "Art and Objective Truth."
103. Rak, *Boom!*, 28.

CHAPTER 3. IMPERIAL DIASPORAS

1. I. Choi, *Kim's Convenience*, 115.
2. I. Choi, *Kim's Convenience*, 26.
3. Daniel Kim, "Bled In," 555.
4. Yuh, "Moved by War," 281.
5. Baik, *Reencounters*, 39.
6. Baik, *Reencounters*, 38.
7. Puar, *Terrorist Assemblages*, 3.
8. Puar, *Terrorist Assemblages*, 31.
9. Puar, *Terrorist Assemblages*, xxxi.
10. R. Kwon, *Incendiaries*, 38.
11. Susan Choi, *Foreign Student*, 317.
12. K. Lee, *Drifting House*, 42.
13. K. Lee, *How I Became*, 110.
14. See Kang, *Compositional Subjects*, 2–5.
15. Chuh, *Imagine Otherwise*, 9–10.
16. Chuh, *Imagine Otherwise*, 11.
17. M. Nguyen, *Gift of Freedom*, 6.
18. N. Lee, *Making of Minjung*, 115.
19. Chuh, *Imagine Otherwise*, 9.
20. Liberty in North Korea (LiNK), accessed April 15, 2023, http://www.libertyinnorthkorea.org/changing-the-narrative/. LiNK, for example, devotes its resources to helping North Koreans undertake the journey from China to Southeast Asia and to supporting North Koreans as they resettle in South Korea. LiNK also makes a concerted effort to shift global perceptions of North Koreans by sharing North Korean stories through documentaries, interviews, and other creative content. Much of HanVoice's efforts are directed toward sponsoring and resettling North Koreans in Canada and providing international human rights training. Past projects include the HanVoice Pioneer Project that provided advocacy, leadership, and ESL training to North Koreans as well as an internship with a Canadian Parliamentarian. HanVoice Pioneers also shared their experiences by giving talks throughout Canada, often at university campuses. While LiNK and HanVoice share with independent documentary filmmakers—like Deann Borshay Liem, Ramsay Liem, and Jason Lee—the desire to change the stories surrounding North Korea and North Koreans, LiNK and HanVoice work with governments and policy makers to enact shifts. It is unclear whether LiNK receives funding from the National Endowment for Democracy (NED) as information about specific grants that fund the organization is unavailable on its website.
21. G. Cho, *Haunting the Korean Diaspora*, 12.
22. G. Cho, *Haunting the Korean Diaspora*, 12.
23. This is not to say that this melancholic longing is completely absent within South Korea, but rather that it does not dominate the affective relation to North Korea; television shows such as Channel A's *Now On My Way to Meet You* (2011–) that showcase North Korean defectors suggests that there is a South Korean audience for such narratives, albeit a limited and possibly older audience with stronger connections. In the

weekly episodes of this show, fourteen North Korean "beauties" (as they are called on the show) and four hosts participate in a format that alternates between talk show and entertainment segments. Discussions, for example, of North Korean cosmetics take place alongside testimonies on prison camps. Here, the goal seems to be to make North Korea seem less foreign while also bringing the plight of North Korea to the attention of South Korea. As Christopher K. Green and Stephen Epstein note, this show, which is supported by South Korea's Ministry of Reunification, shares similarities with another show called *The Person I Miss* that tells stories of people who seek to be reunited with loved ones. They write, "An increasing percentage of those who made their way on to the show were international adoptees, an evolution that encouraged a consciousness that the unhealed wounds of South Korea's past were progressively being played out beyond its borders" (Green and Epstein, "Now on My Way," 6). Reunification within these projects is imagined in physical terms rather than in the economic forms of reunification that have periodically started and stopped with joint projects between North and South Korea. *Now On My Way to Meet You* can be read as also emphasizing the shared Koreanness of those on either side of the border in order to incorporate North Koreans within a South Korean identity and as promoting the need to dismantle the North Korean government.

24. I. Choi, *Kim's Convenience*, 83–84.
25. H. Park, *Two Dreams*, 39–40.
26. H. Park, *Two Dreams*, 28.
27. H. Park, *Two Dreams*, 41.
28. H. Park, *Two Dreams*, 40.
29. H. Park, *Two Dreams*, 46.
30. H. Park, *Two Dreams*, 63.
31. H. Park, "Korean Manchuria," 212.
32. Jin-kyung Lee, *Service Economies*, 15.
33. H. Park, *Two Dreams*, 63.
34. Jin-kyung Lee, *Service Economies*, 32.
35. Morris-Suzuki, *Exodus*, 65–69.
36. Adam Hartzell, "An Interview with Yang Yong-hi," last modified August 14, 2017, https://www.koreanfilm.org/yangyh.html.
37. Morris-Suzuki, *Exodus*, 36.
38. Morris-Suzuki, *Exodus*, 33.
39. K. Lee, *How I Became*, 108.
40. K. Lee, *How I Became*, 176.
41. K. Lee, *How I Became*, 157.
42. K. Lee, *How I Became*, 233.
43. K. Lee, *How I Became*, 234.
44. K. Lee, *How I Became*, 244.
45. K. Lee, *How I Became*, 238.
46. K. Lee, *How I Became*, 227–33.
47. K. Lee, *How I Became*, 235, 243.
48. Chow, *Writing Diaspora*, 14.
49. K. Lee, *How I Became*, 11.

50. K. Lee, *How I Became*, 63.
51. See Jin, *Pluralist Universalism*, for a detailed comparison of Chinese and American pluralist projects.
52. K. Lee, *How I Became*, 107.
53. K. Lee, *How I Became*, 60.
54. K. Lee, *How I Became*, 95.
55. K. Lee, *How I Became*, 60–61.
56. Wang, "Refugee, Returnee, Borderland," 239.
57. Wang, "Refugee, Returnee, Borderland," 245.
58. Jung-Sun Park and Chang, "Contention," 5.
59. Jung-Sun Park and Chang, "Contention," 6.
60. J. Kwon, *Borderland Dreams*, 63.
61. H. Shin and Park, "Regime," 470.
62. Sung Kyung Kim, "Mobile North Korean Women," 123.
63. Wang, "Refugee, Returnee, Borderland," 245.
64. K. Lee, *How I Became*, 110.
65. H. Park, *Capitalist Unconscious*, 4.
66. H. Park, *Capitalist Unconscious*, 8.
67. A. Park, *Sovereignty Experiments*, 14.
68. A. Park, *Sovereignty Experiments*, 7.
69. A. Park, *Sovereignty Experiments*, 14.
70. K. Lee, *How I Became*, 55.
71. Jin-kyung Lee, *Service Economies*, 189.
72. K. Lee, *How I Became*, 28.
73. K. Lee, *How I Became*, 51.
74. H. Shin and Park, "Regime," 464.
75. H. Shin and Park, "Regime," 464.
76. Hartman, "Venus in Two Acts," 13.

EPILOGUE

1. Made prior to the period that I examine, Y. David Chung and Matt Dibble's *Koryo Saram: The Unreliable People* (2006) lays out the history of ethnic Koreans in the former Soviet Union and their deportation under Stalin to Central Asia. Also, Yang Yonghi's award-winning *Dear Pyongyang* (2005) explores her identity as a second-generation Korean resident born in Japan and the daughter of an influential member of Chongryon, an association for Zainichi Koreans with close ties to North Korea.
2. Jackson, "Poetics of Survival," 138.
3. According to *Kim Il Sung's Children*, Kim Il Sung hadn't wanted North Koreans coming back to North Korea from Eastern European countries as highly educated and westernized individuals. The liberalization movements in Hungary, Poland, and Czechoslovakia were concerning as the prospect of having "the nearly 10,000 well-educated young people who had directly experienced the winds of liberalization in Eastern Europe risked destabilizing his system" (Kim Deog-Young, *Kim Il Sung's Children*, 191). In addi-

tion to being exposed to the revolutionary politics in Eastern Europe, the children were introduced to European intellectual thought, art, and lifestyles that "made these North Koreans skeptical of communism" and "changed their way of thinking" (193). This concern relies on a very different conception of what it means to be Westernized as it yokes together the West and socialism, thus unravelling the stability of the West as a signifier. Naoki Sakai argues that, as a mythic term that is routinely used to contrast with places in Asia, Africa, and Latin America, the West is an "ambiguous and incongruous term, yet one that has always been imagined as Western Europe (Sakai, "'You Asians,'" 789, 796). Eastern Europe, by contrast, "is most often excluded from the West" (796).

4. C. Choi, *Healing Historical Trauma*, 170.

5. C. Choi, *Healing Historical Trauma*, 170. Orphans sent to Poland were scattered between facilities in Świder, Golotczyzna, Sloneczko, and Plakowice, and their presence was kept secret from the locals. While the reasons for this secrecy are unknown, Choi speculates that it might be either because the orphans were from elite North Korean families or because Polish officials did not want to jeopardize their relationship with the United States by publicizing how they were caring for North Korean orphans (172).

6. Rangan, *Immediations*, 3.

7. Kim Soyoung, *Korean Cinema*, 44.

8. Kim Deog-Young's journey started in 2004, when he first learned the story of Georgeta Mircioiu and her North Korean husband, Cho Chung Ho. The couple met when Cho was sent to Romania as a teacher for the orphans, and they dated secretly for years before being granted permission to marry. When Cho was called back to North Korea, Mircioiu was permitted to accompany him for a brief period. Kim Deog-Young finally made *Kim Il Sung's Children* in 2020, sixteen years after he learned of Cho and Mircioiu's bittersweet love story. Mircioiu in turn has been waiting to be reunited with her husband since 1962, when she and her daughter were forced to leave Pyongyang. In the decades that they have been separated, Mircioiu has produced by hand a Korean-Romanian dictionary because she "worried that, if my husband returned after so many years, we would not be able to communicate with each other. Because he would have forgotten all the Romanian words" (Kim Deog-Young, *Kim Il Sung's Children*, 117). Mircioiu is not the only person waiting for her North Korean loved one to return. Jolanta Krysowata, a Polish documentary director, shares the story of another woman who married a North Korean man and had a son with him. Even though more than half a century has passed, the woman says that she always looks toward her door when she hears footsteps in case it is her husband is returning (116).

9. Berry, "Documentary Production Process," 139.

10. Berry, "Documentary Production Process," 143.

11. Trinh, *When the Moon Waxes Red*, 34.

12. Kim Dong-won's positioning contrasts sharply with a woman who protests the repatriation of the North Korean unconverted and who wants to see South Korean prisoners of war returned from North Korea. The woman appears on camera in two incidents, the first is when the men attend a service shortly before they are set to be repatriated and protestors confront the men with their cause, and the second is when the buses bearing the men are driving toward the border and a crowd is gathered along their route. Some

of the people standing have come because they want to say goodbye to these men whom they have come to care for. But others are part of the right wing or relatives of South Korean prisoners of war, and they again voice their anger and disapproval that the North Korean men are being repatriated. The woman smirks at those who have gathered to say farewell to those going to North Korea, commenting on what she deems the absurdity of seeing these men as "comrades" (Kim Dong-won, *Repatriation*, 2:13:18 – 2:13:36). The passionate reactions from these various groups speaks to the contentious and polarizing politics that continue to exist in response to the division system.

13. Cheon, "Camera in Pain," 135.
14. Cheon, "Camera in Pain," 136.
15. Cheon, "Camera in Pain," 139.
16. C. Choi, *Healing Historical Trauma*, 177.
17. Chu Sang-mi, *Children Gone to Poland*, 5:38.
18. Chu Sang-mi, *Children Gone to Poland*, 57:05.
19. C. Choi, *Healing Historical Trauma*, 176.
20. Chu Sang-mi, *Children Gone to Poland*, 57:21.
21. Chu Sang-mi, *Children Gone to Poland*, 57:28.
22. Chu Sang-mi, *Children Gone to Poland*, 10:26 – 10:33.
23. C. Choi, *Healing Historical Trauma*, 174.
24. C. Choi, *Healing Historical Trauma*, 174–75.
25. C. Choi, *Healing Historical Trauma*, 181.
26. C. Choi, *Healing Historical Trauma*, 183.
27. Cheon, "Camera in Pain," 136.

Bibliography

Amin, Kadji. *Disturbing Attachments: Genet, Modern Pederasty, and Queer History.* Durham, NC: Duke University Press, 2017.
Aristotle. *Poetics.* Translated by Ingram Bywater. Oxford: Clarendon Press, 1962; Project Gutenberg, 2009. https://www.gutenberg.org/files/6763/6763-h/6763-h.htm.
Arrington, Celeste L. "The Mutual Constitution of the Abductions and North Korean Human Rights Issues in Japan and Internationally." *Pacific Affairs* 91, no. 3 (2018): 471–97. https://doi.org/10.5509/2018923471.
Associated Press. "Kim Jong Un Showed off Executed Uncle's Headless Body, Trump Claims." CTV News, September 11, 2020.
Atanasoski, Neda. *Humanitarian Violence: The U.S. Deployment of Diversity.* Minneapolis: University of Minnesota Press, 2013.
Bae, Jong-Yun, and Chung-in Moon. "South Korea's Engagement Policy: Revisiting a Human Rights Policy." In "Reframing North Korean Human Rights (Part 2)," edited by Christine Hong and Hazel Smith. Special issue, *Critical Asian Studies* 46, no. 1 (2014): 15–38. https://doi.org/10.1080/14672715.2014.863576.
Bahng, Aimee. *Migrant Futures: Decolonizing Speculation in Financial Times.* Durham, NC: Duke University Press, 2018.
Baik, Crystal Mun-hye. *Reencounters: On the Korean War and Diasporic Memory Critique.* Philadelphia: Temple University Press, 2019.
Banton, Michael. "Social Aspects of the Race Question." In *Four Statements on the Race Question,* 17–29. Paris: UNESCO, 1969.
Berry, Chris. "The Documentary Production Process as a Counter-Public: Notes on an Inter-Asian Mode and the Example of Kim Dong-Won." *Inter-Asia Cultural Studies* 4, no. 1 (2003): 139–44. https://doi.org/10.1080/1464937032000060276.
Bonner, Nicholas. *Made in North Korea: Graphics from Everyday Life in the DPRK.* New York: Phaidon, 2017.
Borshay Liem, Deann, and Ramsay Liem, dirs. *Memory of Forgotten War.* Berkeley: Mu Films, 2013.
Borstelmann, Thomas. *The Cold War and the Color Line: American Race Relations in the Global Arena.* Cambridge, MA: Harvard University Press, 2001.

Bow, Leslie. *Racist Love: Asian Abstraction and the Pleasures of Fantasy*. Durham, NC: Duke University Press, 2022.

Boynton, Robert S. *The Invitation-Only Zone: The True Story of North Korea's Abduction Project*. New York: Farrar, Straus and Giroux, 2016.

Brazinsky, Gregg A. "Remembering *Ŏmŏni*: Using Chinese Memoirs to Understand Sino–North Korean Interactions During the Korean War." *Journal of Korean Studies* 26, no. 2 (2021): 251–70. https://muse.jhu.edu/article/820368.

Brooks, Peter. *Reading for the Plot: Design and Intention in Narrative*. Cambridge, MA: Harvard University Press, 1992.

Bush, George W. "President Delivers State of the Union Address." January 29, 2002. https://georgewbush-whitehouse.archives.gov/news/releases/2002/01/20020129-11.html.

Cannan, Rob, and Ross Adam, dirs. *The Lovers and the Despot*. New York: Magnolia Pictures, 2016.

Cheah, Pheng. "Humanity in the Field of Instrumentality." *PMLA* 121, no. 5 (2006): 1552–57. https://www.jstor.org/stable/25501625.

Cheah, Pheng. *Inhuman Conditions: On Cosmopolitanism and Human Rights*. Cambridge, MA: Harvard University Press, 2006.

Cheng, Anne Anlin. *The Melancholy of Race: Psychoanalysis, Assimilation, and Hidden Grief*. New York: Oxford University Press, 2001.

Cheon, Jin. "The Camera in Pain: Memories of the Cold War in East Asian Independent Documentaries." *Inter-Asia Cultural Studies* 16, no. 1 (2015): 134–50. https://doi.org/10.1080/14649373.2015.1007624.

Cho, Grace M. *Haunting the Korean Diaspora: Shame, Secrecy, and the Forgotten War*. Minneapolis: University of Minnesota Press, 2008.

Choe, Sang-Hun. "An Escapee Tells of Life and Death in North Korea's Labor Camps." *New York Times*, May 31, 2007.

Choe, Sang-Hun. "North and South Korea on Alert over Loudspeakers Blaring Propaganda." *New York Times*, August 21, 2015.

Choe, Sang-Hun, and Austin Ramzy. "South Korea and U.S. Begin Drills as North Warns of Rising Tensions." *New York Times*, August 21, 2017.

Choi, Chungmoo. *Healing Historical Trauma in South Korean Film and Literature*. Abingdon, UK: Routledge, 2021.

Choi, Eunyoung Christina. "Introduction: Gender, (In)Securities, and North Korean Migration." *Asian Journal of Peacebuilding* 12, no. 1 (May 2024): 1–12. https://doi.org/10.18588/202405.00a490.

Choi, Ins. *Kim's Convenience*. 2nd ed. Toronto: House of Anansi, 2016.

Choi, Shine. *Re-Imagining North Korea in International Politics: Problems and Alternatives*. Abingdon, UK: Routledge, 2015.

Choi, Susan. *The Foreign Student*. New York: HarperFlamingo, 1998.

Cho Sung-Hyung, dir. *Verliebt, Verlobt, Verloren*. Berlin: Kundschafter Filmproduktion, 2015.

Chow, Rey. *Writing Diaspora: Tactics of Intervention in Contemporary Cultural Studies*. Bloomington: Indiana University Press, 1993.

Chuh, Kandice. *Imagine Otherwise: On Asian Americanist Critique*. Durham, NC: Duke University Press, 2003.

Chung, Byung-Ho. "Between Defector and Migrant: Identities and Strategies of North Koreans in South Korea." *Korean Studies* 32 (2008): 1–27. https://www.jstor.org/stable/23718929.

Chung, Y. David, and Matt Dibble, dirs. *Koryo Saram: The Unreliable People*. 2006.

Chu Sang-mi, dir. *The Children Gone to Poland*. Seoul: Boaz Film, 2018.

Coombe, Rosemary J. "Honing a Critical Cultural Study of Human Rights." *Communication and Critical/Cultural Studies* 7, no. 3 (2010): 230–46. https://doi.org/10.1080/14791420.2010.504594.

Cumings, Bruce. *Korea's Place in the Sun: A Modern History*. Updated ed. 1997. New York: W. W. Norton, 2005.

Cumings, Bruce. *North Korea: Another Country*. New York: The New Press, 2003.

Cumings, Bruce. *Parallax Visions: Making Sense of American–East Asian Relations*. Durham, NC: Duke University Press, 2002.

Cussen, John. "Korea." Review of *Escape from Camp 14: One Man's Remarkable Odyssey from North Korea to Freedom in the West*, by Blaine Harden, and *The Orphan Master's Son*, by Adam Johnson. *Journal of Asian Studies* 72, no. 2 (2013): 477–80. https://www.jstor.org/stable/43553212.

Cussen, John. "On the Call to Dismiss North Korean Defectors' Memoirs and on Their Dark American Alternative." *Korean Studies* 40 (2016): 140–57. https://www.jstor.org/stable/44508431.

Dimock, Wai-Chee. "Introduction: Genres as Fields of Knowledge." In "Remapping Genre." Special issue, *PMLA* 122, no. 5 (2007): 1377–88. https://www.jstor.org/stable/25501790.

Douzinas, Costas. *Human Rights and Empire: The Political Philosophy of Cosmopolitanism*. Abingdon, UK: Routledge-Cavendish, 2007.

"Eun-Joung Lee—Video Excerpt." Legacies of the Korean War, 2015. https://legaciesofthekoreanwar.org/story/eun-joung-lee/.

Fischer, Paul. *A Kim Jong-Il Production*. New York: Flatiron Books, 2015.

Funabashi, Yoichi. *The Peninsula Question: A Chronicle of the Second Korean Nuclear Crisis*. Washington, DC: Brookings Institution Press, 2007.

Green, Christopher K., and Stephen Epstein. "Now On My Way to Meet Who? South Korean Television, North Korean Refugees, and the Dilemmas of Representation." *Asia-Pacific Journal* 11, no. 41.2 (2013): 1–18. https://apjjf.org/2013/11/41/stephen-epstein/4007/article.

Hall, Stuart. "Constituting an Archive." *Third Text* 15, no. 54 (2001): 89–92. https://doi.org/10.1080/09528820108576903.

Han, Ju Hui Judy. "Shifting Geographies of Proximity: Korean-Led Evangelical Christian Missions and the U.S. Empire." In *Ethnographies of U.S. Empire*, edited by Carole McGranahan and John F. Collins, 194–213. Durham, NC: Duke University Press, 2018.

Hanscom, Christopher P. *Impossible Speech: The Politics of Representation in Contemporary Korean Literature and Film*. New York: Columbia University Press, 2024.

Harden, Blaine. *Escape from Camp 14: One Man's Remarkable Odyssey from North Korea to Freedom in the West.* New York: Viking, 2012.

Harootunian, Harry. "Shadowing History: National Narratives and the Persistence of the Everyday." *Cultural Studies* 18, nos. 2–3 (2004): 181–200. https://doi.org/10.1080/0950238042000201473.

Harootunian, Harry, and Naoki Sakai. "Japan Studies and Cultural Studies." *positions: east asia cultures critique* 7, no. 2 (1999): 593–647. https://muse.jhu.edu/article/27930.

Hartman, Saidiya. *Lose Your Mother: A Journey Along the Atlantic Slave Route.* New York: Farrar, Straus and Giroux, 2007.

Hartman, Saidiya. "Venus in Two Acts." *Small Axe* 12, no. 2 (2008): 1–14.

Hartzell, Adam. "An Interview with Yang Hong-hi." Koreanfilm.org. Updated August 14, 2017. Accessed August 30, 2020.

Hong, Christine. "Manufacturing Dissidence: Arts and Letters of North Korea's 'Second Culture.'" *positions: asia critique* 23, no. 4 (2015): 743–84. https://www.muse.jhu.edu/article/602303.

Hong, Christine. "Reframing North Korean Human Rights." In "Reframing North Korean Human Rights (Part 1)," edited by Christine Hong and Hazel Smith. Special issue, *Critical Asian Studies* 45, no. 4 (2013): 511–32. https://doi.org/10.1080/14672715.2013.851154.

Huang, Betsy. *Contesting Genres in Contemporary Asian American Fiction.* New York: Palgrave Macmillan, 2010.

Hwang, Ingu. *Human Rights and Transnational Democracy in South Korea.* Philadelphia: University of Pennsylvania Press, 2022.

Jackson, Earl. "The Poetics of Survival in Soyoung Kim's Exile Trilogy." *philoSOPHIA* 11, nos. 1–2 (2021): 133–44. https://doi.org/10.1353/phi.2021.0022.

Jameson, Fredric. *The Political Unconscious: Narrative as a Socially Symbolic Act.* Ithaca, NY: Cornell University Press, 1981.

Jang, Lucia, and Susan McClelland. *Stars Between the Sun and Moon: One Woman's Life in North Korea and Escape to Freedom.* Madeira Park, BC: Douglas and McIntyre, 2014.

Jang Jin-sung. *Dear Leader: My Escape from North Korea.* Translated by Shirley Lee. New York: 37 Ink/Atria, 2014.

Jin, Wen. *Pluralist Universalism: An Asian American Critique of US and Chinese Multiculturalism.* Columbus: Ohio State University Press, 2012.

Johnson, Adam. *The Orphan Master's Son.* New York: Random House, 2012.

Jolley, Mary Ann. "The Strange Tale of Yeonmi Park." *Diplomat*, December 10, 2014.

Juhn, Joseph, dir. *Jeronimo.* 2019.

Kaiman, Jonathan. "Story About Kim Jong-un's Uncle Being Fed to Dogs Originated with Satirist." *Guardian*, January 6, 2014.

Kakutani, Michiko. "A North Korean Soldier Finds His 'Casablanca.'" *New York Times*, January 12, 2012.

Kang, Laura. *Compositional Subjects: Enfiguring Asian/American Women.* Durham, NC: Duke University Press, 2002.

Kang, Laura. *Traffic in Asian Women.* Durham, NC: Duke University Press, 2020.

Kim, Christine. *The Minor Intimacies of Race: Asian Publics in North America*. Urbana: University of Illinois Press, 2016.

Kim, Daniel Y. "'Bled In, Letter by Letter': Translation, Postmemory, and the Subject of Korean War: History in Susan Choi's *The Foreign Student*." *American Literary History* 21, no. 3 (2009): 550–83. https://www.jstor.org/stable/20638606.

Kim, Daniel Y. *The Intimacies of Conflict: Cultural Memory and the Korean War*. New York: NYU Press, 2020.

Kim, Eleana J. *Making Peace with Nature: Ecological Encounters Along the Korean DMZ*. Durham, NC: Duke University Press, 2022.

Kim, Immanuel. *Laughing North Koreans: The Culture of Comedy Films*. London: Lexington Books, 2020.

Kim, Jodi. *Ends of Empire: Asian American Critique and the Cold War*. Minneapolis: University of Minnesota Press, 2010.

Kim, Minsun. "Inside North Korean Literature: The Hidden Meaning of Narratives." *Journal of Korean Studies* 26, no. 2 (2021): 297–323. https://www.muse.jhu.edu/article/820370.

Kim, Monica. *The Interrogation Rooms of the Korean War: The Untold History*. Princeton, NJ: Princeton University Press, 2019.

Kim, Sung Kyung. "Mobile North Korean Women and Their Places in the Sino-North Korea Borderland." In "Borderlands in Asia: Emergent Conditions and Relations," edited by Yuk Wah Chan and Brantly Womack. Special issue, *Asian Anthropology* 15, no. 2 (2016): 116–31. https://doi.org/10.1080/1683478X.2016.1215540.

Kim, Suzy. *Everyday Life in the North Korean Revolution, 1945–1950*. Ithaca, NY: Cornell University Press, 2013.

Kim Deog-Young, dir. *Kim Il Sung's Children*. Seoul: Docustory Production, 2020.

Kim Deog-Young. *Kim Il Sung's Children: Untold Stories of a Documentary Film*. Translated by Alex Lee. Fort Lee, NJ: Poppypub, 2023.

Kim Dong-won, dir. *Repatriation*. Seoul: PURN Productions, 2003.

Kim-Gibson, Dai Sil, dir. *People Are the Sky*. New York: Women Make Movies, 2015.

Kim Sin-jo. *Na nun minjok ui choein iotta: Kim Sin-jo sugi* [Confessions of a North Korean armed infiltrator who defected to South Korea]. Seoul: Kongbobu [Ministry of Information], 1968.

Kim Soyoung. *Korean Cinema in Global Contexts: Post-Colonial Phantom, Blockbuster, and Trans-Cinema*. Amsterdam: Amsterdam University Press, 2022.

Kim T'ae-jin. *Chiok t'alch'ulgi* [Defecting into North Korea]. P'yŏngyang: Chosŏn Nodongdang Ch'ulp'ansa, 1987.

Kim Yong-gyu. *Sihyo in'gan*. Seoul: Nara Kihoek, 1978.

Kirby, Michael. "Report of the UN Commission of Inquiry on DPRK: At the Door of the Security Council?" 2014. Accessed July 5, 2021. https://www.michaelkirby.com.au/images/stories/speeches/2014/2754%20-%20THE%20REPORT%20OF%20THE%20UN%20COMMISSION%20OF%20INQUIRY%20ON%20DPRK%20-%20AT%20THE%20DOOR%20OF%20THE%20SECUIRTY%20COUNCIL.pdf.

Kirkus Reviews. Unsigned review of *The Orphan Master's Son*. December 18, 2011. https://www.kirkusreviews.com/book-reviews/adam-johnson/orphan-masters-son/.

Klein, Christina. *Cold War Orientalism: Asia in the Middlebrow Imagination, 1945–1961*. Berkeley: University of California Press, 2003.
Krishna, Priya. "Why 'Kim's Convenience' Is 'Quietly Revolutionary.'" *New York Times*, June 1, 2021.
Kwon, Heonik. *The Other Cold War*. New York: Columbia University Press, 2010.
Kwon, June Hee. *Borderland Dreams: The Transnational Lives of Korean Chinese Workers*. Durham, NC: Duke University Press, 2023.
Kwon, R. O. *The Incendiaries*. New York: Riverhead Books, 2018.
Kwon, Vicki. *Mass Games: Nation-Building Spectacles in Postcolonial Guyana and North Korea*. Multimedia archive exhibition, April 15–June 24, 2016. Rutherford Library, University of Alberta, Edmonton.
Lankov, Andrei. "After the Shin Dong-hyuk Affair: Separating Fact, Fiction." *NK News*, June 13, 2016.
Lankov, Andrei. *The Real North Korea: Life and Politics in the Failed Stalinist Utopia*. Rev. ed.. New York: Oxford University Press, 2015.
Lee, Hyeonseo. *The Girl with Seven Names: A North Korean Defector's Story*. With David John. London: William Collins, 2015.
Lee, Hyeonseo. "Life as a North Korean Refugee." Opinion, *New York Times*, May 13, 2016.
Lee, Inyeop. "North Korean Human Rights." In *Politics in North and South Korea*, edited by Yangmo Ku, Inyeop Lee, and Jongseok Woo, 170–91. Abingdon, UK: Routledge, 2017.
Lee, Jason, dir. *Letters from Pyongyang*. Toronto: JSN Omnimedia, 2012.
Lee, Jin-kyung. *Service Economies: Militarism, Sex Work, and Migrant Labor in South Korea*. Minneapolis: University of Minnesota Press, 2010.
Lee, John. "North Korean Defector Yeonmi Park Muddles Human Rights Message with Partisanship." *NK News*, June 23, 2021.
Lee, Krys. *Drifting House*. London: Penguin, 2012.
Lee, Krys. *How I Became a North Korean*. New York: Penguin, 2016.
Lee, Namhee. *The Making of Minjung: Democracy and the Politics of Representation in South Korea*. Ithaca, NY: Cornell University Press, 2009.
Li, Yuk-Sa, ed. *Juche! The Speeches and Writings of Kim Il Sung*. New York: Grossman Publishers, 1972.
Lies, Elaine. "A Fictional Everyman for North Korea." Review of *The Orphan Master's Son*, by Adam Johnson. *Globe and Mail*, January 28, 2012.
Lukács, Georg. "Art and Objective Truth." In *Writer and Critic, and Other Essays*, edited and translated by Arthur D. Kahn, 25–60. Milton Keynes: Merlin, 1970.
Lynn, Hyung Gu. *Bipolar Orders: The Two Koreas Since 1989*. London: Zed Books, 2007.
Lynn, Hyung Gu. "Vicarious Traumas: Television and Public Opinion in Japan's North Korea Policy." *Pacific Affairs* 79, no. 3 (2006): 483–508. https://www.jstor.org/stable/40022088.
Man, Simeon. "Anti-Asian Violence and US Imperialism." *Race and Class* 62, no. 2 (2020): 24–33. https://doi.org/10.1177/0306396820949779.
Mason, Ra. *Japan's Relations with North Korea and the Recalibration of Risk*. Abingdon, UK: Routledge, 2014.

McCormack, Gavan. *Client State: Japan in the American Embrace*. London: Verso, 2007.
McGann, Paul. "Kim Jong-il Part 1: Birth of North Korea." *Real Dictators*, podcast, June 7, 2020. https://www.bbc.co.uk/sounds/play/p0h93n30.
Mignolo, Walter D. "The Many Faces of Cosmo-Polis: Border Thinking and Critical Cosmopolitanism." *Public Culture* 12, no. 3 (2000): 721–48. https://www.muse.jhu.edu/article/26217.
Montagu, Ashley, ed. "Statement on Race." In *Four Statements on the Race Question*, 30–35. Paris: UNESCO, 1969.
Morris-Suzuki, Tessa. *Exodus to North Korea*. Lanham, MD: Rowman and Littlefield, 2007.
Moylan, Tom. *Scraps of the Untainted Sky: Science Fiction, Utopia, Dystopia*. Boulder, CO: Westview Press, 2000.
Moyn, Samuel. *Not Enough: Human Rights in an Unequal World*. Cambridge, MA: Belknap Press of Harvard University Press, 2018.
Neary, Ian. *Human Rights in Japan, South Korea, and Taiwan*. Abingdon, UK: Routledge, 2002.
Ngai, Sianne. *Ugly Feelings*. Cambridge, MA: Harvard University Press, 2007.
Nguyen, Mimi Thi. *The Gift of Freedom: War, Debt, and Other Refugee Passages*. Durham, NC: Duke University Press, 2012.
Nguyen, Vinh. "Mẹ-Search, Hauntings, and Critical Distance." In "Self-Regarding: Looking at Photos in Life Writing," edited by Tanya Dalziell and Lee-Von Kim. Special issue, *Life Writing* 12, no. 4 (2015): 467–77. https://doi.org/10.1080/14484528.2014.915285.
"North Korea: Is Change Really Around the Corner?" *Into the Ether* (blog). Amnesty International UK, April 27, 2018. https://www.amnesty.org.uk/blogs/ether/north-korea-change-really-around-corner.
"North Korea Sends More 'Filth'-Filled Balloons into South, Seoul Says." CBC News, June 1, 2024.
"Not So Splendid Isolation." *Economist*, October 24, 2020.
Nuwer, Rachel. "North Korea Reportedly Executed Pop Singers and Dancers." *Smithsonian Magazine*, August 29, 2013.
Nyers, Peter. *Rethinking Refugees: Beyond States of Emergency*. New York: Routledge, 2006.
Oh, David C. *Whitewashing the Movies: Asian Erasure and White Subjectivity in U.S. Film Culture*. New Brunswick, NJ: Rutgers University Press, 2022.
Onishi, Norimitsu. "Campaigning for Human Rights, and Fishing for Souls." *New York Times*, February 24, 2006.
Paik Nak-chung. "South Korean Democracy and Korea's Division System." *Inter-Asia Cultural Studies* 14, no. 1 (2013): 156–69. https://doi.org/10.1080/14649373.2013.753853.
Park, Alyssa M. *Sovereignty Experiments: Korean Migrants and the Building of Borders in Northeast Asia, 1860–1945*. Ithaca, NY: Cornell University Press, 2019.
Park, Hyun Ok. *The Capitalist Unconscious: From Korean Unification to Transnational Korea*. New York: Columbia University Press, 2015.

Park, Hyun Ok. "Korean Manchuria: The Racial Politics of Territorial Osmosis." *South Atlantic Quarterly* 99, no. 1 (2000): 193–215. https://doi.org/10.1215/00382876-99-1-193.

Park, Hyun Ok. *Two Dreams in One Bed: Empire, Social Life, and the Origins of the North Korean Revolution in Manchuria*. Durham, NC: Duke University Press, 2005.

Park, Jane Chi Hyun. *Yellow Future: Oriental Style in Hollywood Cinema*. Minneapolis: University of Minnesota Press, 2010.

Park, Jung-Sun, and Paul Y. Chang. "Contention in the Construction of a Global Korean Community: The Case of the Overseas Korean Act." *Journal of Korean Studies* 10, no. 1 (2005): 1–27. https://www.jstor.org/stable/41490207.

Park, Yeonmi, with Maryanne Vollers. *In Order to Live: A North Korean Girl's Journey to Freedom*. New York: Penguin, 2016.

Patterson, Christopher B. *Transitive Cultures: Anglophone Literature of the Transpacific*. New Brunswick, NJ: Rutgers University Press, 2018.

Puar, Jasbir K. *Terrorist Assemblages: Homonationalism in Queer Times*. Durham, NC: Duke University Press, 2007.

Quinn, Ben. "Unicorn Lair 'Discovered' in North Korea." *Guardian*, November 30, 2012.

Rajagopal, Balakrishnan. *International Law from Below: Development, Social Movements, and Third World Resistance*. Cambridge: Cambridge University Press, 2009.

Rak, Julie. *Boom! Manufacturing Memoir for the Popular Market*. Waterloo, ON: Wilfrid Laurier University Press, 2013.

Rangan, Pooja. *Immediations: The Humanitarian Impulse in Documentary*. Durham, NC: Duke University Press, 2017.

Rivero, Oswaldo de. *The Myth of Development: Non-Viable Economies of the 21st Century*. Translated by Claudia Encinas and Janet Herrick Encinas. London: Zed Books, 2001.

Rogen, Seth, and Evan Goldberg, dirs. *The Interview*. New York: Columbia Pictures, 2014.

Roh, David S., Betsy Huang, and Greta A. Niu, eds. *Techno-Orientalism: Imagining Asia in Speculative Fiction, History, and Media*. New Brunswick, NJ: Rutgers University Press, 2015.

Ryang, Sonia. *Reading North Korea: An Ethnological Inquiry*. Cambridge, MA: Harvard East Asian Monographs, 2012.

Ryu Seung-wan, dir. *The Berlin File*. Seoul: Filmmaker R&K, 2013.

Said, Edward. *Orientalism*. 1978. New York: Vintage Books, 1979.

Sakai, Naoki. "'You Asians': On the Historical Role of the West and Asia Binary." *South Atlantic Quarterly* 99, no. 4 (2000): 789–817. https://www.muse.jhu.edu/article/30684.

Samuels, Richard J. "Kidnapping Politics in East Asia." *Journal of East Asian Studies* 10, no. 3 (2010): 363–95. https://www.jstor.org/stable/23418864.

Saunders, Patricia J. "Fugitive Dreams of Diaspora: Conversations with Saidiya Hartman." *Anthurium: A Caribbean Studies Journal* 6, no. 1 (2008): article 7. https://doi.org/10.33596/anth.115.

Schmid, Andre. Introduction to "Reconsidering North Korea: Methods, Frameworks, and Sources," edited by Gregg A. Brazinsky. Special issue, *Journal of Korean Studies* 26, no. 2 (2021): 169–86.

Sharpe, Christina. *In the Wake: On Blackness and Being*. Durham, NC: Duke University Press, 2016.

Shih, Shu-mei. "Racializing Area Studies, Defetishizing China." *positions: asia critique* 27, no. 1 (2019): 33–65. https://www.muse.jhu.edu/article/717706.

Shin, Ann. *The Last Exiles*. New York: Park Row Books, 2021.

Shin, HaeRan, and Soyoung Park. "The Regime of Urban Informality in Migration: Accommodating Undocumented Chosŏnjok Migrants in Their Receiving Community in Seoul, South Korea." *Pacific Affairs* 90, no. 3 (2017): 459–80. https://www.jstor.org/stable/44874506.

Shoichet, Catherine E., and Madison Park. "North Korean Prison Camp Survivor Admits Inaccuracies, Author Says." CNN, January 20, 2015.

Simpson, Connor. "Kim Jong-un's Uncle Was Actually (Probably) Killed by Firing Squad." *Atlantic*, January 30, 2014.

Singh, Nikhil Pal. "Culture/Wars: Recoding Empire in an Age of Democracy." *American Quarterly* 50, no. 3 (1998): 471–522. https://www.jstor.org/stable/30042149.

Slaughter, Joseph R. "Enabling Fictions and Novel Subjects: The *Bildungsroman* and International Human Rights Law." *PMLA* 121, no. 5 (2006): 1405–23.

Slaughter, Joseph R. *Human Rights, Inc.: The World Novel, Narrative Form, and International Law*. New York: Fordham University Press, 2007.

Smith, Hazel. *North Korea: Markets and Military Rule*. Cambridge: Cambridge University Press, 2015.

Smith, Sidonie, and Julia Watson. *Reading Autobiography: A Guide for Interpreting Life Narratives*. 2nd ed. Minneapolis: University of Minnesota Press, 2010.

So, Se Pyong. "Note Verbale Dated 1 February 2012 from the Permanent Mission of the Democratic People's Republic of Korea to the United Nations Office at Geneva addressed to the President of the Human Rights Council." UN General Assembly, A/HRC/19/G/1, February 14, 2012. https://documents.un.org/doc/undoc/gen/g12/105/07/pdf/g1210507.pdf.

Song, Dae-Han, and Christine Hong. "Toward 'The Day After': National Endowment for Democracy and North Korean Regime Change." *Critical Asian Studies* 46, no. 1 (2014): 39–64. https://doi.org/10.1080/14672715.2014.863577.

Song, Jiyoung. *Human Rights Discourse in North Korea: Post-Colonial, Marxist, and Confucian Perspectives*. New York: Routledge, 2010.

Subramanian, Courtney. "These Are North Korea's 28 State-Approved Hairstyles." *Time*, February 25, 2013.

Suh, Bo-hyuk. "Controversies over North Korean Human Rights in South Korean Society." *Asian Perspective* 31, no. 2 (2007): 23–46. https://www.jstor.org/stable/42704588.

Suh, Jae-Jung. "Truth and Reconciliation in South Korea: Confronting War, Colonialism, and Intervention in the Asia Pacific." *Critical Asian Studies* 42, no. 4 (2010): 503–24. https://doi.org/10.1080/14672715.2010.515386.

Tadiar, Neferti Xina M. *Fantasy Production: Sexual Economies and Other Philippine Consequences for the New World Order*. Aberdeen, HK: Hong Kong University Press, 2004.

Tadiar, Neferti Xina M. "Ground Zero." *GLQ: A JOURNAL OF LESBIAN AND GAY STUDIES* 22, no. 2 (2016): 173–81. https://www.muse.jhu.edu/article/613185.

Taylor, Moe. "'One Hand Can't Clap': Guyana and North Korea, 1974–1985." *Journal of Cold War Studies* 17, no. 1 (2015): 41–63. https://www.jstor.org/stable/26926183.

Trinh, T. Minh-Ha. *When the Moon Waxes Red: Representation, Gender, and Cultural Politics*. Abingdon, UK: Routledge, 1991.

Troeung, Y-Dang. *Refugee Lifeworlds: The Afterlife of the Cold War in Cambodia*. Philadelphia: Temple University Press, 2022.

Truth and Reconciliation Commission, Republic of Korea. *Truth and Reconciliation* 6, no. 1 (2021). http://www.jinsil.go.kr/upload/211012%20진실화해_소식지_1호%20영문(최종)_1639033346688.pdf.

Ty, Eleanor, and Christl Verduyn, eds. *Asian Canadian Writing Beyond Autoethnography*. Waterloo, ON: Wilfrid Laurier University Press, 2008.

Ŭigŏdan Myŏlgong and Kwisun Yongsahoe. *Sasŏn ŭl nŏmŏsŏ*. Sŏul T'ŭkpyŏlsi: Myŏlgong Ŭigŏdan, 1968.

"UN Dismisses North Korea's Claim That Damning Human Rights Report Is Invalid." *Guardian*, January 21, 2015.

UNESCO. "Building Peace in the Minds of Men and Women." Archived September 9, 2015, Wayback Machine, Internet Archive. https://web.archive.org/web/20161026121124/https://en.unesco.org/70years/building_peace.

United Nations Command. *Armistice Agreement*. Vol. 1. Panmunjom, Korea, July 27, 1953.

United Nations General Assembly. *Universal Declaration of Human Rights*. A/Res/217, December 10, 1948.

United Nations High Commissioner for Refugees. "Convention Relating to the Status of Refugees" (1951). In *Convention and Protocol Relating to the Status of Refugees*, 6–45. Geneva: UNCHR, 2010.

United Nations Human Rights Council (UNHRC). "A Commission of Inquiry on Human Rights in the Democratic People's Republic of Korea Public Hearings in Seoul." Unofficial transcript, August 20, 2013. https://www.ohchr.org/sites/default/files/Documents/HRBodies/HRCouncil/CoIDPRK/PublicHearings/20131219Seoul_Transcripts08.20PMRevised.docx.

United Nations Special Rapporteur. *Situation of Human Rights in the Democratic People's Republic of Korea*. 61st Session. January 10, 2005.

United Nations Special Rapporteur. *Situation of Human Rights in the Democratic People's Republic of Korea*. 66th Session. August 24, 2011.

US Department of Defense. "Exercise Ulchi Freedom Guardian 2017." News release. August 18, 2017. https://www.defense.gov/News/Releases/Release/Article/1282786/exercise-ulchi-freedom-guardian-2017/.

Vollers, Maryanne. "The Woman Who Faces the Wrath of North Korea." *Guardian*, March 15, 2015.

Vukovich, Daniel F. *Illiberal China: The Ideological Challenge of the People's Republic of China*. Singapore: Palgrave MacMillan, 2019.

Walker, Gavin, and Naoki Sakai. "The End of Area." *positions: asia critique* 27, no. 1 (2019): 1–31. https://www.muse.jhu.edu/article/717707.

Wang, Chih-Ming. "Refugee, Returnee, Borderland: The Accidental Activists and Krys Lee's *How I Became a North Korean.*" *Inter-Asia Cultural Studies* 20, no. 2 (2019): 238–56. https://doi.org/10.1080/14649373.2019.1613728.

Waxman, Olivia B. "You Can Send Your Child to Summer Camp in North Korea." *Time*, July 30, 2014.

Weheliye, Alexander. *Habeas Viscus: Racializing Assemblages, Biopolitics, and Black Feminist Theories of the Human*. Durham, NC: Duke University Press, 2014.

White, Hayden. *Figural Realism: Studies in the Mimesis Effect*. Baltimore, MD: Johns Hopkins University Press, 2020.

Wiese, Marc, dir. *Camp 14: Total Control Zone*. Cologne: Engstfeld Filmproduktion, 2012.

Williams, Randall. *The Divided World: Human Rights and Its Violence*. Minneapolis: University of Minnesota Press, 2010.

Wong, Lily. *Transpacific Attachments: Sex Work, Media Networks, and Affective Histories of Chineseness*. New York: Columbia University Press, 2018.

Wynter, Sylvia. "'No Humans Involved': An Open Letter to My Colleagues." *Forum N.H.I.: Knowledge for the 21st Century* 1, no. 1 (1994): 42–73.

Wynter, Sylvia. "Unsettling the Coloniality of Being/Power/Truth/Freedom: Towards the Human, After Man, Its Overrepresentation—An Argument." *CR: The New Centennial Review* 3, no. 3 (2003): 257–337. https://doi.org/10.1353/ncr.2004.0015.

Xiang, Sunny. *Tonal Intelligence: The Aesthetics of Asian Inscrutability During the Long Cold War*. New York: Columbia University Press, 2020.

Yang Yonghi, dir. *Dear Pyongyang*. Santa Fe: Tidepoint Pictures, 2005.

Yao, Xine. *Disaffected: The Cultural Politics of Unfeeling in Nineteenth-Century America*. Durham, NC: Duke University Press, 2021.

Yapp, Hentyle. *Minor China: Method, Materialisms, and the Aesthetic*. Durham, NC: Duke University Press, 2021.

Yokota Sakie. *North Korea Kidnapped My Daughter*. Translated by Emi Maruyama and Naomi Otani. New York: Kodansha, 1999.

Yoneyama, Lisa. *Cold War Ruins: Transpacific Critique of American Justice and Japanese War Crimes*. Durham, NC: Duke University Press, 2016.

Yuh, Ji-Yeon. "Moved by War: Migration, Diaspora, and the Korean War." *Journal of Asian American Studies* 8, no. 3 (2005): 277–91. https://doi.org/10.1353/jaas.2005.0054.

Žižek, Slavoj. *Demanding the Impossible*. Edited by Yong-june Park. Cambridge, UK: Polity Press, 2013.

Zurcher, Anthony. "Did Kim Jong Un Feed His Uncle to Dogs?" BBC, January 3, 2014.

Index

abductions: of Choi Eun-hee and Shin Sang-ok, 23, 45–49, 128n72; of Japanese citizens by North Korea, 23, 42–45, 55, 57–58, 71, 128n72; Kim Jong-il's admission to, 43, 48, 55, 57, 71

affect, 3, 7, 10; of audience, 49; complexity of, 22, 85, 88; happiness as structure of feeling, 75; imperial and diasporic guilt, 89–90; of inhuman subject, 74–80, 134n89; required for recognition as human, 74–75, 80; and state of emergency, 111; structures of feeling, 75, 96, 103, 106, 117. *See also* melancholia

Afghanistan, 1

Amin, Kadji, 10

An Myong Hun, 35

Another World We Are Making (Kim Dong-won), 112

anti-colonial movements, 15, 18–19, 21, 131n38

anti-communism, 5, 19–20, 88, 120–21n26

The Aquariums of Pyongyang (Kang Chol-hwan), 52

archive, 20–22, 106–7

Arduous March, 17, 25, 59, 69

Arrington, Celeste, 43

Asia: Cold War racialization of, 3, 5; complex regional dynamics, 17–18; as inhuman, 7, 12–13; North Korea as metonym for incivility of, 61; struggles within, 50, 91–95, 102. *See also* Japan; Korea; North Korea; South Korea

Atanasoski, Neda, 61

"At the Edge of the World" (Lee), 86–87

audience/reader: credibility of North Koreans defectors questioned by, 29, 31, 50, 51–53, 72–73, 86, 125–26n13; emotions elicited in, 4, 56, 58, 75–76; familiarity, sense of, 36–37; forgetting by, 17, 67, 90, 127n47; intended and unintended, 36, 41, 56–57; interpretive traditions of, 4, 28; knowledge presumed by, 28, 38; morbid fascination of, 22, 33, 89; North Korea as incomprehensible for, 18, 22, 26, 28, 32, 49, 67; North Korea as set of stylized conventions for, 30, 56; and principle of similarity, 79–80; reading practices of, 30, 88, 106; subject not distinguished from, 112; US-centric, 35–36

"Axis of Evil" rhetoric, vii, 1, 55, 59, 71, 119n2

Bae, Jong-Yun, 70

Bahng, Aimee, 34

Baik, Crystal Mun-hye, 11, 19, 84

Banton, Michael, 132–33n61

Berry, Chris, 112

Biserko, Sonja, 54

Black Panthers, 20

Bonner, Nicholas, 32

Borowiec, József, 117

Borshay Liem, Deann, 19, 89, 123–24n87

Borstelmann, Thomas, 6

Bow, Leslie, 3, 13–14

bowibu (North Korean political police), 58

Brazinsky, Gregg, 42, 127n47

Brooks, Peter, 33

Burnham, Linden, 20
Bush, George W., 1, 55, 71

Camp 14: Total Control Zone (documentary), 23, 77–78
Canada: humanitarian organizations in, 89, 135n20; as modern, 2; multiculturalism, 82–84. *See also* diaspora, Korean Canadian; *Kim's Convenience* (Choi)
capitalism, 28, 91, 119n4; and affective state of emergency, 111; hierarchical ordering within, 104; South Korean, 78, 111
Césaire, Aimé, 64
Chang, Paul, 102
Chang, Peng Chung, 60
Chang Myeong-Su, 94
Cheah, Pheng, 3, 68, 131n43
Cheng, Anne Anlin, 7
Cheon, Jin, 112, 114
The Children Gone to Poland (documentary, Chu Sang-mi), 24, 78, 109, 111, 114–16
China: border with North Korea, 87, 100; concerns about ethnic independence movements, 102; Cultural Revolution, 20; divergences and overlaps with US state projects, 99–100; Joseonjok, 95, 99–104; migration to from North Korea, 87, 91, 100–101; nationalism, 91
Chineseness, 75
Cho, Grace, 90
Cho, Miran, 111–12
Cho Chung Ho, 111, 138n8
Choi, Chungmoo, 111, 138n5
Choi, Ins, 81, 82–84, 85
Choi, Shine, 31
Choi, Susan, 84, 86
Choi Eun-hee, 23, 45–49, 128n72
Choi Moon Soon, 124–25n1
Chongryun (community association), 94
Cho Sung-Hyung, 109, 124n91
Chow, Rey, 98
Christians, Korean, 121n28
chuch'e ideology, 124n89
Chuh, Kandice, 87–88
Chun Doo-hwan, 69
Chung-in Moon, 70
Chungmoo Choi, 114, 116
Chun Sun Tae, 19, 123n86

Chu Sang-mi, 24, 78, 109, 111, 114–16
citizenship, 101–2
civil and political rights (CPR), 70
Civil Rights Congress (CRC), 64–65
civil rights movement, US, 6
Cleaver, Eldridge, 20
Cold War: binaries, 5, 9, 10, 31, 71, 110; continuity of in present, 4–5, 7, 16–17, 22, 27, 61, 63, 70, 114; critical studies of, 11; decompositional histories of, 4–5; global order informed by, ix, 7, 50, 61–62; and human rights discourses, 54, 61–63, 68–71; long, ix, 6–9, 26–28, 50, 54, 84, 88–89, 118; minor stories, 112–14; narrative structures of, 3–4; North Korea as first product of, 63; Pacific, struggles within, 50, 91–95, 102; in process of decomposition, 114. *See also* post–Cold War era
Cold War Ruins (Yoneyama), 6
colonialism: anti-colonial movements, 15, 18–19, 21, 131n38; "civilizing mission," 63; continuity of, 7, 12–13; human rights linked with, 15, 62–63; Japanese in Korea, 16, 18, 43, 81, 123n82; North Korea as signifier for, 84; settler, 7–8, 13. *See also* imperialism
comfort women, 44, 71–72, 90
crimes against humanity, 54, 131n43
Cumings, Bruce, 11, 18, 20, 119n2, 123n82, 131n31
Cussen, John, 29

Darusman, Marzuki, 54, 129n4
Dear Leader: My Escape from North Korea (Jang Jin-sung), 46, 66, 74
Dear Pyongyang (documentary, Yang), 94, 137n1
decolonization movements, 6, 60, 63, 124n89
decompositional histories, 4–5
defectors, North Korean, 4; abductees not distinguishable from, 48; "celebrity defectors," 69; credibility of questioned, 29, 31, 50, 51–53, 72–73, 86, 125–26n13; *nihonjinzuma* (escapees), 44; pain of exploited, 115–16; at Seoul hearings, 58. *See also* diaspora, Korean; Jang Jin-sung; life writing/memoirs; Shin Dong-hyuk
dehumanization, 7, 13, 78, 80
demilitarized zone (DMZ), 2, 11, 16, 71, 89

154 INDEX

Democratic People's Republic of Korea (DPRK), establishment of, 16, 60, 87, 101. *See also* North Korea
"democratizing mission," 63
diaspora: diasporic exceptionalism, rhetoric of, 83–83, 85; intellectuals, 98; knowledge from vantage point of, 11–12; nation-state relations with, 82, 85, 88; subjectivity of, 7; subject of allied with project of whiteness, 85; transnational dimensions of, 87. *See also* migration; orphans
diaspora, Asian, 8–9, 90; Koryo Saram, 102, 137n1; model minority narrative, 82–84; queer South Asian, 85
diaspora, Korean: delinked from national frameworks, 90–91; drawn into exploited labor, 83, 92; and ethnic nationalism, 92–93; North Korea as part of, 87–89; North Korea erased from narratives of, 19, 87–88; North Korea in context of, 2, 6, 8, 11, 23–24; privileging of West within discourses of, 101–2; refuge migrants, 84; traumatic effects on, 89–90. See also *Kim's Convenience* (Choi)
diaspora, Korean Canadian, 11, 19, 21, 87; drawn into exploited labor, 83; in *Letters from Pyongyang*, 6, 89. See also *Kim's Convenience* (Choi)
dictatorships, 57, 64, 70–71
Dimock, Wai-Chee, 30
disposability, 7–8, 25, 39
division system, 70–71, 139n12
documentaries, 23, 27, 107, 109–10; alternate history of pain in, 114; exploitation and instrumentalization in, 115–16; independent films made in East Asia, 114; maternal lens, 114–15; negotiations outside of frame, 111–12; new modes of inquiry in, 110; police coercion of filmmakers, 113; Polish, 115; subjects, audiences, and filmmakers, 112–16; as surveillance, 113. *See also* cinema; film (cinema); life writing/memoirs; *specific documentaries*
Douzinas, Costas, 62, 131n38
Drifting House (Lee), 86–87
"Drifting House" (Lee), 86
Du Bois, W. E. B., 5
dystopic speculation, 27, 32–34; as abstract and dehistoricized, 34; fictional and nonfictional representations, 27, 31; move between literary and cultural realms, 30; racialized, 50; Western concepts reinforced by, 22, 27–29, 31, 33, 37, 42. *See also* genre; memoirs

Eastern Europe: orphans sent to, 24, 72, 111–17, 137–38n3, 138n5; Poznań protest, 111
economic, social, and cultural rights (ESCR), 70
emergencies, states of, 49, 111
emergency, lens of, 76
epistemic repression, 7
Escape from Camp 14: One Man's Remarkable Odyssey from North Korea to Freedom in the West (Harden), 23, 29, 51–53, 60, 67, 74–76
ethnic cleansing, "repatriation" as, 94–95
ethnic nationalism, 92–95, 103–4, 106
Exile Trilogy (Kim Soyoung), 109
Exodus to North Korea (Morris-Suzuki), 93, 94

familiarity, 36–37
Fanon, Frantz, 12
fantasy: North Korea as cultural fantasy of the inhuman, 12, 17, 22, 23, 66–67, 80, 119–20n4; of preventing the Korean War, 57; production of, 3
farmworkers, Korean, 91–92
fear, refugee defined in relation to, 65
fiction, 21; fiction and nonfiction binary, 27; knowledge of North Korea as, 30–31; "third North Korea" constructed by outside world, 66–67. *See also* genre
film (cinema): Kim Jong-il and North Korean, 21, 46–50, 128n72; Oriental style in Hollywood, 13; and South Korean states of emergencies, 49. *See also* Choi Eun-hee; documentaries; media; Shin Sang-ok
Fischer, Paul, 46, 128n72
The Foreign Student (Choi), 84, 86
forgetting, 17, 67, 90, 127n47

genre, 23, 25; Aristotle's observations, 4; Asian American and Asian Canadian writing, 30; bildungsroman, 42, 76; comedy and tragedy, 4; propaganda literature, 46, 128n68; readings encouraged by, 30; regenreing, 30;

INDEX 155

genre (*continued*)
  satire, 35; speculative fiction, 34; spy genre, 35; thrillers, 1–2, 27, 33; utopian and dystopian fiction, 27, 33–34. *See also* documentaries; dystopic speculation; fiction; life writing/memoirs; narrative
geographies: distance mapped by long Cold War, 26–27; expansion of, viii, 2, 7–8, 13, 23, 109
The Girl with Seven Names: A North Korean Defector's Story (Lee), 74
global order: informed by Cold War, ix, 7, 50, 61–62; North Korea perceived as threat to global security, 9, 31, 89; prolonged by ideas of North Korea, 4, 21, 50, 74
Global South: fantasy of North Korea in, 3; and human rights discourse, 61, 65; North Korea as socialist model for, 20; representation of by global elite, 31; struggles within, 50, 59
Guardians of Peace, 35
Guyana, 20, 68

Hall, Stuart, 21
Han, Ju Hui Judy, 121n28
Hanawon education facility (South Korea), 59
Hanscom, Christopher, 124n
HanVoice, 89, 135n20
Harden, Blaine, 23, 29; on credibility of Shin Dong-hyuk's narrative, 51, 73; interviewer as absent presence, 78. See also *Escape from Camp 14: One Man's Remarkable Odyssey from North Korea to Freedom in the West* (Harden)
Hartman, Saidiya, 12, 106–7
Haunting the Diaspora (Cho), 90
Hein, Laura, 71
Hirohito, Emperor, 71
Ho, Cho Chung, 111–12
Holocaust, 60
Hong, Christine, 11, 15–16, 52–53, 58, 64, 129n4
How I Became a North Korean (Lee), 23, 85, 87, 95–104; Joseonjok aspirations in, 105–7; Joseonjok-centered reading of, 103; set after economic crisis of 2008, 102
Huang, Betsy, 13–14, 30
human, the: construction of, 67–68, 80; limits of, 3; "*suggestively* human," 14. *See also* inhuman, the
humanitarian organizations, 20, 89, 95, 132n47, 135n20
Humanitarian Violence (Atanasoski), 62
human rights, 6, 14–15, 51–80; and abductions, 43–44, 55; colonialism linked with, 15, 62–63, 67; as composite term, 62; double bind of, 79–80; global Cold War order codified by, 61–62; hypocrisy of US involvement in North Korea, 37; material conditions overlooked by, 15; and memoirs, 53, 56; nonintervention principle, 62; North Korean concepts of, 63–64; political organizations, 55–56; in post–Cold War era, 68–72; post–World War II, 60–68; as privileged epistemic form for political violence, 7; racist and imperial histories, 64; two periods of (1948 and post-1987), 59–60; universality attributed to, 15, 60, 64–65; *We Charge Genocide* petition, 64–65. *See also* Universal Declaration of Human Rights (UDHR, 1948)
Human Rights and Empire (Douzinas), 62
human rights discourse: as apolitical, 66, 132n47; and Cold War, 54, 61–63, 68–71; Cold War–era vernaculars, 15–16; colonialism not taken into consideration, 67, 68; crimes against humanity, 54, 131n43; decontextualization of subjects by, 66–67; Global South critiques erased by, 65; and the inhuman, 54, 60, 72, 79–80; limitations of, 23, 52, 56, 61–65, 72, 76, 80, 132n47; other values disregarded by, 63–66; refugee-ism, narrative of, 65–66; relations with diasporic structures of feelings, 95
Human Rights Watch, 52
Humphrey, John, 60
Hwang, Ingu, 52, 121n28

illiberalism, North Korea as figure of, 2–3, 11, 42, 54, 68, 120n6
imperialism: area studies as resource for, 9–10; continuation of, ix, 5, 22, 62, 112; "democratizing mission," 63; international law as mutually constitutive with, 15; Japanese, 6, 16, 18, 81, 91–93; new forms of, 50; positioned in opposition to the inhuman, 88;

upheld by Korean War narratives, 84. *See also* colonialism

The Incendiaries (Kwon), 86

inhuman, the: and human rights discourse, 54, 60, 72, 79–80; imperialism positioned in opposition to, 88; individual inhumanity, 53, 68, 79; Kim Jong Un depicted as, 36; in life writing/memoirs, 72–78; North Korea as cultural fantasy of, 12, 17, 22–24, 66–67, 80, 119–20n4; North Koreans depicted as figures of, 17, 23, 39–40, 68, 95, 106; not-quite-humans, 7, 12–13; racialization of, 12–13, 27, 67–68; Shin Dong-hyuk depicted as, 60, 74–76, 79–80; "suggestively human," 14. *See also* human, the; minor inhuman; North Korea; racialization; techne

In Order to Live (Park and Vollers), 29

The Interview (film), 22, 27–28, 35–38, 46; Asian stereotypes in, 37, 49; depiction of Kim Jong Un in, 35–38, 126n35; familiarity in, 36–37

In the Absence of Sun (Lee), 53

Jameson, Fredric, 28
Jang, Lucia, 74
Jang Jin-sung, 46, 66, 74, 126n35
Jang Song-thaek, 53–54
Japan: abductions from by North Korea, 42–45, 54, 57–58, 71; colonialism and imperialism of, 6, 16, 18, 43, 45, 81, 91–93, 123n82; "repatriation" of Koreans to North Korea, 93–95; surrender to Allied forces, 93; and UN Commission of Inquiry, 55; as US client state, 23, 28, 44
Japanese Red Cross, 94
Japan–North Korea summit (2002), 57
Jeong Kwang-il, 58
Jeronimo (Juhn), 110
Johnson, Adam, 22, 25–34, 40–42, 46, 49, 124–25n1
Jolley, Mary Ann, 125n13
Joseonjok (ethnic Korean from China), 95, 99–104; aspirations of, 105–7; as survival strategy, 105
Juche! (Kim Il Sung, foreword Cleaver), 20
Juhn, Joseph, 110
Jung Hong Boo, 115

Kakutani, Michiko, 125n10
Kang, Laura, 8, 29, 71, 87
Kang Chol-hwan, 52, 58–59
Kang Dong Wan, 116
Kim, Daniel, 11, 17, 84
Kim, Eleana, 11, 71
Kim, Jeronimo Lim, 110
Kim, Jodi, 8, 11, 61, 63
Kim, Minsun, 128n68
Kim, Monica, 15, 16–17
Kim, Suzy, 119n4
Kim Chol Jun (Kim Young Nam), 130n21
Kim Dae-jung, 70
Kim Deog-Young, 24, 72, 109, 111–12, 124n91, 138n8
Kim Dong-won, 70, 112–14, 138–39n12
Kim Eun Cheol, 58–59
Kim-Gibson, Dai Sil, 110
Kim Hak-sun, 71
Kim Il Sung, 17, 20, 46, 111, 113
Kim Il Sung's Children (documentary, Kim Deog-Young), 24, 72, 109, 111–12, 124n91, 138n8
Kim Jong-il, 17, 25, 33; admission to abductions, 43, 48, 55, 57, 71; as benefit to United States, 44; and cinema, 21, 46–50, 128n72; dystopic speculation on, 33
A Kim Jong-Il Production (Fischer), 47, 128n72
Kim Jong Un, 4, 17, 36–37, 125n3; depicted in *The Interview*, 35–38, 126n35; depictions of, 32, 36
Kim's Convenience (Choi), 81, 82–85; North Korea sidelined in, 83–84; "proud moment Korea history test," 83–84, 91; television and play versions of, 82, 88. *See also* diaspora, Korean
Kim Soyoung, 109–10
Kim Young-soon, 58, 131n23
King, Rodney, 121–22n53
Kirby, Michael Donald, 54, 56
Klein, Christina, 5
knowledge, 129n4; audience presumption of, 28, 38; Cold War as project of, 63; from diasporic vantage point, 11–12; fictional aspects of, 30–31; new forms of production, 110; repressed, 6; shaped by style and genre, 27; West centered in production of, 9–10
Koizumi, Junichiro, 43

Korea: Allied trusteeship imposed on, 15; and complex regional dynamics, 17–18; division system, 70–71, 139n12; ethnic nationalism in, 92; family separation, 2, 85, 89, 103; Japanese colonization of, 16, 18; Kim dynasty, 17; number of Koreans living outside of, 104. *See also* North Korea; South Korea
Korean Americans, 87–89, 99, 101, 103–4, 110
Korean Council, 71
Korean Democratic Party (KDP), 18
Korean War, 5, 16; atomic weapons use contemplated by United States, 61, 131n31; Chinese soldier memoirs, 42; expanded understandings of, 19; fantasy of preventing, 57; as forgotten war, 17, 90; imperialism upheld by narratives of, 84; migration due to, 11; North Korea as signifier of, 84; prisoners of war, 21; responsibility for, 123n78; UN lack of understanding of, 62–63; versions of, 122n74, 123n78
Koryo Saram (ethnic Koreans in Russia and former Soviet countries), 102, 137n1
Krysowata, Jolanta, 138n8
Kusakabe Kyushiro, 48
Kwangju massacre (South Korea, 1980), 70
Kwon, Heonik, 4–5, 17, 114, 123n78
Kwon, June Hee, 102
Kwon, R. O., 86

labor exploitation, 82, 92, 102–3
Lankov, Andrei, 53, 129n7
Lee, Eun-Joung, 5–6, 124n87
Lee, Helie, 53
Lee, Hyeonseo, 74
Lee, Jason, 6, 89
Lee, Jin-kyung, 92
Lee, Krys, 23, 85, 86–87, 95–104
Lee, Namhee, 120–21n26
Lee Hae Kyoung, 116
Lee Min Yong, 19, 123n86
Legacies of Korean War online archive, 5–6
legibility, 8; of North Korea, 26, 125n10; structures of, 23–24, 51–53, 87–88; of subject, 23, 51–53, 56, 65–66, 74, 106
Letters from Pyongyang (documentary, Lee), 6, 89
Liberty in North Korea (LiNK), 89, 135n20
Liem, Ramsay, 19, 89, 123–24n87

life writing/memoirs, 21, 22–23; 1960s to 1980s, 69, 133n65; amplified by political organizations, 55–56; attempts to protect family members, 39; of Chinese soldiers, 42; collaboratively written, 55, 73; credibility of questioned, 29, 31, 51–53, 72–73, 86, 125–26n13; and human rights discourse, 53, 56; increase in during 1990s, 69, 73; inhuman, 72–78; market orientation of, 56, 77, 129n7; as securitized form of writing, 53; South Korean and US support for, 52–53; typicality of, 79. *See also* documentaries; dystopic speculation
The Lovers and the Despot (documentary), 23, 27–28, 42, 47–50, 128n72; Cold War context not addressed, 47; complexity of feeling with respect to North Korea, 48–49; plot, 47–48
Lukács, Georg, 79
Lynn, Hyung Gu, 44

Making Peace with Nature (Kim), 11
Malik, Charles, 60
The Manchurian Candidate (book and film), 1–2
McGann, Paul, 33
media: dystopian tropes in, 32–33; news reports from 2012 to 2014, 32; North Korea narrativized in terms of absolute difference, 32. *See also* documentaries; film (cinema)
melancholia, 7, 22, 85, 95, 103, 135n23; invoked by North Korea, 7, 83, 85; over split of Korea, 89, 103; as structure of feeling, 103, 106. *See also* affect
The Melancholy of Race (Cheng), 7
memory: collective, 89, 95, 117; forgetting, 17, 67, 90, 127n47
Memory of Forgotten War (Borshay-Liem and Liem), 19, 89, 123o124n87
Mignolo, Walter D., 131–32n43
migration: complexity of, 58–59; from Japan, 93; to Japan from Korea, 91; of Koreans to China, 87, 91, 100–101; "militarized migrations," 84; to North Korea, 86; to North Korea from Japan, 58–59, 93; from North Korea to South Korea, 69; repetitive displacement of Koreans, 91–92; to Russia, 104; to South Korea from Japan, 93; from

South Korea to Canada and United States, 11, 19; from South Korea to North Korea, 18–19; waves of, 19, 69, 91, 95, 99, 104; Zainichi Koreans, 93–94. *See also* diaspora; diaspora, Korean; diaspora, Korean Canadian

military occupation, as freedom, 16

minor inhuman: "minor as a method," 14; North Korea as, 8, 14–16, 22–23, 27; North Koreans as, 74–76; toward a genealogy of, 12–16, 60. *See also* inhuman, the

Mircioiu, Georgeta, 111, 138n8

model minority, 82–85, 88, 90, 98; Joseonjok, 101; South Korea as, 71

Moon, Katherine H. S., 71

moralism, liberal, 15

Morris-Suzuki, Tessa, 93, 94

Moscow International Film Festival, 48

mother, nonmaternal, 75, 78

Moyn, Samuel, 15, 61, 64

multiculturalism, 5, 19; Canadian, 82–84

nation (nation-state): and delegitimization of migrations, 101; relations with diasporas, 82, 85, 88; role of, 64; "territorial osmosis," 91–92

National Endowment for Democracy (NED), 38, 130n16

National Human Rights Commission of Korea (NHRCK), 70

nationalisms, affective hold of, 90–91

Neary, Ian, 133n69

neocolonial relations, 3, 93

neoliberal era, 60

New Right (South Korea), 71

Ngai, Sianne, 4, 50

Nguyen, Mimi, 88

Nguyen, Viet, 40

Nguyen, Vinh, 22

nihonjinzuma (escapees), 44

Nishida Tetsuo, 48

Niu, Greta, 13–14

nonaligned nations, 20, 68

North Korea: abductions by, 42–50, 54, 57–58, 71, 128n72; anti-colonial nationalism in, 18; archival sources, 20–22; Arduous March, 17, 25, 59, 69; as bizarre, vii, 3, 22–24, 27, 28, 49, 66–67; border with China, 87, 100; brutality attributed to in fiction and film, 21, 27–28, 125n3; caricatures of, 32, 87, 107; as Cold War product, 63; as comic and tragic, 4; complexity of feeling with respect to, 48–49; Constitution, 63; contextualizing, 16–20; cult leadership attributed to, 13, 45; as cultural fantasy of the inhuman, 12, 17, 22, 23, 66–67, 80, 119–20n4; decolonization project, 63, 124n89; disavowal of, 2, 23, 95; economic and political ties to Russia and China, 19–20; everyday representations of, 1–2, 31–32, 79, 85, 119n4; famine and economic crisis of the 1990s, 2, 13, 17, 25, 59, 69, 71; film and literature used by leaders, 46–48; forgetting in relation to, 17, 67, 90, 127n47; gender inequality addressed in, 18; "grey" and black market activity in, 17, 37; historical context erased, 59, 68–69, 87–88; human rights organizations allowed into, 20; as illiberal, 2–3, 11, 42–43, 54, 68, 120n6; as incomprehensible, 2–3, 18, 22, 26, 28, 42–43, 49, 67, 125n3; industrialization, 68; inhumanity attributed to, 3, 7–8, 23–24, 27–28, 61, 68; internationalization of struggles, 20; Japanese occupation of, 81; locked into Cold War representation, 30; "loss" of, 7; as machine-like figure, 14; melancholia invoked by, 7, 83, 85, 95, 103; as metaphor for alterity, 31; migration to after Korean War, 18–19; as minor inhuman, 8, 14–16, 22–23, 27; as minor villain, 4, 6, 50; and narrative structures of Cold War, 3–4; as not always North Korea, 87; nuclear capabilities, 2, 4, 9, 14, 32, 43, 59, 67, 72, 89; as object for West, 3, 5, 10, 28–29, 34; as Orientalist fiction, 28–29; as outside scope of human rights, 63–64; as part of Korean diaspora, 87–89; perceived as threat to global security, 9, 31, 89; political awareness within, 45–46; "potted history" of, 17, 84; prison camps, 26, 51, 53–54, 57–59, 73–78; produced as threat to West, 44, 72; regime change pushed for, 57, 59, 70; rogue state imagery of, 20, 44, 53, 65; as set of stylized conventions, 30, 56; as site of rescue, 95; socialist countries, relation to, 109–18; as socialist model for Global South, 20;

INDEX 159

North Korea (*continued*)
  state-sanctioned haircuts, 32; terror invoked by, 85; "third North Korea," 66–67; as understandable, 21; United Nations denied access to, 52, 54; values traditions in, 63–65, 95; as villain, 4, 6, 23, 49–50; welfare rights emphasized by, 63–64; Western ideals reinforced by tropes of, 22, 27–29, 31, 33, 37, 42. *See also* defectors, North Korean; demilitarized zone (DMZ); inhuman, the
North Korea Kidnapped My Daughter (Yokota), 58
North Korean Human Rights (NKHR), 43–44
North Korean Human Rights Act of 2004 (United States), 58, 59, 71
North Koreans: depicted as incapable of agency, 17, 39–40, 53, 64, 66, 74; as extensions of Western readers, 42; as inhuman figures, 17, 23, 39–40, 68, 95, 106; as minor inhuman figures, 74–76. *See also* defectors, North Korean
Now On My Way to Meet You (television show), 135–36n23

Obama, Barack, 35, 38, 130n16
Oh, David, 35
Okinawa, 6
oral history, 78
Orientalism, 10, 20, 31; North Korea as fiction of, 28–29; techno-Orientalism, 13–14
The Orphan Master's Son (Johnson), 22, 25–29, 33–34, 46, 49, 124–25n1, 127n47; as bildungsroman, 42; drawn from English translations, 31; generic realness in, 28–31; interrogator's story, 40–42; literary awards, 27; movement between first- and third-person narration, 40–41; plot, 25–26; reading for repetition in, 38–42; value of story referenced in, 126–27n43
orphans: in North Korea, 39; sent to Eastern Europe, 24, 72, 111–17, 137–38n3, 138n5; subjected to "head cleansing" program, 111
Overseas Korean Act (OKA, South Korea), 101–2

Pacific War, 16, 18
Paik Nak-chung, 70–71

Park, Alyssa M., 104
Park, Hyun Ok, 91–92, 104
Park, Jane, 13
Park, Jung-sun, 102
Park, Soyoung, 106
Park, Yeonmi, 29, 96, 125–26n13
Park Chung-hee, 69
Patterson, Christopher, 34
People Are the Sky (Kim-Gibson), 110
plot, 25–26, 30, 46
Poetry Division of the United Front Department, 46
Poland, 115–17; Poznań protest, 111. *See also* orphans
positioning, 22–23, 31, 84, 103, 138n12
post–Cold War era, 3–10, 99, 104; beginning of, 60, 69; as discursive concept, 114; foundations for wars in Asia laid during, 61; global order prolonged by ideas of North Korea, 4, 21, 50, 74; North Korean human rights in, 68–72; read with Cold War era, 7; in terms of racial affect, 16; "transwar connectivity," 6; Western perceptions confirmed by depictions of North Korea, 27. *See also* Cold War
ppalgaengi (빨갱이) (Commie), 19
prison camps, North Korea, 26, 51, 53–54, 57–59, 73–78
prostitution, 71–72, 77, 90
Puar, Jasbir, 82, 85

race: humanity disciplined into hierarchies of humanness, 7–9, 12–13, 121–22n53; UNESCO statements on, 67–68, 132–33n61
racialization, 3, 8, 30; and affective hold of nationalisms, 91; and demonstration of affect, 74–75; and dystopic speculation, 50; of the inhuman, 12–13, 27, 67–68; and political disciplining of Korean migrants, 88; psychic level of, 7; "racist love," 13–14; through incredulity, 28; US imperialism furthered by, 5, 28, 84. *See also* inhuman, the
Rajagopal, Balakrishnan, 62
Rak, Julie, 77, 79
Rangan, Pooja, 66
Real Dictators podcast (McGann), 33, 46
realism: "faux," 29; generic, 28–31
Red Scare, 2

refugee-ism, narrative of, 65–66
Refugee Protocol (United Nations, 1967), 15, 65
refugees, 15, 129n7; Cambodian, 9; stateless people, 65. *See also* diaspora; migration
relationality, 7, 9, 10, 22, 110; documentary focus on, 112–14; legibility of, 87–88; palimpsestic, 27; transnational identifications as ways of refusing national disciplinings, 112
"remote control," 22
René Cassin, 60
repatriation, 93–95, 138–39n12; of orphaned children from Eastern Europe, 111, 117, 137–38n3
Repatriation (documentary, Kim Dong-won), 70, 112–14, 138–39n12
repetition, 30, 38–42, 46
Republic of Korea (ROK), establishment of, 16, 60, 101. *See also* South Korea
reunification discourse, 89, 90, 120–21n26, 135–36n23
Rivero, Oswaldo de, 6
Roh, David, 13–14
Roh Moo-hyun, 70
Roosevelt, Eleanor, 60
Rumsfeld, Donald, 119n4
Russia, 104, 110
Ryang, Sonia, 11, 17

Said, Edward, 10
Sakai, Naoki, 22
Samuels, Richard J., 43
Sanggyedong Olympics (Kim Dong-won), 112
Schmid, Andre, 45, 127n47
scholarship: area studies, 9–11; Asian American studies, 8, 10–14, 90, 101; Asian studies, 10; Black studies, 12; critical Cold War studies, 11; cultural studies, 11; Korean American studies, 11; North Korean studies, 107; queer studies, 10, 85; and techno-Orientalism, 13–14
September 11, 2001, 1
sexual trafficking, 96
Shih, Shu-mei, 9–10
Shin, HaeRan, 106
Shin Dong-hyuk, 23, 29, 66; affect of, 74–78, 134n89; COI testimony, 57, 58, 130n24; credibility of account, 51–53, 73, 125n13; depicted as inhuman subject, 60, 74–76, 79–80; in documentary film, 77–78; legibility of, 51–53; narrative as "bona fide" defector account, 53; public speaking, 52, 67, 69, 129n4
Shin Films, 47
Shin Sang-ok, 23, 45–49, 128n72
Singh, Nikhil Pal, 5
Slaughter, Joseph, 60, 76
slowness, 111
Smith, Hazel, 17, 87, 119–20n4
Smith, Sidonie, 78
Sŏ Chungsŏk, 88
socialist lifeworlds, 11, 20, 109–18; continued persistence of, 114; Eastern Europe, 24, 72, 111–17, 137–38n3; multiplicity of, 110
Song, Dae-Han, 58, 130n16
Song, Jiyoung, 63–64
Songdowon International Camp (North Korea), 20
Songyi (actress), 115, 116
Song-yi (defector), 78
Sony Pictures, cyberattack on, 35
So Se Pyong, 55
South Korea, 4; authoritarian government, 60, 69–70, 133n69; blacklisting in university system, 5–6; capitalism, 78, 111; centering of in scholarship, 11–12; citizenship rights, 102; Constitution, 70; democratization, 60, 69, 132n47; Hanawon education facility, 59; labor exploitation in, 93, 102–3, 105; "lost decade of progressive rule," 70; migration from North Korea to, 69; as model minority, 71; National Security Law, 19; New Right, 71; Overseas Korean Act (OKA), 101–2; police coercion of filmmakers, 113; political repercussions for families remaining in, 19; prisoners in, 70, 112–13; racial capitalist system and mindset, 78; racialized labor underwritten by, 105; social conservatism of, 18; states of emergencies, 49, 111; thriller films, 33; Ulchi Freedom Guardian exercise, 122–23n76; as US client state, 23, 28; US occupation of, 18, 133n69; US support for right-wing groups, 38, 130n16. *See also* demilitarized zone (DMZ)
South Korean Truth and Reconciliation Commission, 124–25n1

INDEX 161

Soviet Union, 4
speculative finance, 34
Spillers, Hortense, 12
Stalin, Joseph, 110
Stars Between the Sun and Moon: One Woman's Life in North Korea and Escape to Freedom (Jang), 74
structures of feeling, 75, 96, 117; melancholia as, 103, 106; shared, 116–18
The Stumps (Chu Sang-mi), 115
style, 27, 30, 56
subhuman, the, 12–13
subject: after 1945, 16–17; bad and good, 85; "compositional," 87; diasporic, 7; of documentary genre, 112–16; imperial, 65; legible, 23, 51–53, 56, 65–66, 74, 106; minor imperial, 95; neoliberal, 15; "subjectless discourse," 87–88
Suh, Bo-hyuk, 129n13
Suh, Jae-Jung, 122n74
The Sympathizer (Nguyen), 40

Tadiar, Neferti, 3, 9, 10
Taliban, 1
Taylor, Moe, 20
techne, 3
techno-Orientalism, 13–14
terrorist, figure of, 1, 82, 85
tone, 6–7
Toronto Fringe Festival, 81, 82
"translegality," 106
transwar connectivity, 6, 44
transwar justice, 8
Troeung, Y-Dang, 8
Trump, Donald, 32, 54
Two Dreams in One Bed (Park), 91–92
Ty, Eleanor, 30

ugly feelings, 4, 50
Ulchi Freedom Guardian exercise, 122–23n76
UNESCO statements on race, 67–68, 132–33n61
United Nations, 14–17; ahistorical approach to North Korea, 59, 68–69; democratic elections supervised by, 16; denied access to North Korea, 52, 54; marginality of colonized spaces codified by, 63–64; as player in staging of war, 60; Special Rapporteur position, 54–55, 71; and US proxy wars, 17. *See also* Universal Declaration of Human Rights (UDHR, 1948)
United Nations Charter, 60
United Nations Commission of Inquiry (COI) on Human Rights in the Democratic People's Republic of Korea (DPRK), 52, 54–56, 129n4; "DPRK Specialists," 58; intended audience for report, 56–57; interplay between text and testimony, 56; public hearings, 57–59, 68
United Nations Commission on Human Rights, 54–55, 72
United Nations Convention Concerning the Status of Refugees (1951), 15, 65–66; signatories allowed to limit obligations, 65
United Nations General Assembly, 59–61
United Nations Human Rights Council (UNHRC), 52, 54
United States: ambitions of furthered by racialized discourses, 5, 28, 84; atomic weapons use in Korea contemplated by, 61, 131n30; civil rights movement, 6; client states of, 23, 28, 44; decentering of, 11; divergences and overlaps with Chinese state projects, 99–100; imperialist expansion, 5; Jim Crow law, 64; media representations of North Korea in 1990s, 20; military presence in Japan justified by threat of North Korea, 44; National Endowment for Democracy, 38, 130n16; North Korea as minor concern for, 4, 6, 50; occupation of South Korea, 18, 133n69; proxy wars in Asia, 5, 17; and UN Commission of Inquiry, 55
Universal Declaration of Human Rights (UDHR, 1948), 15, 59–64, 65; four freedoms, 61; global Cold War order codified by, 61; Global North priorities of, 62–63, 131n38, 131–32n43; political and civic rights emphasized by, 64
universalization, 9; in human rights discourses, 15, 60, 64–65; of shared potential, 67–68
US Committee for Human Rights in North Korea (2002), 59
US North Korea Freedom Coalition (2003), 59

Verduyn, Christl, 30
Verliebt, Verlobt, Verloren (documentary, Cho), 109, 125n91
Vietnam, 4, 17, 20
Vietnam War, 17
violence: "anachronistic" versus Western killings, 77–78; coexistence of with freedom, 88; humanitarian, 62; human rights as privileged epistemic form for, 7; migrants always already touched by, 84; no humans involved (NHI), 121–22n53
Vollers, Maryanne, 29, 126n13
Vukovich, Daniel, 120n6

Walker, Gavin, 22
Wang, Chih-ming, 101, 103–4
warfare: interior locus of, 16–17; nuclear, fears of, 32; as privilege of recognized states, 15; UN as player in staging of, 60; US proxy wars in Asia, 5, 17; war on terror, 1. *See also* Korean War
Watson, Julia, 78
Weheliye, Alexander, 7, 12
welfare states, 15
White, Hayden, 3, 4
White, Kevin, 82
white supremacy, 6, 85

Williams, Randall, 7, 15, 61
Williams, Raymond, 120n6
women, Asian and Korean, 8; comfort women, 44, 71–72, 90; domestic labor performed by, 103; *kkotchebi* woman, 114; sexual labor of, 91
Wong, Lily, 75
"wounded healers," 117
Wynter, Sylvia, 12–13, 121–22n53

Xiang, Sunny, 6–7

Yanbian Korean Autonomous Prefecture (China), 99
Yang Yonghi, 94
Yao, Xine, 74
Yapp, Hentyle, 29
Yokota Megumi, 48, 58, 130–31n21
Yokota Sakie, 58
Yokota Shigeru, 58
Yoneyama, Lisa, 6
Yuh, Ji-Yeon, 84

Zainichi, 93–94
Žižek, Slavoj, 72

www.ingramcontent.com/pod-product-compliance
Lightning Source LLC
Chambersburg PA
CBHW020309170426
43202CB00008B/548